THE AMERICAN WEST

An Appraisal

THE AMERICAN WEST

An Appraisal

Papers from the Denver Conference
on the History of Western America

edited by
Robert G. Ferris

editorial advisers
LeRoy R. Hafen   Allen D. Breck   Robert M. Utley

introduction by Ray A. Billington
preface by James Taylor Forrest

Museum of New Mexico Press
Santa Fe, New Mexico

© MUSEUM OF NEW MEXICO PRESS 1963
Library of Congress Catalog Card Number: 63-22144

This volume was made possible by a grant from the
Museum of New Mexico

Designed by Joseph Haydock

PREFACE

The sharp crack of a bull-whacker's whip and the creaking sound of a dusty prairie schooner carrying its bone-weary occupants westward in the 1850's are in sharp contrast to the smooth hum of a powerful piston-driven engine as it propels its air-conditioned passengers comfortably in the same direction today. Yet there is a common theme—the lure of the Last Frontier, the Great American West. Call it the Great Westward Movement or the Great Westward Tilt, the flow of American history has been ever westward—in the pursuit of national and individual destiny.

Though the two modes of transportation epitomize the West of yesterday and today and the vast historical changes which have profoundly affected not only transportation but all aspects of western life, strong similarities exist between the old and the new West.

Whether the westward-wending pioneer crossed the plains during the 1850's or makes the trek in the 1960's, the motivations are the same: the wide open spaces, economic opportunity, climate, the spirit of adventure, or a desire to share in the robustness and vigor that have always characterized western life.

On the other hand, despite great advances in transportation, business and industry, and all other phases of life, the major problems of the West of today are essentially the same as they were in yesteryear: the critical need for water, the sparse population in many areas and attendant problems in government and business, and the proper retention and development of natural resources.

In the early days, the pioneers—be they miners, trappers, or farmers—battled with the natives and the inhospitable wilderness. But these dangers, now romanticized in text and tale, are of the past. The civilized West of today is part of the great blanket of American culture and economy.

However, it is unique: great distances separate the populated areas; the continued use of Midwest farming and grazing methods adversely affects agriculture; and ranch-farm taxes and financing are not always in accord with economic conditions. These and other differences make for the West's truly unique problems—problems which need further study.

Because of the historical continuity of these problems, the modern, pragmatic historian can contribute significantly to their solution. His interest in doing so is evident from the enthusiasm shown at the two conferences on the history of western America and the formation of the Western History Association.

That interest is also evident from this collection of twenty papers from the Second Conference on the History of Western America—which focus on the major themes and problems of the West. The passing of the cowboy and the changes that have wrought the cowboy of today are chronicled. Fresh light is shed on the Great Surveys. Interesting facets of various fields of business, industry, and transport are explored. The growth and decline of the Missouri fur trade are traced. Activities of the Spanish in the West are evaluated. Territorial developments are related. And finally, the writing of western history itself is examined, along with the allied discipline of historical archaeology.

Certainly all the papers are interesting and pertinent; some provide special insight into the forces that motivate western history and development—then or now or hence.

No matter what the future development of the West, no matter what changes are forged in the crucible of historical change, the West will always be the last American frontier. And it will always intrigue many Americans—whether they be confirmed eastern city dwellers or the westward-wending successors of the pioneers. For this reason, the Museum of New Mexico is happy to make available to the public these outstanding papers on Western Americana.

The efforts of the many individuals who helped produce this volume are deeply appreciated. Special gratitude is extended to the twenty authors, not only for their basic contributions, but also for their splendid cooperation in all phases of production. Invaluable assistance was rendered by the editorial advisers: LeRoy R. Hafen, Brigham Young University; Allen D. Breck, University of Denver; and Robert M. Utley, National Park Service.

The following individuals on the staff of the Museum of New Mexico were also extremely helpful: Joseph Haydock, Ruth Rambo, and Virginia von Schrenk. Robert G. Ferris, the editor of this volume, also prepared the Index.

JAMES TAYLOR FORREST

CONTENTS

THE WEST OF YESTERDAY

AND TODAY—A BROAD VIEW

The New Western Social Order and the Synthesis of Western Scholarship

RAY A. BILLINGTON
The Huntington Library

The formation of the Western History Association provides an opportunity to survey the state of western historical studies, and to venture a few random observations on the effect of the new western social order on future scholarship concerning the West. The remarks that follow are unabashedly personal and unprofessionally subjective; they are based on two decades of reading and research in the field of western history, but bear little relationship to conclusions that might be reached by others more deeply immersed in that fascinating field of study. Yet, if they have the slightest validity, they suggest that the time is ripe for an association of western enthusiasts, and that the future of the newly formed organization is promising.

Perhaps the most heartening feature of the two conferences on western studies, held in 1961 at Santa Fe and now in 1962 at Denver, is the enthusiasm engendered among the participants. The dedicated little band of frontier buffs who organized the Santa Fe conference hopefully dreamed of 50 or 60 registrants; instead, 297 persons responded to their invitation. The enlarged "Organizing Committee" that labored to set the stage for this 1962 Denver meeting wishfully hoped for an attendance as large as the year before; actually, more than 400 enthusiasts listened happily to 31 papers, enjoyed two luncheon and one dinner addresses, and applauded the remarks of 15 commentators and 16 presiding officers. They also attended a business meeting, where they adopted a constitution and elected officers of the Western History Association.

Not even the most optimistic of the conference planners anticipated such results, or dared hope for such unbridled support. Yet, in a larger sense, these enthusiasms might have been expected. Persons of all degrees of learning and all walks of life have for generations succumbed to the lure of the American West. At least three additional forces now serve to heighten that interest.

One is the national attention focused on the trans-Mississippi country by the unprecedented changes currently occurring in the structure of the western social order. What Frank Lloyd Wright described as the "great westward tilt" is today pouring millions of people into that third of the nation lying between the Rockies and the Pacific. During past decades the eleven states there have increased their population at the rate of some forty per cent every ten years, or about twice the national rate; between 1950 and 1960 California alone added five million persons and today hovers at the point where it will soon be the most populous state. This is a migration of breath-taking proportions; beside it all the "great migrations" of the nation's pioneer period sink into insignificance.

The result is the creation in the West of a dynamic new society—a challenge to scholars who would interpret its meaning or venture prophecies concerning its future. This is no stabilized social order, rigidly stratified and easily understood. Instead, the student of western society must deal with an ever-changing land, where a multitude of intruding peoples and a mosaic of differing physical environments defy simple interpretation.

Today, too, the West is following the course of all new societies in its flourishing cultural evolution, as material needs no longer monopolize popular attention. Artists and writers have long trekked toward that land of perpetual sunshine and stark coloration; more recently their cavalcade has been joined by musicians, scholars, and intellectuals of every breed, seduced by the handsome salaries offered by educational institutions. The eleven Nobel laureates who frequent the University of California campuses outnumber those in any university in the world.

This exciting evolutionary pattern is an irresistible attraction to the student who would understand America's social structure. And, perhaps just as important, its very complexity challenges traditional methods of problem-solving in the social sciences. No historian, no anthropologist or sociologist or economist or political scientist, can expect to comprehend the West's unprecedented social evolution without the help of colleagues in allied disciplines. A history student cannot properly write a history of the Sioux wars without enlightenment on Indian psychology by a social anthropologist; a historian of the mining frontier cannot deal properly with his subject until he has tapped the knowledge of geologists and mining engineers; an investigator of vigilance committees cannot be sure of his conclusions without the aid of sociologists and social psychologists. "Do-it-yourself" studies will not suffice to explain the complexities of western society; this is a field made to order for the interdisciplinary approach.

That those seeking to unlock the West's secrets sense this fact seems to be indicated by the enthusiasm with which scholars of all types have welcomed the formation of the Western History Association. Wrote one historian when plans for the new society were announced: "Something of that kind is long overdue. Historical research and the writing of history are both rather lonely tasks at best. Fellowship with others working in the same field would of itself justify such an organization." By uniting all who have a serious interest in the evolution and analysis of western society, whatever their fields of interest, the Association should provide an advantageous means of evaluating and understanding the nation's most complex region.

The second force now heightening enthusiasm for western studies is the emerging realization that they bear a more direct relationship to modern problems than anyone has been willing to admit. Between the 1930's and very recent times, frontier history especially has been in eclipse, no longer capturing national favor as it did in a prior generation. The Great Depression focused scholars' attention on the elements of society that seemed most out of joint: factories and cities and the class structure. So there developed glamorous new fields for historical investigation; economic history blossomed into sudden importance; urban history emerged as a challenging new discipline; immigration and labor history attracted an army of disciples; social and intellectual history swept courses in western history from college catalogues; and contemporary historical studies outshone all others as students focused on the immediate past in their frantic effort to understand the uncertain present.

Before this avalanche of new interests, western history steadily lost ground. Seemingly the historian of the West, committed as he was to the study of remote events in a "distant" land, had little to offer society. What did it matter to a Depression-ridden and then war-torn United States that a wagon train had crossed the plains in the 1840's, that a pony express rider had stayed in the saddle for twenty consecutive hours, or that a man named

Custer had fought a disastrous engagement on the banks of the Little Bighorn? Western historians became reconciled to a defensive role when they associated with the bright young scholars who held the keys to an understanding of modern society. They were, they secretly felt, second-class citizens in the community of scholarship.

Then came the Santa Fe and Denver conferences, and with them the beginnings of a revitalizing new attitude. Suddenly western historians found others who spoke their language, and believed that America's pioneer period was important. Suddenly they could hold their heads aloft and no longer feel ashamed of their enthusiasm. One wrote after the 1961 Santa Fe conference: "So many who have felt apologetic about their historical endeavors—historians described as regionalists, museum people, state historians, and the like—came away with the feeling that they really belonged. They came away inspired to do better things."

This heartening new attitude is well timed, for the changing national temper suggests that western studies will assume even greater importance for the nation in the future. Today America's problems are external rather than internal; the national concern is no longer the revitalization of a faltering economy but peaceful existence in a contracting world containing hostile neighbors. Effective relationship with those neighbors requires us to understand ourselves as well as our friends and enemies; a comprehension of our national character is now vital to survival. The principal duty of historians and other social scientists is to enlighten their country concerning the uniqueness of its traits and institutions.

In this respect, frontier history seems destined for an essential role. Few scholars would disagree with Frederick Jackson Turner's assertion that the most distinctive feature of the American past was the nation's three-century-long pioneering period. If, as Turner maintained, this pioneering experience endowed the American people with different characteristics and institutions than those of other peoples, those differences must be understood before the United States can function effectively among its neighbors, both friendly and hostile.

The long-term evolution of the country's social order, not simply its twentieth-century maturing, assumes a new importance in today's changed international setting. The historian of the West can contribute to the understanding of this evolution as significantly as can the student of the American mind or of the era of the New Deal. Perhaps the students of the West who gathered at the Santa Fe and Denver conferences sensed rather than understood this changing importance of their studies; even this would be enough to engender the enthusiasm that led to the founding of the Western History Association.

The third force evidencing increased interest in the West is a cyclical one: a new groundswell of popular, as well as scholarly, interest in the subject. This can be explained only by the cyclical nature of the public taste. Between the early 1900's and the 1920's, frontier studies captured the imagination of students and laymen alike; Frederick Jackson Turner's frontier hypothesis proved so challenging that a whole generation of historians, sociologists, literary historians, and those in other disciplines reinterpreted their subject matter in the new terms. In the end they went too far, with the result that the inevitable reaction set in during the 1930's; for two decades frontier studies were little regarded. Now the pendulum appears to be swinging in the other direction.

There are straws in the wind everywhere. Popular interest in the West is evident from the persistent popularity of television "Westerns" with their amazing caricatures of cowboys and "gun slingers," from the enduring popularity of the Hollywood fantasies on the same theme, from the acceleration in sales of western fiction (Zane Grey's novels have sold more than 54,000,000 copies and those of Germany's Karl May 15,000,000) and from the blossoming of corrals of "Westerners" in cities of the United States and Europe.

On a more scholarly level, the proliferation of books and articles about the West in recent years staggers the imagination. The first edition of Oscar O. Winther's *Classified Bibliography of the Periodical Literature of the Trans-Mississippi West*, published in 1942, listed some 3,500 articles appearing between 1811 and 1938; the second edition, which appeared in 1961, included an additional 5,500 articles, printed between 1938 and 1957. Thus, in recent years scholars have produced at least 2,000 more articles about the West than in the century and a quarter before. Similarly, the American Historical Association's annual volume, *Writings on American History*, listed all the articles and books about the West published in 1949 on thirty pages; by 1954, sixty-one pages were required.

Should those trends in popular taste and scholarly activity

continue, writers about the West are faced with a sobering challenge in the immediate future. What are their responsibilities to their craft, to their public, and to the nation? And, just as important, how can the newly formed Western History Association play a significant role in the encouragement of sound but readable historical studies?

One answer is apparent: the Association can help effect a reunion of the two schools into which western historical studies are now divided. One of these is the "History of the West" school; the other is the "History of the Frontier" school. What do these schools represent? And why is more cooperation between them essential?

The designation "History of the West" as it appears in college catalogues suggests a regional orientation which, if carried to extremes, can only bring discredit upon its disciples. Regionalists of this school are too often guilty of three cardinal sins: they overemphasize local events at the expense of the national, they are lured by antiquarianism, and they forget their responsibilities as historians in their eagerness to cater to popular tastes. A more detailed examination of these three faults will illustrate the pitfalls that threaten such overzealous historians of the West.

The tendency toward provincialism is understandably, but nonetheless regrettably, apparent in too many writers of the "History of the West" school. Their concern is with local events, without regard to the larger significance of the problems with which they deal. Their energies are squandered on obscure characters whose influence failed to reach beyond the confines of the locality where they lived. This is not to say that the most trivial details of the past are unimportant, for every event is a stone in the giant mosaic of human progress. It is to say that those who polish their individual stones endlessly and fail to fit them into the larger pattern fail in their principal duty as historians: to interpret the past as a means of understanding the present. Each episode in human behavior has some relationship to every other episode; the historian must discover and explain these relationships. Western regionalists often have failed to do so, and have earned the disrespect of scholars having a broader vision.

Akin to localism among the sins of the "History of the West" school is antiquarianism—a preoccupation with details that contribute little to the main stream of history. That an explorer opened part of the West to settlement is important; that he went up one side of a river rather than the other in doing so may be totally unimportant. Yet hours of patient research are frequently squandered on such a problem. This tendency has been accentuated by the scarcity of certain types of source materials dealing with the West.

For example, because the Mountain Men left few personal records, students have raked over the same few diaries and reminiscences again and again, and told the same old stories in the same old way (in how many books does the tale of Hugh Glass and the grizzly appear?)—even though the largely untapped records of such important fur companies as the American Fur Company and the Hudson's Bay Company still await complete analysis. Again this is not to say that minor events are of no significance. It is to say that scholars should not waste time upon them so long as more meaningful problems await solution, as they do so urgently in the largely untold story of the American West.

Finally, writers of the "History of the West" persuasion are sometimes inclined to cater to a sensation-seeking public, rather than to grapple with more important topics. Considering the influence of public taste, this is understandable. The reading public possesses an insatiable taste for tales of desperadoes and badmen, cowboys and "gun slingers," Indian fighters and vigilantes. Yet these swaggering types were not the men who built the West; instead, their lawless behavior hindered the coming of civilization. Historians who glorify such unimportant characters fail in their duty to their craft, for the function of the scholar is not to amuse but to explain the evolving social structure. Too often regional historians have forgotten this obligation in their desire to entertain. Little wonder that they have fallen into disrepute in the eyes of more analytical scholars.

Extreme regionalists of the "History of the West" school, then, stand indicted in the eyes of their profession for provincialism, antiquarianism, and popularization. For these reasons, they have failed to win the confidence of their fellow craftsmen and they have added little to the knowledge of the West as a molding influence in the social order of today's world.

At the opposite end of the scale stand historians who label their college courses "The History of the American Frontier," and whose emphasis differs in two ways from that of the regionalist school: they are concerned with the spread of population across the entire continent rather than with the evolution of one section, and they are obsessed with the task of testing and retesting the frontier hypothesis of Frederick Jackson Turner in their writing and teaching. Members of this school have also failed to meet their obligations to the profession; they are guilty of advancing unsupported generalizations, they squander their energies in time-wasting semantic arguments, and they adopt an attitude of intellectual aloofness that repels those who might be attracted to western history. An examination of each of these points will reveal the extent of their guilt.

Since that July day in 1893 when Frederick Jackson Turner read his seminal paper on "The Significance of the Frontier in American History," frontier historians have shown a deplorable tendency to theorize rather than to test their generalizations. Turner himself was perhaps justified; he was advancing a hypothesis for subsequent proof or disproof. Instead of accepting the challenge and subjecting the Turnerian theories to the rigorous analysis they deserved, many of his disciples continued to stress interpretation rather than testing, often in fields where their master himself had not dared tread. The painful process of searching out the truth by laborious digging in the records appeals to but few of this school; instead they continue to spin out their fine-webbed theories, even in the face of contrary evidence.

To make matters worse, extremists within this group have squandered their energies in endless semantic arguments among themselves, or with their opponents. Many pages have been wasted in an effort to determine exactly what Turner meant by "frontier" or "democracy" or "individualism." This is understandable; windmill tilting is a less trying occupation than the painful extraction of facts, and has always appealed to academicians who find verbal juggling a soul-satisfying substitute for hard work. Yet all the empty phrases contained in their many books and articles have failed to prove or disprove the frontier hypothesis, and thus help explain one force among the many creating modern American society.

Finally, the Turnerians have failed in a cardinal duty of the historian: to make his studies palatable to a wider audience. History, especially western history, is a fascinating subject, alive with the color and motion that appeals to the reading public. The true historian has an obligation to cater to this audience, for he can enlighten as he entertains. No one needs to be told that a sound grounding in history is an essential ingredient of effective citizenship. The scholar who fails to recognize this, and who clouds his works with meaningless theorizing on a level unsuited for popular consumption, is neglecting one of his basic duties as a historian and citizen.

What does this superficial, and perhaps exaggerated, comparison of the regional and Turnerian schools of western history suggest concerning the future role of the Western History Association? The answer is obvious. The Santa Fe and Denver conferences happily demonstrated that members of both groups can benefit by rubbing intellectual elbows, one with the other. Regionalists, brought face to face with enthusiastic theorists, can be taught that their array of facts takes on new meaning through generalization and interpretation. And theorists, emerging from their speculative clouds, can learn that historians who master facts have a world of information to offer toward the proof or disproof of generalizations. From this merging of interests and purposes can emerge a truly significant western history, one blending fact and theory, and of genuine importance to a nation seeking to understand itself in its emerging international role.

If this valued end is to be achieved, both regionalists and theorists must learn one practical lesson. Neither can afford to ignore the wider implications of his subject if western history is to win its proper place among the scholarly disciplines. The day has passed when unessential trivia or unrealistic interpretation can command the respect of the historical profession. Instead, western history must adjust itself to the commanding needs of a United States urgently seeking to establish a meaningful relationship with its heritage.

To the regionalist, this means a greater stress on the enduring phases of western history. He must concentrate increasingly on the important and the essential, less on the glamorous and ephemeral. He must recognize that remote events or trivial occurrences, no matter how fascinating, are less essential to an understanding of modern America than more pertinent happenings and lasting influences. The wandering prospectors whose wild "rushes" founded short-lived mining camps contributed far less to civilization than the San Francisco capitalists or the engineers who began the long-term process of extracting precious metals from the earth.

Wild Bill Hickok played an insignificant part in the development of the modern West when compared with the nameless Ole Olsons and Patrick Kellys whose plows broke the plains of Nebraska and Kansas. George Custer did less toward hurrying the occupation of western America than the little-known commanders who won rather than lost engagements with the Indians. Yet thousands of pages have been wasted on the mining rushes, Wild Bill, and the Battle of the Little Bighorn, while few other than serious students of the West are aware of the importance of the tides of immigration that swept civilization toward the Pacific.

Similarly, disciples of the Turnerian school must cease their meaningless quibbling and apply themselves to the serious business of testing the validity of the frontier hypothesis. As a recent writer has suggested, we are entering the third generation in our appraisal of the frontier as a molding force in our civilization; complete acceptance that was universal during the first generation, or unreasoning rejection that sufficed during the second, have already been outmoded. Already there are signs that a healthy new viewpoint is gaining strength. A handful of economists are applying wage theory and the concept of sequential growth to test the correctness of the "safety-valve" theory; a few sociologists are studying the impact of the pioneering past on modern social and physical mobility; at least one competent historian has experimented with statistical techniques to appraise the role of the frontier in shaping democratic institutions. These are encouraging developments; generations of such testing are needed before we can fully understand the frontier's role in the evolution of today's social order.

If the various signs in the wind have any meaning, they suggest that the Western History Association was organized at an opportune time. Interest in the West is increasing steadily, among laymen and professionals alike. Scholars are turning toward the use of new techniques and an emphasis on the enduring features of the past that should command both interest and respect among readers. Students are accepting the necessity of cooperative enterprise between historians, ethnologists, economists, and other specialists if Americans are to understand their pioneering past and its relation to the present.

If the Western History Association can provide a meeting ground for those with such interests, and if it can inspire and help direct western studies into meaningful areas of investigation, it should help bring new meaning to America's past and new understanding to the present.

THE COWBOY—THEN AND NOW

The Old-Time Cowhand

RAMON F. ADAMS
Dallas, Texas

There's an old saying that "a cowboy's a man with guts and a horse," and that's about as good a definition as anyone could give. If he didn't have guts he wouldn't last long; if he didn't have a horse he couldn't be a cowboy.

Some of us know him as a man who followed the cattle business as a profession. A few generations ago the East knew him as a bloodthirsty demon of disaster, reckless and rowdy, weighted down with enough artillery to make his horse sway-backed, and ever ready to shoot. Today he is mostly known as the hero of Wild West stories, as the eternally hard-riding movie or television actor, as the guitar-picking yodler of the radio, or the loudly dressed rodeo follower. The West, which knew him best, held him to be "just a plain, everyday bowlegged human," carefree and courageous, fun loving and loyal, uncomplaining and doing his best to live up to a tradition of which he was mighty proud.

No class of men was ever so unfaithfully represented, and in consequence so misunderstood and unfairly judged by people generally, as the old-time cowhand. He suffered severely from the bad publicity of ill-informed writers who had no real conception of his life and work. They pictured the rough, crude, brutal aspects of the cattle country; the reckless, happy-go-lucky visits to town; the careless use of the six-shooter; the drinking; the fighting; the rough practical jokes; the gambling; and the profanity. All these things were subjects for the writer who painted, in the most lurid colors, slanderous accounts for his eager eastern readers.

So thorough was the misrepresentation that part of the public, even today, will have no other way of looking at him. They see the wide hat but not the honest face beneath it. They remember the wild stunts he pulled in a moment of relaxation, but forget his lifetime of hard work and enduring faithfulness. It is utterly unfair to judge a whole class by what a few individuals do in the course of two or three days spent in town, instead of by the long months of weary, honest toil, common to all alike. One might as well judge all college boys by the one who turned out to be a drunkard or a thief. To appreciate properly his real qualities, this wild rough rider of the plains should have been seen in his own bailiwick. There he passed his days; there he did his life's work; there, when he met death, he faced it, as he had faced all other perils, with quiet, uncomplaining fortitude.

The real cowhand's typical day was anything but romantic. There was no romance in getting up at four o'clock in the morning, eating dust behind a trail herd, swimming muddy and turbulent rivers, nor in doctoring screw worms, pulling stupid cows from bog holes, sweating in the heat of summer, and freezing in the cold of winter.

If, when he got to town, after long months out in the brush, on the lone prairie, or on the long, long trail, the cowboy "cut his wolf loose" and had a little fun, he could hardly be blamed. He was a robust animal, full of vinegar and pride, and generally came from venturesome ancestors.

The old-time cowhand lived in the saddle. He was strictly a riding man, and detested walking, even for short distances. A self-respecting cowhand would never be going far on foot. This is why he was mighty particular about a straight riding job. When he was out of work and rode to a new range seeking a job, he was careful to inquire about the outfit before he arrived. He didn't want to sign up with some little "three-up" outfit that didn't own enough beef to hold a barbecue. On such an outfit there would be chores to do that were beneath his dignity, such as feeding, digging postholes, or cutting stove wood, and the only place a cowhand could cut wood and not hurt his pride was at a line camp where it was chop wood or "no eat."

When he "hit" a fenced ranch for a job, he hoped that all the fencing and cross fencing had been done and no more postholes needed to be dug. He didn't want to be caught on the blister end of no damned shovel. High-heeled boots weren't made for foot work, and he wouldn't be caught in a low-heeled shoe. But he didn't shirk any duty as long as it could be done from horseback. He worked without complaint long hours through flood and drought, heat and cold, and dust and blizzard, never once thinking of his own discomfort if the cattle and the welfare of his boss demanded his attention.

Fighting prairie fires, the dangers of stampedes, the loneliness of range riding, the discomforts of standing guard in the rain or sleet—none of these things seemed unusual if he could do them from the back of a horse. On the other hand, he didn't even want to open a gate unless he could lean over and do it from the saddle. His profession was born of necessity, and with it was born a tradition that he followed jealously until he became the most colorful and picturesque hired man ever known. About the only footwork he considered honorable was roping in the corral, or doing the branding.

A lot of sunshine put that squint in the old-timer's eyes, and a lot of prairie wind tanned his face. That ten-gallon hat and those fancy boots were not what made him look like a cowman. It was the elements, the corral dust, the horse smell, and the cow-camp chuck that branded him. He could go away from the cow country and dress in fancy society togs, and another cowman would still know him to be a cowman.

After the fences came, most of these old-timers were always bellyaching with a yearning to go somewhere where they could spread a loop without getting it caught on a fence post. Most of the real old-timers have now saddled a cloud and ridden into the Great Beyond, and their like will never be seen again.

When so many of the ranches got to be small pasture outfits with their fencing and footwork, many an old-time cowhand quit and got a job in town as a bartender or a livery stable chambermaid. Here he could still be with cowhands and horses. He still claims that bob-wire and bib-overalls were what ruined the cow country. By the time modern ranching, with its flivvers and helicopters, had caught up with him, he had passed over the Great Divide, or was too old to care.

The radio has developed a lot of cowboy crooners in the past few years, and even if they don't know which end a cow quits the ground with first, they have done a lot to make cowboy songs popular. But, with all this ballyhoo, there are mighty few folks who have heard cowboy songs as they were really sung on the range.

Most outdoor men have developed the custom of singing at their work. It lightens the job and entertains them. Back in the beginning of the cow business it didn't take the cowman long to savvy that the human voice gave cattle confidence, and kept them from juning around. The singing probably started when the herder got to humming a tune to keep himself from getting as lonesome as a preacher on paynight. The practice got to be so common that night herding was spoken of as "singin' to 'em." Some claimed talking would have been just as effective because it was the human voice that kept a cow from being nervous. But talking out loud to yourself never got to be a popular custom, for no man wanted another to think he was so feather-headed he needed a wet nurse because he talked to himself by the hour.

Most folks think that cowboy songs are what they hear over the radio sung by some New Jersey cowboy. Judging by the singing of these drugstore cowboys, you'd think a real cowhand yodeled all the time, but you didn't hear all that gargling on the range. It seems like every fellow who could yodel and claw a guitar duded himself up in hair and leather and got himself a job bawling into a microphone, sounding like a sick calf lost from its mammy until it became as monotonous as a nagging woman. He could sure punish the air with a noise like he was gargling his throat with axle grease. Some of the tenderfoots that came West seemed disappointed when they didn't find cowhands riding around with a guitar strapped over their withers.

One reason the cowboy doesn't like the radio singer is because he represents himself to be a cowhand when he isn't. Perhaps, too, he is a little jealous because this radio singer has a better voice than he has. Some of the songs he sings are real pretty, but the trouble is, when a song makes a hit they sing all the nap off of it until you get the trigger itch and want to shoot the singer where he looks biggest.

A lot of folks make the mistake of thinking a puncher sang his cows to sleep. He was only trying to keep himself awake, and was not trying to amuse anyone. In the first place he had no motherly love for those bovines. All he was trying to do was keep them from jumping the bedground and running off a lot of tallow. In the second place, these brutes had no ear for music, which was a good thing because the average puncher's voice and the songs he sang were not soothing. Mostly when he opened his mouth to sing some kind of noise came out, but his voice usually sounded like a burro with a bad cold, and the noise he called singing would drive all the coyotes out of the country.

A lot of the songs he sang were mighty shy on melody and a lot strong on noise, but a man didn't have to be a born vocalist to sing when he was alone in the dark if he had a clear conscience

18

and wasn't hiding out. When I say strong on noise I'm not speaking of his singing on night herd. These had to be songs that were melancholy and fitted the walk of his horse. He loved to use religious tunes because they had this melancholy, but the words he used would surely shock the clergy. It seemed like most cowhands wanted to convince you that something had surely swiped the silver lining off their clouds. They liked to be knee-deep in pathos and picture themselves as having more troubles than Job had boils.

But the trouble with most cowhands was they had lost their voices yelling at contrary cows, sleeping in the wet, or trying to explain to some judge how they had come to have their brand on somebody else's cows. Usually they had an E-string voice that sounded like a rusty gate hinge, and when they opened their mouths to sing it sounded like the long-drawn squeak of a slow-running windmill crying for oil. When one puncher I knew started singing, I thought it was a scrub bull in a canebrake in cockleburr season. His singing made me forget all my other troubles. You didn't notice trifles when a calamity like the sounds he let out hit you full in the face. Once when we were moving camp and one of the boys was pouring forth his soul in song, the cook got off the chuck wagon to look for a dry axle.

When cowhands went to town, perhaps three or four of them, after nosing their way to the bottom of a few glasses of joy juice, they might feel like exercising their tonsils in song if the barkeep wasn't a music critic and didn't have a bronc disposition. But you would never see them standing on a street corner singing like a bunch of college boys. Somebody would be apt to build a smoke under their hoofs and make them light a shuck without waiting to kiss the mayor goodbye.

There is an underlying humor in nearly every utterance of the cowboy. The country he lived in was vast and vivid; the life he lived was hard and lonely. This loneliness, his lack of education, and a certain restrained lawlessness all had their influence. His natural dislike for rule and restraint, his hatred for all authority, his extravagant and often grotesque humor, his exceptional capacity for word pictures—all these attest the spirit of the West, and from such qualities its language is nourished.

Though he led a hard and dangerous life, he could usually see the funny side, even if the joke was on him. His humor grew out of what he knew and observed. It expressed itself in picturesque, full-flavored, fertile, and vigorous speech, in practical jokes and rough horseplay, and in the tall tales he spun around the campfire. His capacity for humor was largely due to the fact that he was a young man, full of prank and play. His kind rarely considered the problems of life seriously. His humor was not merely an occasional flash of mood; it was a way of living, a standard reaction to the problems of life. Even in his ordinary everyday speech, his humor was evident.

A typical example is Bud Puryear, an old cowhand of the Texas Panhandle. The ranch had sent several cowboys to drive in a small bunch of cattle to the home ranch. They had to drive these cattle through a desert section nearly all day before reaching the ranch, and both cattle and men suffered extremely from thirst. By the time they reached the southern edge of the ranch where there was a surface tank, the cattle were frantic and the men's tongues were swollen. When the cattle smelled the water of the tank they made a run for it, and the men followed.

Bud rode right in among the cattle, lay down on his belly, and stuck his muzzle in the water. The other boys had ridden over to the other side where the water wasn't muddied.

"Hey, Bud!" one of them yelled over, "Why don't you come over here where the water's clear?"

"Hell," answered Bud, "what difference does it make? I'm goin' to drink it all anyway."

The early West was a man's country. Until it became more settled, range calico was as scarce as sunflowers on a Christmas tree. This scarcity of women made her kind of awesome to the cowboy and he looked upon her as being something holy and plumb precious.

In later years more married men came out to the range, bringing their families. If there was a pretty daughter the whole range would soon be suffering with Cupid's cramp, and some favored puncher would be calling on her as regular as a goose goes barefooted. The fewness of women didn't lessen a cowhand's wish to go courting.

That naked little runt with the bow and arrow we call Cupid could surely booger up a peeler. Once he was shot with that weapon he started camping on the trail of some filly until he'd slapped his brand on her and had her tied to the snortin' post, or she had him walking the fence.

When the nesters began drifting into the cattle country, some of them would bring a daughter pretty as a painted wagon. It didn't take a cowhand long to find out where she lived. He'd find some excuse to ride over her way and somehow every time he'd ride by he'd develop a burning thirst and stop to ask for water. No matter how gyppy it was, he'd drink it like it was nectar. When he looked into her eyes over the rim of that tin dipper and found 'em soft and leathery as blackstrap molasses poured onto a tin plate, he'd take to her like honeysuckle to a front porch.

Her old man was usually kind of religious and didn't like cowboys. They drank and gambled, were wild and quick to fight, and spent their money as free and easy as suicide. But the daughter found them more attractive than the sodbusting boys. She liked their jingling spurs, their gaudy dress, their broad grin and free-heartedness. When a nester boy came a-courting he thought he was a sport when he bought her a ten-cent bag of gumdrops. The cow-hand brought her the biggest box of candy he could find in town, and apologized because he couldn't find a bigger one. Anyway, a riding man has always been more romantic than a man on foot.

As the West became more settled, wisdom-bringers, or school teachers, were imported to teach the range yearlings their three R's. Some of them were from the East, educated to a feather edge, and as full of information as a mail-order catalogue. Being soft and pretty as a young calf's ear, they never lacked a good saddle horse and a willing escort to ride home with them. Some admiring puncher just happened by with an extra horse or in a buckboard as school was turning out.

Sometimes she had left her heart back East and was as aloof as a mountain sheep. A cowhand didn't have any more show with her kind than a stump-tailed bull in fly time. But it often happened that she fell for one of those bowlegged range riders. If she did, he wasn't long in mortgaging his here and hereafter for the papers necessary to file a permanent claim on her affections, and hunting a sky-pilot to weld him to the neck yoke.

Many an old alkali became dissatisfied with the boar's nest he'd been living in when some filly cut his trail. Most unmarried men are as homeless as a poker chip. Some of them would like to settle down and stay in one place until they rust, but nearly all cowmen are skittish of widows, both grass and sod. It was the voice of experience against the amateur. Some of those widows might have a short rope, but they sure threw a wide loop. Once she had gotten a man in her trap you couldn't turn her any more than you could a runaway hog.

The grass widow was a dangerous critter. Being of the grass

variety didn't mean she was letting any of it grow under her feet. When she adjusted her sights for a poor male she didn't seem to have any trouble getting a rake to gather her hay crop.

The *Heart and Hand* woman was another who sometimes came west to shake her rope at some lonely batch. She got his name from that old magazine put out by a matrimonial agency. Some love-hungry cowboy'd get a copy through the mail and read it with a lot of interest—that is, those who could read. His simple soul believed all those descriptions. Hell, wasn't it printed? He didn't believe you could print anything that wasn't the truth.

Sometimes he started a letter of courtship with one of these catalogue widows who wanted her weeds plowed under. Maybe it started out of curiosity, to pass the time and learn the news from the outside, or just for a joke. But he often found out too late that he'd put a spoke in his wheel, and some gal was on her way out, ready to surrender like a willow to the wind. He'd find himself driving a buckboard fifty miles to the railroad station to meet a lady love he'd really never intended seeing him in his home corral. He knew such a wife was a gamble, but the suspense was what fascinated him.

There was always that thrill of expectancy, like opening a box of crackerjack to see what prize was inside. Those prizes usually turned out to be something you wouldn't want if you had seen them first, like a little wooden whistle or some such gadget. The chances were when this catalogue woman stepped off the train the photograph she'd sent didn't show up all the blemishes, and she'd forgot to tell him that she owned enough kids to start a public school. Maybe she had a face built for a hackamore and wasn't anything for a drinking man to look at, but, as a rule, he wasn't any parlor ornament either.

You shouldn't get the impression that he was like those television cowboys who spend all their time in town. True—after weeks on the trail, fed up with the dangerous, monotonous work and their own company—the boys were pretty apt to be on edge and in search of what excitement and good times the town offered. As the night wore on and the liquor began to take hold they were more than likely to resent the authority of some marshal. Being young, healthy, and reckless cusses, they proceeded to get noisier than a Mexican revolution until they were a thorn in the marshal's shortribs. The law never knew whether they were going to fight or frolic, sing or shoot. More than likely the marshal kept behind cover until things got out of hand, for he had no craving to be fingering music out of a harp.

At the bar, the first thing the cowhand did was plant his boot heel on the brass rail like he intended it to take root. After asking the aproned man on the sober side to set out a bottle, he proceeded to lap up liquor like a fired cowhand. He didn't have an educated thirst that called for bottles with pretty labels and silver foiled bonnets on 'em, and he didn't have any truck with drinks that called for olives or red cherries or fizz water. And he sure didn't waste any ice putting it in the drinks to weaken the whisky. He'd never do that.

Using his rope arm to hoist a glass, the newly arrived cowhand proceeded to take the first layer off his tonsils and let his weakness for booze run wild. Sooner or later he zigzagged off to the next saloon looking like somebody had stolen his rudder. Feeling his way along the buildings like his legs were a burden, he wondered why these buildings didn't stay put and why they had never thought to build those board walks wider. To watch him, you'd have thought walking was a lost art.

Though most cowhands drank when they hit town, some of them were regular walking whisky vats, and could hold more liquor than a gopher hole. But there were others like watched Puritans who stayed sober as a muley cow. Others just took enough joy juice to get a talking load. If their tongues did get too thick to talk they resorted to sign language, but they stayed as peaceful as a church. Drinking was a means of relaxing from a season of hard, dusty, and dangerous work, and it gave them a chance to blow off steam. Most of them drank in the spirit of fun and for a friendly get-together with others of their breed.

The next morning a cowhand was apt to feel like the frazzled end of a misspent life, and had one of those headaches built for a horse. His head felt so big he wouldn't bet he could crowd it into a corral. He usually had a brindle taste in his mouth like he'd had supper with a coyote, and felt like going out and burying his teeth on the prairie.

But don't think he spent all his time like this. He had to sweat a little to stay on the payroll. He had to ride something besides a brass rail, and he had to accomplish something besides filling a flush or a full-house. Life was something besides blood, bullets, and bar-rooms. Town was a mighty poor place for a man of his small finances, and where there were no cows to punch his credit soon ran out. After the gamblers got through with him all he had left was something to talk about.

Sure, he wanted to have his fun before that old fellow with the hay hook came along, but he had to do a lot of work between times. From seeing too many television westerns some folks get the idea that he was the kind to take a long squint at the sun and a quick squat in the shade. They get the idea he was so lazy he had to lean against a building to spit, but he wasn't the kind that had nothing to do all day except sit around on his one-spot. When he was sitting on the south side of his pants, he was in the saddle doing the work he was hired to do.

I'm not trying to make a hero of the old-time cowhand, but I want to show some of his virtues, too. Maybe I've waited too long, for they say it's only after a man's dead that folks dig up a lot of virtues to pin on him. Some folks think that he was a double-dyed villain with an everlasting thirst and a finger with the trigger itch. He had his faults, but in my opinion his virtues outnumbered these, and for sure we will never see his like again on the American scene.

I hope that you have enjoyed these highlights from my book *The Old-Time Cowhand*. The book itself was written in the vernacular in an attempt to preserve the cowhand's lingo, but for your educated ears this paper has been put into more sophisticated grammar. Yet, you should now have a little better picture of the working cowboy.

Let me say in closing that I have been interested in the cowboy and his lingo for more than sixty years—way back, as the cowboy would say, since I was "fryin' size." My real interest probably started when Jim Houston, a typical Texas cowboy, told a group of other cowmen, into which I had poked my young ears, of the time he had a narrow escape from a cow on the prod while he was afoot in a branding pen:

"There's no love-light in that cow's eyes as she makes for me," said Jim. "I fogs it across that corral like I'm goin' to a dance, an' she's a-scratchin' the grease off my pants at ever' jump. Seein' I can't make the fence in time, Brazos Gowdy jumps down off the fence an' throws his hat in the old gal's face. Seein' a cowboy come apart in pieces like that makes her hesitate till I climb the fence without losin' anything more'n some confidence, a lot o' wind, and a little dignity. You can take it from me, a cow with a fresh-branded calf might be a mother, but she shore ain't no *lady*."

The Modern Cowboy—An Image

CLIFFORD P. WESTERMEIER
University of Arkansas

The story of the old-time cowboy during his brief reign of two decades, 1865 to 1885, has been well recorded. But how can one account for his phenomenal rise as an adventurous and romantic figure and the continuance of this concept for more than three quarters of a century? Certainly, if it had been left to the cowboy to carve his niche for immortality and to chronicle his story, our roundup would have been mighty slim.

Simply stated, the old-time cowboy was a product of a big-time frontier business—the cattle industry. However, the present image of him came, for the most part, from the pen of the frontier journalist who made him known to the nation. As this image appeared in periodicals and newspapers, the readers demanded more; then, at the close of the nineteenth century, a new note crept into the reporting. For the journalist had witnessed the change in the cow country—the influx of farmers, the breakup of the range, the rise of towns, the collapse of the range cattle industry—and he predicted the passing of the cowboy.[1]

Thus, at the peak of his career, the old-time cowboy was dismissed by the frontier journalist. But this image, this hero, was no legendary one to be consigned only to the realm of folklore, and in the minds of his admirers the man on horseback did not ride into the sunset.[2]

The cowboy had emerged as a hero. Essential to the creation of a hero are his noble qualities but, more important, hero worshippers, and, as in "days of old when knights were bold," the admirers not only publicized the hero but, in addition, fabricated myths around him. In the twentieth century the hero worshippers, or "troubadours" if you will, are—according to Mody C. Boatright—journalists, novelists, biographers, script writers, and historians. The written and spoken word, visual images, and sound effects are their media; newspapers, magazines, books, motion pictures, radio, and television are their instruments.[3]

In 1885, there appeared in print *A Texas Cowboy*, an autobiography by Charles A. Siringo, which heightened interest in, and admiration for, the hero of the West. Furthermore, the climate was congenial for the birth of a folk hero. The Wild West Shows of Buffalo Bill, Pawnee Bill, and Charlie Meadows all featured the cowboy. As agriculture steadily gained ground in the nineties, county fairs and agricultural exhibits featured cowboy contests, which continued in popularity.[4]

Furthermore, the works of W. S. James (1893), Emerson Hough (1897), and Andy Adams (1903) strengthened the hold of the cowboy on his admirers. Although Owen Wister had said in *The Virginian* (1902), "[the cowboy] will never come again. He rides in his historic yesterday,"[5] the book still has wide circulation, and its immortalized hero still gallops over motion picture and television screens.[6] Two decades later, *The Cowboy* (1922), a monumental volume by Philip A. Rollins, joined the classics of Adams and Hough. And then the literary roundup began, with reminiscences and contemporary observations on one hand and scholarly research on the other—a split-level image wherein the cowboy of the "historic yesterday" is kept alive. This, in turn, has been bolstered by a passionate desire on the part of Americans to cherish the virile and adventuresome aspects of the Old West.[7]

The main objective of this paper is to point out that the cowboy, whether old-time or modern (with emphasis on the modern), whether of the range, ranch, rodeo, or motion picture, continues to be the center of interest in so much of our literature and entertainment because he was, and is, the product of big business—the cattle industry, motion pictures, radio, television, advertising, and journalism—all resulting in an image, greatly exploited and overexposed.[8]

We must grant that as long as there is a cattle industry in the United States there will be cowboys to do the work involved. True, the lone-riding, six-shooting, town-painting cowboy of myth and reality has disappeared, along with the long trail drives, stampedes, endless months of isolation, and the open range. Our highly technical age has alleviated the conditions of life and work in the cow country. The present-day cowboy may go to town in a fast-speeding car over improved roads and superhighways, or he may sit in an up-to-date bunk house and let the "one-eyed monster" mesmerize him with endless portrayals of his predecessors.[9]

The popular literature of the last two decades reveals that the work of the modern ranch cowboy has been tempered by the signs of progress in the twentieth century[10]—jeeps, airplanes, helicopters, foam-rubber-cushioned saddles, battery-charged prods, and belly-dragging, high-quality cattle. Nevertheless, the men are active in the art of "cowboying," and, as earlier, there are journalists who mourn the passing of the cowboy.[11]

David Brinkley, the NBC news commentator, recently devoted fifteen minutes of his half-hour television program to the life of the modern ranch cowboy. The program was filmed on the 200,000-acre Kendrick ranch in northern Wyoming and supports the common knowledge that the work of the cowboy is violent, hard, dangerous, hot, and dirty—even in 1962.

The old cowboy cook of the outfit prepared three meals a day—all consisting of beef, beans, and potatoes, dished up at 3:00 A.M., 9:30 A.M., and 6:00 P.M. Asked what he did when he had time off, he replied, "I git to town—git drunk—an' throw a wingding!" According to this old hand, the modern cowboys have "too much rodeo stuff in 'em today."[12]

Doug Douglas, a twenty-three-year-old cowboy on this ranch, who began working at fifteen at a salary of $90 a month, plus room and board, is now earning $150. He spends fourteen hours a day in the saddle, riding approximately forty miles; his excursions to town include drinking beer, watching television, and eating chicken. According to him, most of the modern cowboys are natives of the range country, and some seldom go beyond 200 miles from home. "I've seen a lot of sorry Hollywood Western movies" was his comment regarding his impressions of western film fare.[13]

Obviously, a program of this calibre plants an almost ineradicable image in the minds of the millions of viewers, regardless of the norm. "The only people Brinkley has ever presented as heroic in his weekly series are the American cowboys who work a seven-day, 100-hour week for wages that 'would make a union business agent cry like a baby' and who leave the world as devoid of personal wealth as when they enter it."[14] Brinkley is a crusader against "the pressure of conformity" and says that cowboys "instead of togetherness, demand personal freedom."[15]

This modern cowboy does not differ from his predecessor in matching his skills with men of another outfit, but he does more of it. Today, instead of waiting until the big western holiday, the Fourth of July, a cowboy may engage in several competitions within riding distance (meaning, of course, by car—usually air-conditioned—and horse trailer) from the home base. And, he may be so successful that he will give up nursing cattle and become a rodeo cowboy, aiming to have a "spread of his own," once the competitive fever cools.[16] The old-time cowboy sought a good string of ponies from the *remuda* for his use—and he appreciated good food and drink, and a "sweet smellin' gal," as is evidenced by his brief and often explosive visits to town. The fact that his chroniclers perpetuate the hardships of his life does not mean that he would not have accepted more comforts if they had been available.[17]

As for the man himself, a cowboy is a cowboy. Changes in the way of life and work in the cattle industry itself do not permit a just comparison;[18] however, the modern cowboy is often more of a westerner than his predecessor, who came from all parts of the United States and, in some instances, from Europe. If this was the origin of the old-time cowboy, why should it seem unusual that the modern cowboy hails from New Jersey, Pennsylvania, or Florida?[19]

For example, almost a hundred years ago, on the Fourth of July 1869, Emilnie Gardenshire, of the Mill Iron Ranch, rode Montana Blizzard from the Hashknife Ranch at an inter-camp cowboy competition in Deer Trail, Colorado, and won the title "Champion Bronco Buster of the Plains" and a suit of clothes as a prize. This cowboy was an Englishman![20]

More recently, Harry Tompkins, five times World Champion Bull Rider (1948, 1949, 1950, 1952, and 1960) and World Champion Bareback Rider (1952) hails from Peekskill, New York.[21] Pete Knight, one of rodeo's greats, from Philadelphia, was four times World Champion Saddle Bronc Rider (1932, 1933, 1935, and 1936) and outright winner of the famous Prince of Wales Trophy.[22] Jim Shoulders, holder of the largest number of world championship titles, is a city boy—a native of Tulsa, Oklahoma, who, as a fifteen-year-old high school youngster, entered his first rodeo at Oilton, Oklahoma.[23]

The rugged aspects of the range cattle industry were in evidence in the nation-wide publicity on the trail drive of last January, in South Dakota, when rancher Don Hight, ex-paratrooper of World War II and ex-rodeo cowboy, trailed his herd seventy miles from his ranch near White River to Winner.

In the old days this would have been just a normal event on the range, but midway in the twentieth century it was news via every means of communication. By noon of the fourth day, following severe blizzard conditions, U. S. Highway 183 (17 miles from Winner) was lined with ranchers, townspeople, and out-of-state sightseers to view the herd at the point of crossing. As the 1,800 head of cattle appeared, portable television units, photographers, and reporters were on hand to record for the world the story of a cowboy in trouble.[24]

But, in order to complete the image of the modern cowboy, one must look on the other side of the coin, which represents him as he is best known to millions of admirers through the media of mass communications. The cowboy, old-time or modern, is, let me repeat, the product of big business—whether it was, and is, the cattle industry or the various areas of entertainment.[25]

The cowboy has been an entertainer and sportsman from his very beginning. The inter-camp contests were local sports events; his appearance in the Wild West Shows proved him to be a daredevil performer. The community and pioneer celebrations of the early twentieth century—Cowboy Tournaments, Frontier Days, Cowboy Reunions, Roundups, Stampedes, Pow-wows, and finally the Rodeos—are all classic examples of the cowboy in this capacity.[26]

With the great tourist migrations to the West following World War I, practically every western community with a semblance of historical background began to celebrate some occasion or other. By the late 1920's and the early 1930's, cowboy contests reached from Madison Square Garden in New York City to the towns and cities across the country to cowboy-conscious California. Rodeo and the rodeo cowboy were here to stay.[27]

This cowboy soon became aware of his hold on the American public, and gradually a plan of organization was developed. In 1929, because of inherent weaknesses in rodeo concerning advertising, prize money, judging, and lack of standards, the managements of several leading contests formed the Rodeo Association of America.[28] Because this organization was not represented at all rodeos and because the cowboys were professional contestants, they boldly aimed for further protection, and in 1936, at the Boston Garden Rodeo, went on strike until their demands for larger purses and added entrance fees were met.[29] This group, the Cowboys' Turtle Association, was the predecessor of the Rodeo Cowboys' Association (R.C.A.) of today, [30] which has an official publication, *Rodeo Sports News*,[31] and a Rodeo Information Commission for press and public relations affairs.[32] All this is a far cry from

29

the Fourth of July 1869 cowboy contest at Deer Trail, Colorado, or from the Rough Riders Reunion, in 1899, at Las Vegas, New Mexico,[33] but so are the astronauts from the Wright brothers.

Rodeo is big business. In 1955, according to the Rodeo Cowboys' Association, more than 3,000 cowboys competed for $2,-829,984 in purses and entry fees in 421 R. C. A.-approved rodeos in 35 states and Canada.[34] In 1961, the rodeo records show $3,013,213 in purses and entry fees in 542 rodeos in 37 states and Canada.[35] The annual average number of paying spectators is estimated at 14 million.[36] Financially, all communities, both large and small, do very well in their promotion of this cowboy sport. The annual Cheyenne Frontier Days Rodeo in Wyoming brings in approximately $2,000,000. Gate receipts are estimated at $200,000, or ten per cent of the total amount spent by rodeo fans during the five-day period.[37]

In December 1959, the First National Finals Rodeo was held in Dallas, Texas, and offered the largest five-day rodeo purse, of $50,000, plus entry fees of $100 per event. The top fifteen contestants in each of the seven regulation events were candidates for this "Rodeo World Series," which, with much fanfare, was another bid for recognition of the profession as a sport in a sport-conscious country.[38] Earlier, in the 1930's and 1940's, efforts had been made to attract the sports world's attention, but only a modicum of success was achieved.[39]

Rodeo abroad is not new. In 1925 a contest was featured at the British Empire Exposition and again in 1934.[40] Furthermore, the American cowboy, as a member of the armed forces, carried with him the spirit of his occupation and the "soldier-cowboys" staged contests in France, Italy, India, and China, on Okinawa and Guam, and in Hawaii.[41] More recently, exhibition rodeos have been held in Venezuela, France, Switzerland, Mexico, Cuba, and at the World's Fair in Brussels in 1958.[42]

What about the average rodeo cowboy? Too often attention is focused on the successful individual—the man who makes the grade. For example, Jim Shoulders is, as yet, the biggest money winner in any one year—$43,381 in 1956;[43] Casey Tibbs won $42,065 in 1955;[44] Benny Reynolds, $31,309 in 1961.[45] But what about just plain "ole Smokey Joe"—the average rodeo cowboy? Actually, there is no such individual. The rodeo cowboy cannot be tied down to statistics, for he is an individual and continues to remain so under all circumstances.[46]

Many contestants are successful and make a satisfactory livelihood on a year-round basis. A comparison of their expenses is so varied that an average figure is impossible. The contestant who does not travel far and works events that require little equipment and no horses, such as the bronc and bull riding contests, may win only half as much as the man who must haul horses for bulldogging or calf roping, but his net winnings may be higher. Some men have their own ranches or are engaged in allied occupations and contest only part of the year; however, they could probably make a living by contesting alone.

The largest group includes those who depend entirely upon rodeo in its various phases and consists of both old-timers and newcomers. In addition to contesting, they work as stock contractors, rodeo producers, and at the numerous jobs associated with rodeo, such as stock men, pickup men, judges, arena managers, and the like. These combined efforts sustain them at various financial levels.

Of course, there are many young hopefuls on the fringe of the profession. They lack experience, they do not win consistently, and they are unable to get paying rodeo jobs because of their limitations. Frequently, they eke out their existence by teaming up for traveling, by sharing expenses and splitting winnings, and by much borrowing and begging to keep going. They live on the hope that they have what it takes to become "big time."[47]

The most notable feature of rodeo is the lack of enough prize money, even with entry fees added, to go around. Of the $3,013,213 in winnings in 1961, $1,461,715 was the amount of entrance fees paid by the contestants—almost one-half of the grand total.[48] Since rodeo is highly competitive, the Rodeo Cowboys' Association expects that this problem will continue and, as approved rodeos in various communities become more successful financially, it constantly makes a plea for more prize money. The R. C. A. does not assure *every* rodeo cowboy of a living in professional rodeo; it is the individual contestant who wins, and for each winner there must be several losers.[49]

The growing interest in rodeo on the part of young America during the past twenty-five years should dispel any fear that this sport will die out in the future.[50] Today, the American Junior Rodeo Association[51] and the National Intercollegiate Rodeo Association[52] make it possible for teenagers and collegians to get an early start in rodeo. Furthermore, innumerable other organizations are interested in and devoted to rodeo—both on the amateur and the semi-pro levels.[53]

Recently, a number of "training schools" in various rodeo events have been established by some of the best rodeo professionals and are proving to be a success.[54] Thus, a new breed of performers is developing, who with this basic training and participation in local or state amateur contests assure rodeo of an even more promising future.

So far, we have been concerned with the modern cowboy and his continuance of the actual work and sport of the old-time cowboy. But far more important is the overexposed image of this American hero which, through all forms of communications, has been deeply entrenched in the hearts of his worshippers.

The "six-gun Galahads"[55] who appeared early in this century and their persistence in western story, on motion picture screen, radio, and television provide the source for much comment and speculation on the part of psychologists, sociologists, and some historians.[56] Since the introduction of Broncho Billy Anderson as the first of the great horse-opera heroes in "The Great Train Robbery" (1903), there has been a long list of "Perseus' of the purple sage."[57] William S. Hart followed in Anderson's tracks; then came Tom Mix, "who looked like a mail-order cowboy, but was a genuine rough-string rider"[58]—after much practice, it might be added.[59] Both Tom Mix and Will Rogers were members of the "Wild Bunch" from Miller's 101 Ranch outfit.[60]

Art Acord, Buck Jones, Jack Hoxie, Hoot Gibson, Tim McCoy, Ken Maynard, Fred Thompson, Harry Carey, and Bill Boyd were the forerunners of John Wayne, Randolph Scott, Gary Cooper, Ward Bond, Chuck Connors, Clint Walker, Dale Robinson, Robert Fuller, and, may God forgive us, the strummin', hummin' cowboys, Gene Autry and Roy Rogers.[61] Some of these men had western backgrounds; others were cowboy entertainers and contestants in Wild West Shows and early cowboy competitions; still others are from television's "beef trusts," but all are fabrications of publicity departments,[62] which, like the skalds of old, embellish and exaggerate the prowess of the hero with each recital of the saga.

Among hundreds of western motion picture films, only a few deal with the cowboy, his work, and his problems. Of these, "Red River," "Shane," "Cowboy," "Bus Stop," and "Lonely Are The Brave" are worth mentioning. The latter film was recently adapted from an obscure book, *The Brave Cowboy*, by Edward Abbey.[63]

The theme concerns a weatherbeaten cowboy who rebels against progress and conformity. In his attempt for survival, he and his horse meet death on a much-traveled highway, but "the symbolic question is clear: Is the untamed free spirit an outlaw that must learn to toe the white lines of the modern world or perish?"[64] In striking contrast is "The Lusty Men," an RKO film about hell-raising and hard-drinking rodeo cowboys, which features more sex-play than horse-play.[65]

Since January 1953, professional rodeos have been televised, and annually several outstanding contests have brought the sport to an estimated audience upward of 20 million for each telecast.[66] Furthermore, rodeo has been the theme of episodes on such weekly programs as "Bus Stop," "Dr. Kildare," "Route 66," and "Check-mate."[67]

This overexposed image of the cowboy as the hero of the West has spread far beyond our shores. Particularly in Germany, long before the advent of films portraying *"die wilde West,"* translations of the works of Cooper and London had a firm hold on the reading public.[68]

The most lasting influence, however, still strongly evident after a century of existence, was created by the *Winnetou* series of Karl May (1842-1912), a prolific writer, who depicted the opening of the frontier without ever having been to this country. Winnetou is a legendary Apache Indian chief whose adventures take him to Colorado, New Mexico, and Wyoming, and Old Shatterhand is the typical cowboy hero who fights against and, of course, wins over evil.[69]

For the past ten years an annual Karl May festival has been held in Germany, attracting more than 800,000 cowboy and Indian fans. *Time* magazine reported on the 1962 festival under the caption "Schnell on the Draw":[70]

> Ten thousand Germans were in their places in Bad Segeberg's outdoor amphitheater . . . to see Old Shatterhand make his grand appearance. Shatterhand slithered down a sheer rock wall and armed only with moral courage set out to defeat Brave Buffalo, chief of the Shoshone. In the end, it was no surprise that Old Shatterhand had triumphed again, and no surprise that the leader of the bad guys fell into a geyser and was parboiled.

Time does not permit us to follow this cowboy craze abroad, where the word "cowboy" falls from every tongue. The fad for levis, boots, and cowboy hats and holsters is evident everywhere, as are also western films both home-produced and *a la* Hollywood. Cowboy clubs are very popular, such as the "Arizona Boys" in Munich, Germany (1935)[71] and the *Club Hippique du Lasso* in Paris (1905).[72] Japan has made its own westerns and views twenty American western serials on television;[73] Finland, on the facade of a school in Helsinki, immortalizes the cowboy as representative of America in a huge world-mosaic.[74]

Thus, the cowboy in a variegated image—old or new, ranch, rodeo, dude, or entertainer, true to form or highly exaggerated—is here to stay.

But what is there about him that makes a halo of his Stetson and a dragon-slaying sword of his six-shooter? The West had other heroes with traits just as admirable—the explorer, the trapper, the prospector, the homesteader—all of whom laid the toil of their hands on its altar and, unassumingly, took their place among its children. Why in this age of space and urbanized society does the cowboy still have that magic hold on millions, both young and old, as is evidenced in the numerous riding clubs, posses, dude ranches, and western outfits which give his admirers an opportunity to give vent to the feeling of adventure?

It is quite possible that this "something" is not any particular trait nor a combination of several, but is rather his trusted companion—his horse. For, among our forebears, it was the horse that lifted man into the realm of the demi-gods or heroes. The Knights of the Round Table, the Paladins of Charlemagne, the Crusaders—all ride before us on their charging steeds. And so now, centuries later, in a highly mechanized world, those avid followers of America's favorite hero seek the sense of the living moment and the feeling of affinity which a rider has when his hands are on the rein and he sits firm in the saddle.

Whether the horse or the cowboy is king, we must admit that they have been, and will continue to be, inseparable. Perhaps Goethe, the great German poet (1749-1832), had this in mind when he wrote: "God created the horse as comrade of the wind and companion to the storm, to carry man wherever he wills,"[75] and more than a century later, Paul Coze, a French author, summed it all up in a few words, more aptly fitted to the modern age: *"Sans cheval, pas de cowboy* [without a horse, no cowboy]."[76]

34

THE GREAT SURVEYS—

PROBING THE WEST

The Wheeler Surveys and the Decline

of Army Exploration in the West

WILLIAM H. GOETZMANN
Yale University

According to American tradition, the civil authorities always take precedence over the military; the individual citizen is more important than the military establishment. One can hardly quarrel with this principle as a statement of value, stemming as it does from a long-standing republican aversion to the aristocratic military despotisms of Europe. But the very persuasiveness of this principle has done much to obscure the important role played by the United States Army in our history, and especially has it tended to prevent an accurate assessment of that role. Nowhere is this more evident than in the histories of the American West, where the stereotype of the "Indian-fighting Army" has prevailed over all attempts to assess the Army's more constructive role in the development of the West.

This paper, therefore, concentrates on a less flamboyant and bellicose soldier, one who was not part of the "Indian-fighting army," Lt. George Montague Wheeler, who despite his great labors in the West died in 1905 virtually unnoticed, even by the *Army and Navy Journal.*[1] In focusing upon Wheeler and his story to the exclusion of the many other soldiers[2] who operated beyond the Mississippi after the Civil War, this paper stresses a constructive aspect of Army work in the West and suggests that it was a vital part of what might be called the nineteenth-century American imperialistic experience. As a functioning part of the administrative apparatus for the recently subdued domain, Wheeler's views and those of the Engineer Office represent one of the varieties of imperialistic experience that has perhaps gone too long unnoticed.

The whole historical episode represented by the rise and fall of the Wheeler surveys also illustrates clearly a fact often overlooked by regional historians: the West did not grow up in isolation. It was always closely related to the rest of the nation and of deep concern to people in other parts of the Union. An examination of this concern, along with a brief description and assessment of the Wheeler surveys, is the purpose of this paper.

Wheeler began his career at an inopportune time. He belonged to an earlier generation of Army explorers who, from the time of Zebulon Pike down to the Civil War, explored and mapped the Far West.[3] He might have been as famous as Frémont the Pathfinder, but he was born a generation too late, in Hopkinton, Massachusetts, in 1842—the year of the Pathfinder's first dramatic trip to the Rocky Mountains. And he began his work in the West just as John Wesley Powell was completing his voyage through the last unexplored region of the West, the canyons of the Colorado and the "Plateau Province" of Utah and Arizona.

When Wheeler graduated in 1866 from West Point, where he had spent the war as a cadet, he was a newly minted second lieutenant at a time when experienced officers were the most common commodity on the national labor market.[4] Thus as a soldier he was one among many, and as an explorer he was born a generation too late.

In spite of these odds, Wheeler did become a soldier and an explorer. Certainly he was an explorer in the technical sense of the word—which means "one who *seeks* discoveries"[5]—even though his wilderness marches were frequently in the wake rather than in the van of previous excursions. He sought, or was perhaps forced to seek, his discoveries in the less obvious and more esoteric realms of science and public policy as they were related to what he saw in the West.

As a new second lieutenant, he was assigned to General E. O. C. Ord's command in California. In 1869, he got his first independent assignment as an explorer. He led an expedition southward from Camp Halleck, Nevada (near Halleck on the Central Pacific Railroad), along the eastern boundary of Nevada, to the Mormon settlements near present-day Las Vegas in the southern part of the new state.[6] He was in search of a military road over which troops could be transported from the Central Pacific line to posts in Nevada and Arizona.

But when he marched southward at the head of his picturesque train of cavalry, engineers, surveyors, canvas-topped wagons, and the curious one-wheeled odometer vehicles that looked like old-fashioned spinning wheels being pulled by horses across the desert,[7] he was really following in the wake of, and assisting, the latest mineral rush, which had brought miners by the droves eastward from Washoe into central Nevada in 1868.

Charged with extending the protection of the Federal Government over these prospectors and pioneers, Wheeler was on the lookout for hostile Indians and points at which forts or outposts might be built. He was also under orders to make a general resource survey of the whole area, including especially the mineral sites and mining camps. In his spare time he was to complete an accurate topographic map of southern Nevada. Thus, from the outset of his career Wheeler's work was to have a broad significance that was as much civil as military.

His first reconnaissance was a grueling one that took him five months, or until the end of November 1869. When he finished, he had completed the first important north-south traverse of the Great Basin since the fur trade days of Peter Skene Ogden, and he had reached the Colorado River at Callville not long after Powell had ended his epic canyon voyage at that point; thus Wheeler and Powell arrived in the "Plateau Province" almost simultaneously. Along the way, too, Wheeler paused in eastern Nevada, and in a modest gesture assured himself of immortality the first time out by naming the most prominent peak in that region Wheeler Peak.

But even this was not enough to gain him the kind of sudden fame that Frémont and others had obtained before the war. Competition in the field of exploration was stiff. During that same year (1869) Clarence King, also operating under the War Department, extended his Fortieth Parallel Surveys along the line of the transcontinental railroad east of the Wasatch Mountains, and virtually completed the whole survey along that line from Washoe to the Rockies.[8] And, because he was primarily interested in mining, King produced results that had some direct value for prospectors and speculators.

In 1870, J. D. Hague, geologist of the King surveys, compiled his important work, *The Mining Industry*, based on a series of studies of the Comstock Lode and other Nevada mines.[9] By 1869, too, the experienced geologist F. V. Hayden had shifted his work from Nebraska and Wyoming to Colorado and the Salt Lake Valley of Utah.[10] By 1873 he managed to secure his own geological empire, "The United States Geological Surveys of the Territories," under the direction, not of the War Department, but of the Interior Department. Then too, in 1870, Powell was able to secure backing for a land reconnaissance of the "Plateau Province" from Salt Lake City to the Colorado River. And in 1871, after another voyage down the river, he began his topographical and geological work in a thoroughly scientific and large-scale manner.[11]

With so much competition it is still somewhat of a mystery just how Wheeler managed to parlay his reconnaissance of 1869 into the large-scale survey operation he later commanded. He did not take the field at all in 1870, thereby losing priority to Powell in the "Plateau Province," and when in 1871 he once more took to the field he had been thoroughly "scooped."

Though it is impossible to be certain, it seems clear from small pieces of evidence that Wheeler owed his rise to several factors. First, though the King survey was Army sponsored, it consisted entirely of civilians. This rankled such officers of the Regular Army as General A. A. Humphreys, Chief of Engineers, who recalled the proud prewar tradition of the Topographical Corps. They regarded western exploration as their own prerogative, especially because it was one of the few paths to fame in the peacetime Army.

Secondly, Wheeler was able to capitalize on the backing of the scientists who supported King on a *quid pro quo* basis, as his correspondence with King's patron, Professor O. C. Marsh of Yale, clearly indicates.[12] These two factors, plus the real need for military information about the Southwest—where Apaches, Navajos, Utes, and Paiutes were as yet unsubdued—were enough to place Wheeler, scarcely thirty years of age in 1872, at the head of his own elaborate bureau, "The United States Geographical Surveys West of the 100th Meridian."

Contributing also to his early success was his spectacular expedition of 1871, which included, besides a survey of central Nevada, the repeated crossing and mapping of Death Valley; and a harrowing boat trip up the Colorado River from Black Canyon to Diamond Creek, where he and his men emerged from the river in a state of complete exhaustion and near starvation.[13] Along with Wheeler's party on this expedition was Tim O'Sullivan, whose photographs, made with cumbersome wet-plate cameras, were a spectacular introduction to the fantastic landscape of the basin, range, and canyon country.

And, even more important, that year Wheeler introduced one of the greatest of all American geologists, Grove Karl Gilbert, to the barren, lake-bed landscapes of the Great Basin. Building on this experience, Gilbert was able to compose his classic treatise on the prehistoric Lake Bonneville. Though others before him— notably Capt. Howard Stansbury in 1850, Henry Engelmann on Capt. James H. Simpson's expedition of 1859, and Clarence King— had surmised that the Great Basin was an enormous ancient lake bed, it was left to Gilbert to demonstrate this scientifically. The first seeds of this discovery were all in Wheeler's otherwise businesslike report for 1871.[14]

In his report for 1871, too, Wheeler had recognized that, as he put it, "the day of the path-finder has sensibly ended," and he proposed a broad plan for the "complete reconstruction of the engineer map of the Western Territories," which led to the creation of his surveys the following year.[15] Yet in 1872 his field operations were still largely of the pathfinding or reconnaissance variety rather than the accurate surveys of broad regions he was proposing.

Though he recognized the value of base-line and trigonometrical surveys and actually established six astronomical stations that year, his chief concern seems to have been to meet his competition by re-exploring the Colorado Plateau and Grand Canyon region. The most interesting results of this work were the photographs of Bell and the drawings of John E. Weyss, the former Mexican Boundary Survey topographer and Civil War mapmaker who accompanied the field parties. Weyss's drawings of the Grand Canyon country, such as his famous portrayal of the Crossing of the Fathers, though hardly in a class with W. H. Holmes' super-accurate studies of the same mesa and canyon country, nevertheless were impressive renditions of that remote locality, visited by Escalante nearly one hundred years before.[16]

In his prospectus for 1873, Wheeler again declared that "the time has come to change the system of examination, from that idea of exploration which seems to attach itself to a linear search for great and special wonders, to a thorough survey that shall build up from time to time, and fortify our knowledge of the structural relation of the whole."[17] What he meant was that the day of the great individual explorer like Frémont and Powell was over. But just when he actually began to lay out the entire trans-Mississippi West in ninety-four enormous mapmaker's quadrants is not clear.

As early as the summer season of 1873 he had two distinct parties in the field beginning work on a systematic trigonometrical and astronomical basis. One party, which he led personally, operated out of southern California, while the other party, commanded by Lt. W. L. Marshall, began its work from Denver, Colorado, having as its duty the survey by triangulation of Colorado south of the Union Pacific line and west of the front range.[18] But that summer, near the headwaters of the Arkansas, Lt. Marshall ran into parties of the Hayden survey, and before long four out of five of Hayden's geological field parties were operating in the Twin Lakes region.[19] Thus occurred the absurd spectacle of two sets of surveying parties, their instruments placed on the same remote mountain peaks, surveying the same wilderness territory. Congress, however, saw no humor in the situation at all.

In 1874 the Townsend Committee on Public Lands of the House of Representatives met to consider the problem of duplication in western surveys, and the clash between the Powell, Hayden, and Wheeler surveys first became a national issue. Though real evidence is lacking, the matter was probably instigated by the War Department in an effort to assert its authority over all the surveys, but the political pressure was by no means one-sided.

According to Wheeler's geologist, H. C. Yarrow, Hayden declared in 1873: "You can tell Wheeler that if he stirs a finger or attempts to interfere with me or my survey in any way I will utterly crush him—as I have enough congressional influence to do so and will bring it to bear."[20] Hayden did, indeed, have enormous influence in Congress. His letter files reveal that for several years he had been supplying members of Congress with the explorer's equivalent of the railroad pass—free sets of lavishly illustrated books, geologists' reports of value to would-be prospectors, and sets of sun pictures and stereopticon slides of the marvels of the West—enough to delight anyone's favorite nephew.[21]

Indeed, throughout the seventies the various surveys vied with one another in producing these lavish propagandistic, photographic works—for which, incidentally, the historian has reason to be thankful.[22] In this cut-throat competition between the various surveys, and in a number of other related cases, such as the bitter scrap between E. D. Cope and O. C. Marsh over old dinosaur bones, the age of the robber barons was perfectly mirrored.[23] These competing surveys, it should be stressed, were backed by important scientific and academic pressure groups, each of which had something to gain if its candidate's survey prevailed.

In the 1874 hearings, the Army was immediately put on the

defensive. Wheeler's haughty refusal to testify on matters of War Department policy did nothing to aid his cause, and his intemperate exchange with Hayden caused them both to be censured for bad manners in the committee report.[24] Moreover, most of the civilian scientists stood together against the military because they felt that the western surveys could better be staffed by their protégés than by men from West Point, to whom the civilian scientists were subordinated.[25]

Powell, deliberately picking the worst example of Wheeler's work, declared flatly that his maps were inaccurate and useless for geological purposes.[26] Hayden asserted: "There is not a single square mile of the Rocky Mountain region sufficiently accurate and in detail on the engineer maps that we could use for geological purposes."[27] And, despite Clarence King's protest, his assistant James T. Gardiner turned against his Army employers and alleged that Wheeler had "marched around and looked into but did not enter . . . great regions as large as Connecticut and Rhode Island together," forcing "a large amount of the topography" to be "left to the imagination of the draughtsman."[28]

Based on half-truths and differences of opinion, these statements were nevertheless stunning blows to Wheeler's survey. This was especially true because they were backed by a whole series of academic protest letters, the most prominent of which was one from Yale College signed by President Noah Porter, O. C. Marsh, and all the scientists except James Dwight Dana, who was under some obligation to Wheeler because he had received permission to incorporate Wheeler's researches in his new textbook on geology.[29]

In 1874, however, Wheeler mustered enough strength, possibly because he enjoyed the support of President Grant, to stave off the opposition.[30] In fact, all the surveys were left in the field stronger than ever. The Yale letter was quietly replaced by another which denied opposition to Wheeler,[31] and the Townsend Committee concluded that, though the Hayden and Powell surveys were more accurate, "there is an abundance of work for the best talent of both the War and Interior Departments in the scientific examinations of the Western Territories for many years to come." Characteristically for its time, it felt that there was a public value in encouraging unrestrained competition between the various branches of government service.[32] Perhaps, then, it was out of pure gratitude and nothing else that the following year Wheeler named a mountain peak for James G. Blaine.[33]

In response to the charges brought out in the hearings, however, Wheeler paid more attention to the latest scientific techniques in his surveys. He set up three separate astronomical observatories, including one housed in a lavish building in Ogden, Utah. He abandoned entirely the meander system based on measurement by odometers in favor of base-line and trigonometric triangulation, and he began experimenting with contour maps instead of representing topography in vague hachured sketches.

He further addressed himself to problems of settlement in the arid lands, branching out into irrigation surveys, and attempts at land classification and the redirection of settlement patterns, clearly anticipating by several years Powell's celebrated and influential *Report on the Lands of the Arid Region*, published in 1878.[34] However, in concerning himself with these matters, Wheeler was no pioneer. As far back as Kearny's Mexican War reconnaissance of 1846, Lt. William Hemsley Emory had looked at the arid Southwest and called for new settlement patterns based upon the realities of topography and water courses rather than upon the 160-acre grid pattern of the public land surveys.[35]

Each year, from 1874 on, the Wheeler surveys became more extensive, and their atlas of maps grew. In 1874, two field divisions were operating in California and Colorado.[36] Under these divisions were two and five field parties, respectively. One provided the famous paleontologist E. D. Cope with the opportunity to make his greatest discovery, the Eocene beds of northern New Mexico, in which were found distinctive remains of early mammals.[37]

In 1875, seven parties were in the field, including a special expedition operating out of Santa Barbara which made archaeological and ethnological collections for the Smithsonian Institution.[38] In 1876, Wheeler's work became more "practical," and one of the six field parties concentrated on a detailed study and map of the Comstock Lode, though King's survey had already provided this service and Dan De Quille's *Big Bonanza*, surely a more famous work, came out that same year. Another of the parties "explored" and mapped Lake Tahoe and Carson City; the survey was apparently beginning to run out of wildernesses to conquer.[39]

In 1877 and 1878, in an operation perhaps grown too elaborate for its own good, Wheeler sent *nine* parties into the field in three divisions: Colorado, California, and Utah; and his surveyors triangulated from five separate base lines, checking their results against those obtained at astronomical observatories in Ogden, Utah, in Fort Bliss, Texas, and in the Dalles in Oregon. Survey parties trekked over the entire eastern slope of the California Sierras and moved northward into Oregon, while other groups surveyed parts of Idaho, Wyoming, Colorado, Nebraska, Montana, and New Mexico.[40]

A certain sign of their waning enthusiasm for exploration, however, was evident in the decline in quality of the reports received. Lt. Symons, exploring in northern California, began one section of his report with the memorable travelogue phrase, "Bidding adieu to Rabbit Creek and its myriads of little scampering inhabitants. . . ."[41] and a journalist accompanying one of the Colorado divisions described how they all intently studied "a sprightly humming bird [which] stole among the flowers and robbed them of their honey with his dainty bill."[42]

Thus, in the spring of 1878, the House Committee on Appropriations, noting that all the western surveys were growing at a rate somewhat faster than that of Parkinson's Law, refused to vote funds for their continuation until an investigation was made as to possibilities for consolidation and condensation.[43] This was really a vote of no confidence in Wheeler's work, and it marked the beginning of the end of large-scale Army exploration in the West.

Nevertheless, as commander of the "Surveys West of the 100th Meridian," Wheeler could look back with some pride in his achievements in promoting the study and settlement of the West. He had been one of the first—though admittedly not *the* first—scientific explorers of Nevada and the "Plateau Province." His astronomical work, which involved literally thousands of observations, "ranked with the best that has ever been done," as even Powell admitted. By his own count Wheeler had supervised some twenty-five publications, including his annual reports and seven large volumes of final reports on geography, astronomy, geology, paleontology, zoology, botany, archaeology, and history.

By the time he finished he had produced some seventy-one maps, including a geological as well as a topographical atlas, seven economic or land-use maps, and special maps of the Comstock Lode and the Grand Canyon.[44] To be sure, however, many, though not all, of these maps were on too large a scale to be useful to geologists, but for military operations and for a general basis of information leading to settlement they were more than adequate. In addition to this, his artists and photographers had made some of the best of all the pictures of the old West; and the Smithsonian Institution profited richly by the 43,759 specimens of natural history received from his collecting parties.[45]

Individually, the geological work of Gilbert, the paleontological work of Cope, and the archaeological work of Cope and Loew were of first-rate importance; and the geological work of J. J. Stevenson, the zoology of Coues, and the ethnology of Yarrow were by no means unimportant. And in a modest way Wheeler himself had been a pioneer, though not an innovator, in advocating land classification and planned settlement in the West.

Nevertheless, taken altogether, the Wheeler surveys, despite his attempts to match his rivals, were essentially only a great reconnaissance reminiscent of pre-Civil War days, and as such they were clearly overshadowed by the more useful, practical, and theoretical work of scientists from other surveys who were interested in the particular and profound problems of an age of increasing specialization. Wheeler's work in the final analysis was too broad and superficial. In a tactical sense, it represented a false tunnel, one of the abandoned mine shafts of learning—a clear case for the most part of the discontinuous and the non-cumulative in science.

Though the Army continued to send out the usual scouting parties, many of which produced important results, and though it maintained an interest in Alaska, all official large-scale Army exploration ended in 1879, when the western surveys were consolidated under Clarence King, director of the United States Geological Surveys. By 1878 President Grant was gone, and the military had lost its preponderance in Washington. No western party, or so-called "land ring," wished to defend the Army surveys, though the parties likewise disapproved of the centralized and federalized geological survey.[46]

Thus times had changed, and Wheeler, his surveys, and the Army suffered a signal defeat at the hands of Powell, King, and especially King's patron, Professor O. C. Marsh, who reappeared as the head of the special committee of the National Academy of Science chosen to recommend a consolidation policy to Congress. That committee produced a report which condemned the Wheeler surveys and called for centralized civilian control of the Far West, its exploration, and indirectly its exploitation and settlement.[47]

In accordance with American tradition, the military gave way to the civil. The scientific patronage of the western surveys, though ultimately not the Land Office surveys themselves, was placed firmly in the hands of the Academy—a clear indication of the East's continuing "interest" in the West. Perhaps, as far as the Army was concerned, this was all for the best because the "starving time," when the West was but sparsely settled and the danger from Indians still necessitated the clanking cavalry escort, was over. As some of the more recent explorers' accounts were already suggesting, and perhaps as a direct result of the influence of these accounts, the day of the spa and the tourist was about to begin.[48]

John Wesley Powell and the Great Surveys:

A Problem in Historiography

RICHARD A. BARTLETT
Florida State University

A year or so ago Walt Disney released a nature-adventure film entitled "Ten Who Dared." It purported to be an authentic pictorial narration of Maj. John Wesley Powell's trip down the Green and Colorado Rivers in 1869. The one-armed major was costumed quite splendidly in what appeared to be blue denim overalls and a blue flannel shirt. After he had navigated nearly 900 miles of foaming river, his costume still looked like correct apparel for a Saturday night barn dance.

Many other incidents of the first trip down the Colorado were "re-enacted." The missteps of an alcoholic caused the wreck of the *No-Name*, which was followed by a bitter struggle over a keg of whiskey. A murder nearly resulted because of bad blood between two members of the expedition, a Yankee and an ex-Confederate. One of the members was bitten by a rattlesnake. Three others, who deserted and climbed out of the canyon, were killed by beautifully attired Indians, who were mounted on magnificent spotted ponies.

Despite the numerous historical inaccuracies, the film has grains of truth. An incident did occur involving a keg of whiskey, but no quarreling over said keg of *elixir vitae* is recorded, nor were any of the crew alcoholics. Some intense feeling did exist between certain members of the crew. And three members of the party did leave the canyon, and were killed by Indians—but by unmounted, dirty, disheveled, desert Indian slum dwellers called Shivwits, not by handsomely attired pony riders.[1]

The historian's problem is exactly the opposite of Hollywood's: truth is abundant in historical writing, but with grains of falsehood. After all, history is subject to the whims of those who write it. Historians sometimes distort the activities of men and the events of history because of personal feelings, prejudices, whims, or perhaps sheer laziness. Though these distortions do not appear on the silver screen, they do even greater damage, presenting as they do an incorrect record for future generations.

Biographies present a special problem in this regard. Although biography and history are closely related, the former has some built-in weaknesses against which the historian must ever be on guard. The biographer tends to glorify his hero, to commit the sin of omission, and he may fail to relate adequately his subject to the contemporary events of history. As a result, the subject may become the symbol of an age, or of a movement, or of a profession, when he was really no such thing. If, when the historian comes along, there already exists a personality fortunate enough to have commanded a biographer, the historian may be confronted with the unpleasant task of destroying a personality image, or at least changing it in order to present an accurate history.[2]

A case in point is the lionizing of Maj. John Wesley Powell at the expense of other explorers. The result has been an inaccurate picture of government-sponsored scientific exploration in the American West in the decade, roughly, of the 1870's. The major's image is that of a lone giant in the field. In point of fact, he and his survey had three strong rivals. Each of these rivals made contributions which should have earned for them some kind of recognition in the history of science or of the government service. Yet, if they have been mentioned at all, it has been in Powell-oriented works and in an adverse or negligible light. Their side of the power struggle which preceded the creation of the United States Geological Survey has never been adequately recorded.[3]

To better demonstrate this problem, a brief review is in order of the situation in science and western exploration in the period of the Great Surveys, from 1867 until 1879, when the U. S. Geological Survey was created and other government surveys were consolidated with it.

The first "forgotten scientist" with a "forgotten survey" was Dr. Ferdinand Vandiveer Hayden. Born in 1829 in Massachusetts, he was a teacher at sixteen and a student at Oberlin two years later. Graduating from there in 1850, he went on to Albany Medical School, but spent his leisure time learning geology from an irascible old paleontologist, James Hall.[4] Instead of establishing a medical practice when he had completed his courses, young Hayden grabbed at the opportunity to accompany the invertebrate paleontologist Fielding Bradford Meek to the White River Bad Lands of Dakota, under Hall's sponsorship.[5]

For the next thirteen years, with some time out serving the Union during the Civil War, Hayden was busy exploring the upper Missouri country. During these years, he reported his discoveries so prolifically that two or three issues of *The American Journal of Science and Arts* rarely passed by without some report from him—and that was just one of many publications which recorded his discoveries.[6]

In 1867, when nearly forty years of age, he was appointed Geologist of Nebraska, his investigations being financed with about $5,000 of unexpended federal funds, left over when Nebraska achieved statehood.[7] From this first foothold, he proceeded to advance professionally until before many years he was Geologist in Charge of the United States Geological and Geographical Survey of the Territories. He maintained offices in Washington, D.C., and gathered about him a team of highly capable men, many of whom remained loyal to him until his death.

His professional aides included his executive officer, James Stevenson, who later held the same position on the U. S. Geological Survey;[8] Henry Elliott, who later became an authority on the fur seal industry and was the author of the fur seal treaty ratified in 1911 by the United States, Japan, Russia, and Canada;[9] Henry Gannett, later a chief topographer for the U. S. Geological Survey, a statistician for the Census Bureau, and one of the six founders of the National Geographic Society;[10] James Terry Gardiner, a leading topographer and conservationist, who had worked with King on the Fortieth Parallel Survey and who in later life became director of the state survey of New York;[11] and William Henry Holmes, master topographer and later the Director of the National Collection of Fine Arts.[12]

Several leading geologists worked with Hayden, including Frederick Endlich, Archibald Marvine, A. C. Peale, C. A. White, and Orestes St. John; in botany there was John Merle Coulter; and, in entomology, W. L. Carpenter. The most capable journalist to be attached to any of the surveys, Ernest Ingersoll, accompanied Hayden,[13] as did also the most capable of the early western photographers, William Henry Jackson, whose 2,000 and more photographs and stereopticon slides helped convey to the world at large a more accurate concept of the West than that given them by the pretty lithographs of Currier and Ives.[14]

Besides the men in the field, Hayden made use of men in the laboratory and the study, sending fossils and all manner of collections and specimens to them. They in turn wrote up their findings, and Hayden, using government funds, published them under the auspices of the Hayden survey. Thus did Edward Drinker Cope, Joseph Leidy, Fielding Bradford Meek, Leo Lesquereux, J. A. Allen, Asa Gray, and a host of other quiet men of science get their work published under circumstances by which it would be available for decades to come in most parts of the world.

Most of Hayden's choices in all professional categories indicate that he was an excellent judge of men. He appears to have hired mainly on the basis of competence. Many of his men returned to him season after season, even his camp men and mule packers. The charge so often leveled against him—that he filled his ranks with political appointees—appears to be founded upon jealousy rather than fact, barely a dozen such employees being listed in the records, most of whom lasted for just one season.[15]

Having enlisted such capable men both in the field and in the laboratory, Hayden obtained annual appropriations in increasing amounts. The Hayden survey—the United States Geological and Geographical Survey of the Territories—explored the Yellowstone and contributed materially to the creation of the national park there, explored the Grand Tetons, and mapped mountainous Colorado. It discovered cliff dwellings and photographed the Mount of the Holy Cross. At a cost of about $690,000, it laid the foundations for much of our knowledge of the geology, paleontology, paleobotany, zoology, botany, entomology, and ornithology of the Rocky Mountain West.[16]

In short, the Hayden survey accomplished a phenomenal amount of scientific work.[17] Its collections and classifications of flora and fauna alone should have earned for it a place in the history of American science. But who today has ever heard of Dr. Ferdinand Vandiveer Hayden and his survey? They have been almost totally forgotten by historians, as have also the achievements of the dedicated men who were involved.

Something less needs be said about the second of the surveys, the King survey, officially known as the United States Geological Exploration of the Fortieth Parallel. It was the inspiration of Clarence King, a New Englander who was a very close friend of Henry Adams. At the age of twenty-five, King, who was a graduate of the Sheffield Scientific School at Yale and had been with Whitney's California Geological Survey, was appointed Geologist in Charge of the proposed survey of the fortieth parallel. The survey followed the route of the Pacific Railroad, proceeding eastward from the crest of the Sierras to Cheyenne. Under the administrative supervision of A. A. Humphreys of the Army Engineers, King surrounded himself with a small coterie of experts, most of whom were New Englanders like himself and better than half of whom were his personal friends.

In the late spring of 1867, the Fortieth Parallel Survey commenced operations in western Nevada, working eastward. The professional staff consisted essentially of Samuel Franklin Emmons, James D. and Arnold Hague, James T. Gardiner (later with Hayden), the botanist Sereno Watson, and the seventeen-year-old ornithologist Robert Ridgway. King devoted most of the next six years to the survey, and a portion of his time through the succeeding years until 1879 in completing the final reports.[18]

These reports, in seven volumes and an atlas, constitute not only, as King said, "a stepping-stone worthy to be built into the great stairway of science," but they also represent a successful attempt to raise the standards of American scientific investigation and writing.[19] "The day has passed in geological science," King wrote to General Humphreys, "when it is either decent or tolerable to rush into print with undigested field operations. . . . It is my intention to give to this work a finish which will place it on an equal footing with the best European productions, and those few which have redeemed the wavering reputation of our American investigators."[20] King accomplished his lofty task well, and the format of his final reports became a model that was emulated by Hayden, Powell, and Wheeler.

In addition to raising the standards of American science, King's survey raised the stature and improved the image of the much-maligned American civil servant. King exposed the Great Diamond Hoax in northwestern Colorado, thus saving an unknown number of investors from losing a large quantity of money. The San Francisco *Bulletin* thanked King for the exposure, calling him a "cool-headed man of scientific education who esteemed it a duty to investigate the matter in the only right way." The newspaper further pointed out that the diamond exposure sharply emphasized the practical value "in the ordinary business of society, of scientific education and research."[21]

Well educated, honest, and dedicated, the Fortieth Parallel men were in the vanguard of the many government men who later conducted their investigations with dispassionate efficiency, protecting the people and their natural resources alike for their own generation and for generations to come. Yet who has heard of Clarence King's Fortieth Parallel Survey? Who can deny that the $600,000 it cost were not American taxpayers' dollars wisely spent?[22]

The third of the Great Surveys was the Powell survey, officially known during most of its existence as the United States Geographical and Geological Survey of the Rocky Mountain Region. Powell is, of course, well known, and so is his survey if we consider it as embracing the early years of his western explorations.

A Wisconsin farm boy and teacher, Powell, though hindered by the loss of an arm for the Union at Shiloh, persevered and led privately sponsored expeditions into the West in 1867 and 1868. He climbed both Pike's Peak and Long's Peak, camped in Colorado's Middle Park, and finally planned a trip down the Green and Colorado Rivers in 1869. In May of that year he started down the Green with nine other men—friends, relatives, and drifters who had joined him out West. One man left the party early in the trip, and three others climbed out of the canyon and died at the hands of the Indians. But the major and five of his men did make the journey, reaching the mouth of the Virgin River, not far from the Mormon village of Rioville.[23]

The next year Powell explored the plateaus of southern Utah and northern Arizona, and in 1871, increasingly with funds from the government, he made a second trip down the canyons. He was determined to make a general geologic and geographic survey of the Colorado River country, but he found himself a Johnny-come-lately in Washington; Hayden, King, and Wheeler were already there, entrenched, knocking on Congressmen's doors for continuing appropriations. Powell observed their methods, grasped the weakness of the situation—too many surveys—and shrewdly charted his course. A congressional hearing in 1874 resulted in Powell's gaining his own survey, although his aim of a consolidation was not realized for another five years.

Meanwhile he had gathered together a group of inexperienced men and set them to work mapping the plateau and canyon country. They had a hard time of it at first, Professor Almon Harris Thompson once writing to the major about the maps, "Swear on the outside about it—Old Boy—but thank God in your heart that I have not chucked the whole business into the fire."[24] But the men did learn, and eventually accomplished remarkably good work.

For the major, these were years of trial and error, years of learning. The work of his men improved each season. By 1876 he was hiring outstanding geologists, such as Grove Karl Gilbert and Capt. Clarence E. Dutton, to add to his own abilities in that field. These men could write as well as do field work, although none were as good writers as the major himself, whose *Exploration of the Colorado River of the West* has fascinated armchair explorers for three generations and will continue to do so for ages to come.[25]

By the time of the consolidation, Powell's talents were being directed toward improvements in the land laws, as his noted *Report on the Lands of the Arid Region of the United States* (1878) suggested. He was also interested in ethnology, and it was due to his efforts that the Bureau of Ethnology was established, and of which he became the first director. This, then, is what the American people received from Powell and his survey, at a cost of about $259,000.[26]

The fourth of the Great Surveys was the Wheeler survey, officially called the United States Geographical Surveys West of the One Hundredth Meridian. Up to the time of the Civil War, the United States Topographical Engineers had assumed the task of scientifically exploring the West. They passed out of existence during the war, and early in the 1870's the Army Engineers set out to regain the position which their late brethren had once held. Lt. George M. Wheeler was placed in charge, and from 1871 until the consolidation in 1879 he administered an ambitious scientific and mapping program in the West. The primary aim of the Wheeler survey was the mapping of the West with sufficient accuracy for Army purposes. Plans called for completion of such a map by 1885, at a cost of *not more than* $2,500,000.[27] Natural history observations were also to be made.

The tragic part of the story is that in 1879, when Wheeler was well on his way to accomplishing his aims and had spent a half million dollars, his survey was discontinued and all the plans and most of the maps were shelved—much of the half million dollars being virtually wasted. However, he could list 41 reports and 164 maps as accomplishments of his survey. Many of the reports were prepared by Edward Drinker Cope; Grove Karl Gilbert, who had been with him before joining Powell; Archibald Marvine; the geologist John J. Stevenson; the paleontologist H. C. Yarrow; and the botanist J. T. Rothrock.[28] Their contributions were of substantial value to science. That many of the scientists did not get along especially well with Army rules and regulations is, perhaps, beside the point.[29] Surely it is in view of the relationship of science with the military services in the present day.

But who has ever heard of Lt. George M. Wheeler or his survey? Or of the Hayden and King surveys, for that matter, or of their leaders? Yet the record is clear: in the decade of the 1870's, vigorous scientific exploration was conducted of the West; it was concentrated in four government-sponsored surveys; and it was led by four rather remarkable men. For history to record anything differently constitutes error.

An error has been committed. A survey of ten recent college-level American history textbooks reveals that none of them mention Hayden or Wheeler or their surveys, four of them mention Powell, and two of them also mention King.[30] None of the four most successful textbooks on the westward movement even mentions Powell, let alone the others.[31] Hence, an error by omission has occurred, as well as by undue adulation of one explorer at the expense of the others.

Why has one man, Major Powell, received so much more credit than Hayden, King, and Wheeler? The answers are of course relatively simple, but the implications should concern historians regardless of their areas of specialization. First, Powell did the romantic thing. Adventure-minded America was intrigued by the daring one-armed major who conquered the terrible and mysterious Colorado River of the West. Nothing else accomplished by the Great Surveys—not even the descriptions of geysers and cliff dwellings, nor the exposure of the Great Diamond Hoax—so fired the imaginations of the American people. Powell's name became a household word.

Second, history pays little attention to the "also-rans." In the struggle for the creation of the U. S. Geological Survey, Powell won—with some aid from King—while Hayden and Wheeler and their surveys were literally destroyed. Third, Powell remained active for another two decades, molding the policies of the new Geological Survey and the Bureau of Ethnology. Hayden, however, died in 1886; Wheeler's health failed and his career ground to a halt; and King busied himself in private enterprise. For Powell, then, the decade of the 1870's—the decade of the Great Surveys—was prologue; for King, Hayden, and Wheeler, it was postlogue. The major is best remembered, from the point of view of accurate history, for his achievements after 1879; the others must be remembered for their achievements before that year.

Fortunately, historians today seem to be more correctly evaluating the work of the four men of the Great Surveys. Taking the lead in this respect is the new fifth edition of Morison and Commager's *Growth of the American Republic* (page 122):

> First in the field was the army-sponsored Geological Survey of the Fortieth Parallel under the leadership of Clarence King. . . . Meanwhile the Corps of Engineers launched a large-scale expedition to explore the territory west of the 100th meridian; this was entrusted to an army engineer, George M. Wheeler. . ┆ . The Hayden Geological Survey of the Territories . . . mapped much of the *terra incognita* of the Far West and uncovered much of its mineral and botanical resources. Easily the most dramatic of the Western expeditions was that headed by the remarkable John Wesley Powell.

Let us hope that other historians will follow the lead of Professors Morison and Commager and give deserved credit to Hayden, King, and Wheeler, as well as to Powell. For after all, did not all four of these men contribute to our knowledge of the West?

Why have historians, who are always searching for new research topics, been so lax in researching these men of science? Most of the research has been done by English professors and physical scientists—but for whose work the record of our men of science would have nearly disappeared.

The answer seems to be that until recently it has rarely occurred to historians that the march of science constitutes excellent historical material. About twenty years ago an article appeared in a historical journal entitled "The Scientist in the West, 1870-1880."[32] The author had taken a superficial glimpse of the reports of the Great Surveys, had apparently blown the dust off a few of the volumes and, to the sound of cracking bindings, had even read a few pages here and there. He then passed off the reports as containing very little information of value about western society, institutions, and settlement, adding that what they did contain was "successfully hidden in an almost impenetrable mass of technical language." He concluded dryly: "The scientist does not make a good reporter of historical material."[33]

It never occurred to him that the surveys themselves constituted a chapter in the history of science. And too many historians still think as this one did, in terms of wars and politics, of economics and census statistics. The history of science is a field wide open to the competent researcher. It is a challenging and rewarding field. But, unless historians act, the English professors and the physical scientists will fill the vacuum. Surely, in these middle years of the twentieth century, our profession should be more aware of the march of science.

ECONOMIC DEVELOPMENT—

INDUSTRY AND TRANSPORT

Research in Western Economic

History—Problems and Opportunities

GERALD D. NASH
University of New Mexico

The organization of a new association of western historians provides an opportune time for an appraisal of present and future trends in western economic history.[1] Such an appraisal requires not only an examination of the scope and content of the field but of its problems and methodology as well. And it makes appropriate an investigation of the opportunities for research which might help to shape the future dimensions of the subject.

Even a cursory survey of books and articles in western economic history written during the past decade reveals that few are oriented toward contemporary problems, either in choice of topic or in chronological emphasis. The themes selected—and the questions posed—have not changed greatly in the past fifty years. The areas of inquiry first outlined by Turner, Paxson, and the pioneers in the field still occupy many of today's historians as they write about the exploration of the West, the coming of the railroads, the cattle industry, overland migration, and the various mining booms.

Moreover, as John Caughey had already noted in 1947, most works in western history are still concerned with the nineteenth century. The generation of town founders, state builders, prospectors, and Indian fighters still figures prominently in most accounts, which focus on the initial settlement of the West before 1900 rather than on its consequent patterns of growth. Like the historians of the South, who only recently turned to the history of their region after Reconstruction, students of the West have slighted western development in more recent times.[2]

Yet, unlike Turner and his generation, scholars now can look back over a half-century of western industrial expansion and can study topics related to western economic development and still-vital issues which it raised during more recent times. This period, and its problems, does not deserve to be ignored in favor of undue

61

emphasis on the romantic era of exploration and settlement. Few would argue that research in the earlier era is exhausted, but a plea should be made for greater emphasis on the history of the past fifty years. Extended breadth in subject matter and greater balance in chronology would do much to stimulate the study of western history.

Of the subjects related to industrialism which still have many gaps, western transportation history is prominent. Because the railroads played a dramatic role in the opening of the West, they have attracted much attention from historians. Several excellent railroad histories have been published in recent years. The Santa Fe, the Burlington, and the Denver and Rio Grande have fortunately attracted able historians. Unfortunately, the same cannot be said of the history of state railroad regulation, which still needs to be studied in most states.

Throughout the trans-Mississippi West after 1870 legislatures created state railroad boards to stabilize competition and to regulate corporate abuses, such as discrimination, high rates, and poor or unsafe service. With few exceptions, the history of these commissions still needs to be written. Who were the men who served on them, what were their problems, and how did they develop the reasonably adequate regulatory system that prevails in the twentieth century? The technical difficulties which the early commissioners faced were staggering, especially in light of the small and inexpert staffs and the inadequate funds which lawmakers allotted.

The popular assumption that railroad corporations controlled many of these state commissions, often by corruption, will not bear the test of closer scrutiny. Certainly a detailed study of the California Railroad Commission between 1876 and 1911 reveals that such an assumption is only partially valid, and the same is true in Alabama. It may well be that as detailed histories of state railroad commissions are produced, revealing the complexity of problems, the agrarian protest movements of the late nineteenth century will be seen in an altered if less sympathetic perspective.[3]

But the railroads were only one of the important forms of transportation in the West, and after 1900 their influence steadily declined as roads became increasingly important. Why is the history of highways shrouded in obscurity? Needed are histories of individual roads and turnpikes, and their impact on localities and regions. Few have studied the road construction and maintenance programs of county supervisors. How well did western local governments perform their responsibilities of maintaining roads and bridges? In California between 1850 and 1900, they turned in a very poor performance. But only detailed and scholarly studies of selected areas and states will provide accurate information.

After 1900, additional problems arose with the Good Roads Movement. What groups in the western states participated in it? How did they influence federal and state policies? How did the new highway departments, established throughout the trans-Mississippi West by 1920, carry out their tremendous responsibilities in creating new road systems for their states? What were the problems which they faced—in finance, in technical matters, and in determining routes?[4] Good studies of local and state automobile associations would do much to clarify the specific impact which a new generation of American motorists had in shaping public policies and institutions.

A related subject is the rise of the trucking industry after World War I, when the Federal Government disposed of a large surplus of vehicles. Although the boom was as dramatic as the burgeoning of the railroads in the 1850's, this story has not attracted much attention. The jitney bus had its origins in Los Angeles in 1919 when some enterprising operators charged five cents for a ride; the vehicles came to be designated as "jitneys," a southern slang expression for five cents.

Who organized the new bus and truck lines after 1919? How did they fare during their difficult early years? What changes did they effect in business locations and transportation patterns? How, within a mere decade, did they obtain a large share of the freight and passenger traffic once exclusively that of the railroads? More recently the appearance of another competing carrier, the airlines, has evidenced the need for similar historical studies of this industry, its origins, its problems, and the development of federal and state regulation.[5] The West may have been opened by the railroads, but since 1900 it has expanded only because of the emergence of these newer forms of transportation. Historians cannot fail to take notice of the fact.

Much work remains to be done in the history of western natural resources and their development. This is a much discussed but generally little studied subject in which many important questions are still unanswered. Especially is this true of the history of forests. The conservation and forestry policies of large corporations and associations of lumbermen between 1900 and 1950 need to be studied in detail. The assumption that many of these corporations and associations were composed of greedy speculators will not always stand the test of evidence. Large corporations often assumed the leadership in seeking scientific exploitation and preservation of forest resources in their own and the public domains.

A good example was the Diamond Match Company, in California, which pioneered in 1901 by appointing fire wardens on its properties. It also adopted reforestation policies and pursued scientific forest research projects in cooperation with the U. S. Bureau of Forestry. Such actions were, of course, in the company's own best interests. However, the detailed story of these actions and those of other companies need to be told to gain a clearer conception of private natural resource exploitation since the turn of the century.[6]

Historians have not written much about state forest policies in the West. By 1914 almost every state had established a forest commission or commissioner to deal with various problems of lumber depletion. What problems led to the creation of these agencies in each state? Who were the men who shaped state policies? How successful were the commissions in accomplishing their aims between 1900 and 1950? What was their relationship with federal agencies operating in their states, such as the U. S. Bureau of Forestry?[7] Before the outlines of public forest policies are clear, histories of state forestry commissions must be written.

An important but neglected aspect of conservation history is the story of fish in western waters. The movement for fish conservation began shortly after the Civil War when the prospects of exhaustion first alarmed scientific groups such as the American Fish Culturists Association and its adherents in the West. As a result of its efforts, and those of sportsmen's groups, which historians have yet to study, every western state between 1865 and 1900 established fish and wildlife commissions to regulate the propagation as well as the catch of fish and game.[8] Histories are needed of federal and state fish and game commissions, of the influences which led to their creation, and of the impact of electric power development and stream pollution upon wildlife with the spread of industrialization since 1900.

Though the development of water resources in the West has given rise to a vast literature, paradoxically very little of it is historical. Between 1870 and 1900 almost every western state created an office of State Engineer to deal with water disputes among individuals, the conservation of water resources, irrigation, and the improvement of the navigability of streams. These engineers had a profound impact upon resource development in their states and regions, yet historians know almost nothing about them. Some are among the neglected heroes of the West. Who has heard of William H. Hall, State Engineer of California from 1877 to 1887; of Elwood Mead in Wyoming; John Wade in Montana; Lamar Cobb in Arizona; or Robert C. Gemmell in Utah? Hall, an outstanding example of a devoted public servant, fought courageously for the adoption of an integrated state water plan such as the legislature of California adopted after World War II. No study has been made of Hall, and even less is known about his colleagues in the other western states.[9]

Similarly, historians have not studied the great debate over alternative water policies which took place at the beginning of the Progressive Era. Scores of individuals and organizations—individuals such as Hall and Mead and organizations such as the California Water and Forest Association—offered plans and proposals for the solution of western water problems. Many progressives believed that the problems of an industrial society could be solved by rational planning and administration, and in few spheres did this belief manifest itself as strongly as in proposed water policies.

Scholars have also neglected histories of the policies and activities of western state water commissions created during the Progressive Era. These commissions came to take on major responsibility for the adjudication of disputes over water distribution and the recording of water rights and claims. Nor are there many histories of irrigation districts. Under what circumstances was public rather than private development of irrigation projects feasible? What were the reasons for the success or failure of districts in western states such as Utah, Colorado, and California between 1870 and 1950? The history of western water problems and public policies provides fertile ground for new research opportunities.[10]

Although several books on the history of western mining have been published in recent years, much research remains to be done. A comprehensive study of the California Gold Rush in its varied economic manifestations still needs to be written. The Comstock Lode was reputed to have been the most lucrative silver mine the world had seen, yet 100 years after its discovery an adequate historical account of its exploitation is still lacking.

The history of the petroleum industry in western states, such as California, Montana, and New Mexico, since 1870 also awaits study. Because of increasing over-production of oil after 1920, oil-men, state and federal governments, and various "pressure" groups undertook a great variety of experiments to promote conservation and restriction of output. Students of the West have neglected the history of these efforts, of voluntary agreements between groups of producers to regulate production between 1920 and 1939, of a mass of individual state laws and regulations, and of interstate compacts. Although the significance of these activities far outweighs that of the Teapot Dome scandals, the full story of these activities still needs to be told. Similarly, the western coal industry is worthy of study from its beginnings in the 1870's, when the western steam railroads desperately sought to acquire deposits closer than Pennsylvania. And, for those interested in more recent years, an interesting and significant story could be related about the rise and fall of the uranium industry in New Mexico, Utah, Colorado, and Nevada in the perspective of earlier mining booms.[11]

Encouraging beginnings, but beginnings only, are being made in the business history of the West. This broad field embraces the history of important individual entrepreneurs, of firms and corporations, and of business associations. Needed are biographies of prominent western businessmen, such as the paper magnate Isaac Zellerbach; the banker A. P. Gianninni; Caspar T. Hopkins, the father of Pacific Coast insurance; the lumber baron T. B. Walker; and the telegraph kings James G. Fair and James C. Flood.

Scholarly accounts of corporations important in their localities or regions are likewise lacking. Especially neglected are studies of chambers of commerce and boards of trade, which had a profound impact upon the development of urban communities and of states, although very little is known about them. The Denver Chamber of Commerce, for example, by 1890 included in its wide range of interests matters such as immigration, transportation, the development of manufacturing, and better harbors on the Gulf of Mexico. On the Pacific Coast, the San Francisco Chamber of Commerce was one of the most important organizations in the state after 1870 in shaping local and state legislation, especially with regard to harbors and finance.[12]

Little information has been published on the history of business techniques that were used in the economic development of the West. Were interest rates charged by mortgage companies excessive? Allan Bogue has shown that, contrary to popular belief, the rates of a Kansas money lending firm were really quite moderate. Detailed studies of other companies and other states are needed. No one has studied the mass of legislation enacted in western states between 1850 and 1950 to regulate interest rates. The usual maximum was six to seven per cent, in the absence of private contracts. The persistence of usury laws, from their beginning to the present, points to a subject having broad economic and social implications which deserves the attention of western historians.[13]

Much the same can be said of the enactment of homestead exemption and bankruptcy laws between 1870 and 1950, which affected a large portion of the population in addition to business groups. The story of negotiable instruments and various types of commercial paper, which facilitated business transactions in the West, remains to be told. Nor have the functions of middlemen received much attention—wheat brokers and speculators like Isaac Friedlaender in the California of the 1870's, mail order houses and general stores in the later period.[14]

The history of agricultural industries in the western states is neglected. Where can one find a scholarly history of horticulture, or any variety of fruit, in California, Arizona, Colorado, Utah, or other western states? Who has traced the impact of urbanization on the creation of a western dairy industry after 1890? Where are the histories of agricultural cooperatives and other marketing associations? Even the largest of these, the California Fruit Growers Exchange, has not had an adequate historian.[15]

What has been the historical development of government responsibilities toward agriculture? Histories of state agricultural societies after 1860 would shed much light on this question, as would also monographs treating the development of state agricultural agencies, weather departments, and boards and commissions dealing with special crops. Who has studied the enormous subject of disease prevention in western agriculture and livestock raising and the development of state and regional quarantines? A revealing book could readily be written about the hoof-and-mouth disease epidemic of 1924, which created a severe crisis throughout the West and mirrored many aspects of voluntary and state and federal disease control programs.[16]

Virtually unexplored is the history of banking in the West. Needed are histories of individual banks within particular localities before broader studies can be made comparing practices on a state-wide, regional, and national scale. The phenomenal rise of branch banking in the West after 1920 merits special study. Books have been written about log cabins and sod houses but none about the role of western savings and loan associations after 1890 in enabling millions to acquire homes.[17]

The history of insurance is almost totally neglected, although insurance companies in the last fifty years have become major purveyors and suppliers of capital for investment. Here, too, are needed histories of individual firms and of boards of underwriters and the techniques and policies which they developed. Moreover, the growth of state regulation of insurance, involving the creation of a commissioner or official in every state, needs to be detailed, as well as the complicated web of relations and negotiations between insurance men and state legislators and officials.[18]

Though much of the economic development of the West between 1850 and 1950 was speculatory, the absence of any reliable histories of stock trading and exchanges is surprising. In California, Nevada, Colorado, and Utah, stock speculation on a large scale became rife, especially after the Civil War. The history of the three stock exchanges founded in San Francisco in 1863 or of the Salt Lake City Stock and Mining Exchange remains unwritten. After 1860 most states sought to regulate stock transactions, with varying results.

By 1900 the growth of business magnified corporate problems and within two decades led to more comprehensive control measures, especially the Blue Sky Laws of the Progressive Era. The most detailed regulation appeared in California after 1917, but many of the other western states developed similar, if less ambitious, programs. Corporation commissioners usually issued permits allowing stock issues, checked on the honesty of promoters and their literature, and sought to prevent fraud.[19] If problems of stocks and stock regulation are to be viewed in proper perspective, thorough histories of the experience in the western states are needed.

A field just now evoking interest from scholars is the history of labor in the West. As yet, impartial, objective, and reliable histories of state federations of labor and of individual unions and brotherhoods, and their impact on members, employers, and communities, are lacking. Similarly, the influence of unions on state and local policies needs to be delineated more precisely. In California, for example, the State Federation of Labor virtually dictated legislative policies on labor matters between 1870 and 1920 through its paid lobbyist in the state capital, and very probably this was true in other states as well. Laboring men may have suffered defeats in the courts during this period, but they were singularly successful in obtaining the introduction and enactment of laws.

Moreover, state labor policies deserve detailed study. Almost every western state had created a bureau of labor statistics by 1920. The activities of these bureaus needs to be carefully examined, for they included the regulation of hours, working conditions, and employment agencies, and many other related subjects. Study of the development of workmen's insurance and compensation programs, private and public, would reveal much about such programs at a time when their expansion is a burning contemporary public issue.[20]

The subjects suggested above are not among those that have been traditionally considered as within the realm of western history.

Almost seventy years ago Frederick Jackson Turner provided new directions for the study of western history. His impact came not only from his mental brilliance, not only from his superlative imagination, but also from the relevance of his ideas to his own times. Turner himself, and his generation, were concerned with the closing of the frontier in 1890, with the Populist reaction against an industrialism which threatened the mid-nineteenth century agrarian society which they knew, with the submergence of the individual in the face of large and powerful organizations, and with a questioning of what they had thought to be established values.

Although some of these issues are still pertinent, they are now placed in a very different contemporary setting and are no longer of the same relevance as they were toward the close of the nineteenth century. Thus, a searching reexamination of the objectives and dimensions of western history is needed and of the research trends within it. The present generation of historians might well ask itself: "Have students of the West since Turner turned their attention to problems of importance to their own age?" The future direction of western history depends on the answer which every scholar in the field gives to this question.

The Development of Air Transportation in the West

LEE SCAMEHORN
University of Colorado

One of the more persistent themes in American history has been continuing improvements in transportation. A century ago major advances in surface travel hastened the settlement of the West. The stage, freight wagon, and railroads—and the business organizations dedicated to their efficient employment—expedited communications, broadened markets, promoted specialization, encouraged exploitation of mineral wealth, and opened formerly inaccessible agricultural resources throughout the high plains and mountains in what is today a fourteen-state area.[1]

Like the West itself, transportation facilities have changed radically since the close of the frontier era. Railroads, once the principal carriers, began declining in economic importance more than forty years ago as motor-carriers gradually captured a larger proportion of the passenger and freight market. Even greater changes resulted from the almost universal adoption of the private automobile as a vehicle for business and pleasure. Another new major force of change appeared when the private airlines emerged in the second quarter of the century.

Commercial aviation in the West has passed through six distinct phases of development. The first, from about 1900 to 1920, was characterized by experiments with aircraft and attempts to establish airlines. During the second, from 1920 to 1926, actual intercity flights were made on regular schedules along the Post Office Department's transcontinental airmail route. The third, from 1926 to 1935, was devoted to the formation of private companies by holders of airmail contracts. The fourth, from 1935 to 1946, was dominated by revolutionary equipment changes, sharp increases in traffic, and reduced dependence on mail payments for operating revenues. During the fifth, from the close of World War II to the middle

1950's, the air carriers made major improvements in their service which enabled them to outstrip all rivals in a contest for the long-haul passenger market. They also re-entered the local market, which they had largely abandoned a decade earlier, and made rapid progress in developing freight traffic on a volume basis. The final phase, from about 1955 to the present, has been characterized by the introduction of revolutionary new sources of power—the turbo-prop and turbo-jet.

The West was interested in air travel at an early date because it represented a feasible method for overcoming vast distances and rugged terrain—serious impediments to surface travel. The discovery of gold at Sutter's mill in 1848 produced the first scheme for air travel west of the Mississippi. In the late winter of 1848-49, as thousands of fortune seekers prepared for the overland journey, an eastern inventor announced plans for an "Aerial Railway," along which balloons would span the continent in from two to five days, when the wind was fair.[2] Though the proposal probably received a great deal of attention from men anticipating a four-month trip by ox team or pack animal, it was quickly abandoned—perhaps because the cost of constructing the wire-way, an estimated $1.3 million, discouraged investors.

The balloon, man's first vehicle for air travel, was unsuited for commercial ventures in intercity transportation. A hydrogen-filled cloth bag with attached basket or car for passengers, it lacked motive power and the proper directional controls; it was always at the mercy of prevailing winds. Nor were there effective methods for regulating height or duration of flight. These obvious short-comings served, however, as an important stimulus to experiments with both lighter- and heavier-than-air craft.[3]

The mounting volume of research devoted to mechanical flight by 1900 generated new interest in air travel. Almost a year before the Wright brothers completed the first powered flight at Kitty Hawk, a Denver newspaper reported that George O. L. Davidson, a local resident, would soon inaugurate overnight passenger service to New York in a giant airliner of his own design.[4] Six years later he secretly departed for his native land in the British Isles, leaving behind a heavily mortgaged home, staggering personal debts, and a flying machine of questionable merit.[5]

Other schemes were even more ambitious. The International Aerial Navigation Company of San Antonio, Texas, reportedly a million-dollar venture, planned airship operations commencing in

1909 to cities throughout the United States, Mexico, and other countries.[6] A year later one of the Texas promoters withdrew to form a rival concern in St. Louis, the Universal Aerial Navigation Company, which planned to operate 100-passenger gyroplanes—curious vehicles combining the features of a gyroscope, helicopter, and airplane.[7] Similarly, Dr. A. Brodbeck of Salt Lake City organized the Globe Airship Company for the purpose of creating a world-wide system of dirigible routes.[8]

The flying machine remained an unwanted stepchild of modern technology until transformed during World War I into a powerful, dependable instrument for long flights with surprisingly heavy loads. Prewar aircraft were fragile, unreliable, inefficient, and mechanically crude by comparison to accepted vehicles then employed in surface transportation. Proposals for intercity commercial flights were highly speculative, unrealistic, and for the most part ignored by the public.

Like all new modes of travel, aviation was initially viewed as a supplement to existing transportation routes. As early as 1910 the Post Office Department became interested in the airplane as a means of maintaining all-season service to remote communities, especially those in mountainous regions isolated by winter snows. Four years later, following a series of experiments throughout the country, postal officials requested funds from Congress for limited airmail service. Airlines were projected in the western mountain states, which would provide flight service to forty-three communities in Colorado alone; in the Southwest; and elsewhere.[9] Advertisements for bids from private contractors for routes in Alaska and New England brought a disappointing response in 1916 and the program was temporarily abandoned. Manufacturers and operators of aircraft who, under normal conditions, would have been eager to foster airmail flights were largely absorbed in supplying World War I European belligerents with equipment and trained personnel.[10]

The delay, although unappreciated at the time, was a blessing to commercial aviation. Within a year English and French engineering knowledge, much of it originally secret, created a revolution in American aircraft design and performance, greatly accelerating the trend away from the "stick and wire" features of prewar United States models. By the final year of World War I, manufacturers were mass-producing sturdy, dependable, streamlined models having speeds, ranges, and carrying capacities thought impossible a few years earlier. In addition, the U. S. Air Service trained thousands of pilots, mechanics, and technicians, many of whom turned to the fledgling aviation industry for jobs after demobilization.[11]

Commercial aviation's postwar growth fell short of wartime predictions. Private airlines, unable to cope with public apathy and unsupported by subsidies, were still-born or short-lived. While the forerunners of British Overseas Airways, Air France, K.L.M., and other prominent European carriers charted successful routes beyond the Atlantic, only a single enterprise of importance appeared in the United States—the Post Office Department's transcontinental route, completed in 1920.[12]

Until the middle of the following decade, the air transportation industry, except for the government airmail service, was dominated by former military pilots and surplus aircraft. The fliers were so-called "gypsy" pilots, who moved about in search of meager business, and used a few established fixed bases for charter flights, instruction, sales, and service. The instability of the industry was indicated by the rapid company turnover. A directory of operators compiled by the Aeronautical Chamber of Commerce reported seven companies in the eight-state mountain region in 1920; three years later all were out of business and four new companies had taken their place.[13] Equipment was inadequate, and manufacturers capable of producing planes for commercial service were reluctant to do so because the market remained glutted with military castoffs.

The one promising development during a period otherwise characterized by confusion and lack of progress was the transcontinental airmail experiment. For nine years the postal service pioneered in air transportation on a scale unduplicated elsewhere in the world. At a total cost which was estimated to be between $10 and $12 million—a small amount compared to subsidized programs in Europe—the government airline maintained a vast route system, developed valuable operational techniques and procedures, and created the foundation for a domestic private industry.[14]

The success of the airmail service prompted Congress, in 1925, to enact legislation designed to foster commercial air enterprises throughout the United States. The Kelly Act of that year authorized the carriage of mail by private contractors between cities approved by the Postmaster General with compensation to carriers "at a rate not to exceed four-fifths of the revenues."[15] Companies quickly organized in anticipation of profits from airmail while developing the facilities and equipment necessary to lure passengers to the airways.

Seven of the twelve airlines formed in 1926 served communities west of the Mississippi River, and three were located in mountain states. Western Air Express organized C.A.M. 4—600 miles from Los Angeles to Salt Lake City. Varney Air Transport established C.A.M. 5—435 miles from Elko, Nevada, to Pasco, Washington. Colorado Airways operated C.A.M. 12—199 miles from Cheyenne to Denver and Pueblo. All the new companies were "feeders" for the transcontinental route, which remained for another year under government control.[16]

After a halting start, most carriers experienced phenomenal growth. They rapidly acquired the necessary experience and equipment which permitted diversification of services after Charles A. Lindbergh's epic trans-Atlantic solo flight created widespread support for air travel. During aviation's first boom year came the demise of government air service; Boeing Air Transport, a subsidiary of the manufacturing firm, acquired the Chicago-San Francisco segment, and National Air Transport took over the eastern portion of the coast-to-coast system.[17]

Prior to the abrupt cancellation of all contracts in 1934, the number of domestic air carriers increased to twenty-three. Three giants—United Air Lines, Transcontinental & Western Air, and American Airways—afforded western cities direct access to either coast. Ten other companies, including three in continuous operation since 1926, served six plains and eight mountain states.[18] Passenger traffic volume throughout the entire domestic system exceeded half a million, compared to six thousand eight years earlier, and mail soared to 6.7 million pounds, more than a fivefold increase over the first year of operations.[19]

Public support of air travel permitted the western airlines to keep pace with industry-wide expansion. The original "feeders" became combination regional-local carriers catering to intercity as well as interline movement of passengers, express, and mail.[20] Western Air Express extended its route to San Diego and formed from the Cheyenne-Pueblo contract (pioneered by Colorado Airways) an elaborate system stretching into Oklahoma, Texas, and New Mexico.[21] Varney Air Transport, a division of United Air Lines, moved its southern terminal to Salt Lake City and expanded into the Northwest, connecting with the north-south coastal lines at Seattle.[22] Northwest Airways, destined to become a transcontinental carrier, lengthened its Chicago-Minneapolis service, reaching out to Bismarck, North Dakota.[23] Other airlines opened new territory: National Park Airways established direct flights between Salt Lake City and the upper tier of mountain and plains states; and United States Airways provided direct service between Denver and Kansas City, Missouri, with intermediate stops throughout western and central Kansas.[24] A number of "independent" companies, which did not have mail contracts, provided needed air communications in the plains states, from the Dakotas to Texas.[25]

A reorganization of domestic airlines by the Post Office Department in 1934 reshuffled routes but left the basic structure intact. Transcontinental operations were not appreciably altered, remaining assigned to the original companies.[26] On the regional and local level, Western Air Express, under the temporary name of General Air Lines, lost its lines in Colorado and the Southwest, but retained the lucrative Salt Lake City-San Diego route as a base for future growth. The Pueblo-El Paso contract went to Varney Speed Lines, reorganized three years later as Continental Air Lines.[27] Three independents—Braniff Airways, Wyoming Air Service, and Hanford Tri-State Air Line—entered the ranks of subsidized carriers and acquired territories in competitive bidding from older companies.[28]

Despite the dual blow of forced reorganization and the Depression, commercial aviation prospered in the seven years prior to World War II. Western companies experienced rapid expansion, healthy competition, and rapid technological advances. The adoption of modern equipment greatly stimulated the development of passenger traffic, which in turn lessened dependence on mail. The Boeing 247-D, introduced on United Air Lines' Chicago-San Francisco route in 1933, set new standards for speed, comfort, and safety. Donald Douglas, William Boeing's chief competitor, followed with the famous DC (Douglas Commercial) series, which set the stage for a revolution in air transportation.[29]

The adoption of more efficient aircraft inevitably led to major changes in the industry. Western carriers had been developmental; they had penetrated regions where surface modes of transportation were inadequate or nonexistent. The typical company was small, and it was short of capital, equipment, and personnel. Its operations centered around airmail service, and maximum revenues required flights to many communities with little regard to size. Boeing and Douglas transports encouraged airlines to become more exploitive;

operations shifted to passenger service between larger cities, and schedules were altered to increase speed by reducing the number of intermediate stops.[30]

The impact of modern airliners on the route pattern may be illustrated by the case of Denver. Although the principal metropolitan area between the Middle West and the Pacific Coast, Denver was initially denied transcontinental air service, as it had been by-passed sixty years earlier by major railroads. For more than a decade, it had access to coast-to-coast routes only by secondary carriers flying to Cheyenne, Kansas City, Albuquerque, and El Paso.[31] The airlines and the Post Office Department refused to alter the airways system until it became obvious that a financially stable industry depended on passenger traffic between major population centers.

United Air Lines began negotiations in 1934 for direct access to Denver. The Post Office was sympathetic, but Wyoming Air Service, the operator established that year on the inter-connected Pueblo-Billings routes, refused to surrender its major city without compensation.[32] Three years later United Air Lines gained its objective by purchasing the Denver-Cheyenne segment. At the same time, Continental Air Lines strengthened its Pueblo-based system by extending operations to Denver.[33]

Denver became the aviation hub of the high plains and mountain region, providing a sense of balance for the first time to western air travel. Flight to and from its municipal airport formed a pattern of coordinated national, regional, and local services. Passengers, express, and mail moved to and from the small, intermediate, and metropolitan cities in a twelve-state area with a minimum of delay and inconvenience. The north-south operations of Continental Air Lines and Wyoming Air Service (reorganized as Inland Air Lines) provided needed facilities because of inadequate or nonexistent surface modes of travel and placed remote or isolated communities within a few hours of the Pacific Coast, Middle West, and East by way of airports on transcontinental lines. However, the industry's inability to exploit the vast region effectively with one national and two regional carriers led to modifications initiated during World War II and completed after the close of hostilities.

The drama attached to commercial aviation's role in transportation exaggerated its actual contributions. Airlines remained a relatively insignificant element of the nation's economy on the eve of World War II. In 1940, nineteen domestic air carriers accounted for only 0.37 per cent of all intercity travel, compared to

8 per cent for railroads, and the remainder for highway motor-carriers and private automobiles.[34] Less than 0.01 per cent of inter-city freight moved over the airways that year. On a sectional basis, western companies probably improved upon the national record, particularly in the long-haul passenger market because of the rugged terrain and vast distances which separated communities and inadequate surface modes of travel in some areas.[35]

World War II marked a major turning point in the development of commercial aviation. The decisive role of air power on a global scale exerted a profound psychological impact upon the American people; the nation emerged from the conflict prepared for an "Air Age," the war itself providing almost unlimited personnel and equipment for future expansion of domestic and international flight.[36]

Wartime advances strengthened commercial aviation for the postwar contest with surface modes of transportation for existing and potential traffic. Surplus Douglas DC-4's, four-engine transports already obsolete by the time they reached the private carriers, were cheap, plentiful, and fast by prewar standards.[37] Boeing 307 *Strato-liners* and Lockheed *Constellations*, which manufacturers rushed from newly established assembly lines to meet the demand for airliners, offered passengers the comfort of pressurized cabins.[38] In addition, military-sponsored research afforded improved communications, radar, Instrument Landing System (ILS), Ground Control Approach (GCA), and other improvements which reduced many of the hazards once associated with air travel.[39]

By 1958, the final pre-jet year for the industry, thirty airlines surpassed all other common-carriers in domestic intercity operations. Air travelers that year exceeded forty-eight million. In the decade 1948-58, aviation's share of scheduled passenger traffic jumped from 14 to 43 per cent; the proportions for railroads and motor-carriers fell from 48 to 30, and from 38 to 26 per cent, respectively.[40]

Western companies shared the industry's remarkable prosperity. Transcontinental carriers multiplied and expanded beyond the continental limits to Hawaii, Alaska, and to many parts of the world. Regional carriers—Continental Air Lines, Western Air Lines, and Braniff Airways—extended operations throughout the West, and the last two entered the Latin American market.[41] Two prewar companies disappeared: Inland Air Lines was purchased by Western in order to gain access to the northern mountain and plains states; and Mid-Continent Airlines (formerly Hanford Tri-State) was merged with Braniff in 1952, adding to that company's Chicago-Dallas and southwestern routes a vast system covering the northern plains.[42]

The short-haul passenger market became the exclusive domain of the local service airlines, postwar additions to the air transportation industry. Demands from communities bypassed in the prewar drive for longer route segments prompted Congress to enact laws providing for new carriers designed specifically for areas where national and regional carriers did not, or would not, provide adequate air service. Initially the newcomers were "feeders" for the older companies.

By 1958, 13 of these "feeder" companies served 547 communities, of which 334 depended exclusively on the local carrier for Air Age communications.[43] Operations were largely concentrated west of the Mississippi River. North Central Airlines and Ozark Air Lines operated in Nebraska, the Dakotas, and Minnesota, in addition to six other Middle Western states.[44] Central Airlines and Trans-Texas Airways centered activities, respectively, in the central and southern plains.[45] Farther west, Frontier Airlines, the largest in its class, criss-crossed the mountain states (except Nevada), and penetrated northward and eastward into the Dakotas, Nebraska, and western Missouri. Bonanza Air Lines limited its flights mainly to southern California and Arizona, but one route extended northward to Reno and two to Salt Lake City. West Coast Airlines, oldest of the local lines in point of continuous service, linked its base-city, Seattle, with communities in five northwestern states, plus British Columbia.

Local service provided the only Air Age link for small and intermediate communities. A large proportion of schedules were north-and-south, where surface modes of travel were deficient; others penetrated remote regions where terrain had retarded the development of highway and rail facilities. Twin-engine, short-haul operations greatly strengthened an industry otherwise dominated by four-engine craft engaged in non-stop and limited-stop operations in the long-haul market. In developing a neglected field of enterprise, the new companies suffered the handicaps of light traffic and heavy dependence on subsidies, but they played a vital role in breaking down barriers of distance and terrain which once isolated many communities and provided a needed stimulus to economic and social growth.

The Jet Age enhanced aviation's competitive position with

respect to surface modes of travel. The greater speed and comfort of turbo-jet and turbo-prop models adopted by trunk and local carriers attracted passengers in record-smashing volume. By 1960, airlines transported almost half of all persons who utilized common-carriers in intercity travel; railroads and highway motor-carriers each controlled about one-fourth of the market.[46]

In less than forty years business efficiency and technology combined to fulfill the air pioneer's dream—fast, economical city-to-city and coast-to-coast travel. In the year of its demise, the government airmail service scheduled flights from New York to San Francisco in 31 hours and 45 minutes.[47] Three years later Transcontinental & Western Air operated two different passenger services daily to Los Angeles: one by air in 36 hours and one by plane and train in 48 hours. All flying was restricted to daylight.[48] The DC-3 in the late 1930's reduced elapsed time to about 20 hours, day and night. Postwar refinements in aircraft shortened the east-west flight—to about eight hours with the DC-7, introduced in 1953, and to about six hours with turbo-jets, introduced six years later.[49]

More recently, technical refinements, as well as economic forces, have produced important modifications in air transportation. The balance achieved with the formation of local service in the immediate postwar years proved transitory; high costs and public pressure for more airline self-sufficiency and improved operations prompted a gradual shift from local- to limited- and non-stop flights. In fact, if not in name, the newer companies have become regional carriers. Frontier Airlines, for example, serves an eleven-state area, providing essentially north-south schedules from Montana and the Dakotas to New Mexico and Arizona. It hopes to link the rich Missouri Valley with the Pacific Northwest.[50] Service designed fifteen years ago to "feed" traffic from small communities into important traffic centers has shifted to intercity and interairline business in the volume market.

The conditions which brought about local service after World War II still largely exist today. Recognition of the need for an airways system catering to the local market has given rise to serious consideration of "third level" enterprises which will supplement national and regional networks. Small, twin-engine aircraft with accommodations for as many as eight passengers may provide local-stop service at a fraction of the costs incurred by existing airlines. The recent application of Hi-Plains Airways of Hill City, Kansas, for certificates permitting stops at forty-six cities in Kansas, Colorado, Nebraska, and the Dakotas may well open a new era in air travel.[51]

The record indicates that commercial aviation has fallen short of its potential. Continuing advances—technical and economic—may dwarf by comparison past achievements. Expansion in local service and increased efficiency in transporting air cargo are required to stabilize and strengthen the industry's position in the national economy. Whatever the trend of the future, the West, because of its reliance on air travel, will play an active role in shaping transportation history.

The Role of Russell, Majors & Waddell in Western Overland Transportation

RAYMOND W. SETTLE

Monte Vista, Colorado

This paper might well be entitled "The Rise and Fall of William H. Russell," for he, more than anyone associated with him, was responsible for the swift rise, dazzling success, and tragic failure of the giant overland freighting company of Russell, Majors & Waddell. That firm, composed of Russell and William B. Waddell, both of Lexington, Missouri, and Alexander Majors of Westport, Missouri, was for about six years the largest and most financially able company of its kind ever known upon the Great Plains. Its purpose was to take advantage of a unique opportunity which seemed to promise a fabulous profit. As later events showed, that promise was not empty.

This opportunity was created primarily by the War with Mexico, 1846-48. Col. (soon Brig. Gen.) Stephen Watts Kearny was ordered to assemble the diminutive, 1,700-man "Army of the West" in record time, make a swift forced march of 900 miles across the unsettled Great Plains, capture Santa Fe, and occupy New Mexico.[1] Thus, he was confronted with the difficult problem of supplying his army on the march and transporting enough supplies to last it a year. The magnitude of his task is revealed by the fact that he requisitioned 900 wagons; enough supplies and munitions to load them; 10,000 horses, mules, and oxen; and 1,000 civilian drivers.[2]

In the making of these preparations, Kearny followed the old system whereby the Army operated its own supply lines, and hired civilian teamsters. It had always been successful, but it proved to be a costly, tragic failure upon the Great Plains. Trains of twenty-five wagons without military protection, or even arms, were not dispatched on schedule, hostile Indians harassed them, captured some, and killed a staggering number of the greenhorn drivers. By the end of 1847, the Santa Fe Trail was strewn with $5,000,000 worth of supplies, the remains of burned wagons, and the bones of oxen.[3]

In contrast to the chaotic, inefficient Army system, the merchant trains made the trip in comparative safety, on schedule, and encountered only a minimum of trouble with the Indians. The reason was that they were combined into a single caravan of 300 to 400 wagons and led by a captain experienced in travel on the plains. The bull-whackers and mule-skinners were professionals. Every man in the caravan had a gun and knew how to use it.

Because of the success of the civilian freighters, the Quartermaster Department let a contract in 1848 to James Brown of Pettis County, Missouri, who agreed to transport 200,000 pounds of military supplies to Santa Fe.[4] The experiment was so successful that in 1849 he and William H. Russell contracted to deliver an unspecified amount of supplies to the same place. This was Russell's introduction to military freighting. In the fall of 1849 Brown, Russell, and John S. Jones, also of Pettis County, contracted to transport 600,000 pounds of supplies (135 wagon loads) to Santa Fe.[5] In 1852, Russell became a partner with William B. Waddell in the general merchandising firm of Waddell & Russell.[6] In 1853, the firm contracted to transport military supplies to Fort Union in New Mexico, but the quantity was not large.[7] This was Waddell's introduction to the freighting of military supplies.

During 1854 the Quartermaster Department decided to abandon the old, complicated system of letting contracts piecemeal to the lowest bidders, and make only one assignment to a single firm or individual covering all the supplies destined for all the Army posts west of the Missouri River. In other words, the Department granted a tight monopoly on military freighting.

Meanwhile, Alexander Majors had entered the freighting business in 1846, when he transported one wagon-load of trade goods to the Pottawatomie Indians north of the Kaw River. By 1848 his outfit had grown to 6 wagons, 8 or 10 bull-whackers, and 35 to 40 oxen. He transported military supplies to Santa Fe for the first time in 1849, and in 1850 his contract with the government required 10 wagons, a dozen bull-whackers, and 130 oxen. That fall he made a second trip, to Fort McKay near Dodge City, Kansas, using 20 wagons. In 1851, he used 25 wagons, as many bull-whackers, and 300 oxen. In 1853, he freighted military supplies to Fort Union. A contract requiring 100 wagons, 120 drivers, and 1,200 oxen was awarded him in 1854.[8]

When the new plan for letting a single contract covering all the Army supplies was made public, Russell, Majors, and Waddell got together and formed a co-partnership agreement, which became effective January 1, 1855.[9] The firm thus created was capitalized for $60,000, one-third of which was furnished by each of the partners. On March 27, 1855, under the name of Majors & Russell, they signed a two-year contract with the government to transport from 50,000 to 2,500,000 pounds of supplies from Fort Leavenworth to all Army posts and depots in Kansas, Nebraska, Utah, and New Mexico, and to El Paso, Texas.[10]

Headquarters of the concern was established in the infant town of Leavenworth, Kansas, a mile from the fort. They bought 500 wagons, enough for 20 trains, hired 1,700 men, most of whom were bull-whackers, and equipment for the vehicles. When ready for the road, the rolling stock, and 7,500 oxen, represented an investment of some $360,000 to $400,000.[11]

In financing their new firm, the partners relied upon the common frontier expedient of credit. They bought oxen, wagons, supplies, and equipment by giving notes, drafts, or acceptances, payable in three to nine months as they collected pay for transportation from the War Department. The firm's credit was good, it held a lucrative monopoly on government freighting for two years, and anyone who had money to lend was glad to lend it.

With Majors superintending the loading of wagons, hiring drivers, and supervising the movement of trains upon the road, the work of fulfilling the contract for 1855 was carried on without a hitch. Majors said the profit for that year was $150,000. Presumably it was no less in 1856. They took up their drafts as they matured, paid for their wagons, oxen, and equipment, and earned a profit of $300,000 in two years.[12]

On February 25, 1857, they signed a one-year contract with Quartermaster Capt. Thomas L. Brent at Fort Leavenworth, again under the name of Majors & Russell, to transport from 50,000 to 5,000,000 pounds of military supplies to Army posts and depots in the West.[13] By the middle of May, 48 trains, composed of 645 wagons, were loaded and on the road.

On June 19, Quartermaster Brent informed Russell that the firm would be required to transport an additional 2,500,000 pounds of supplies to Salt Lake City for the Army of Utah. This was an expeditionary force of 2,500 officers and men, sent there in a hurry to maintain the authority of the United States among the Mormons.[14] Because the firm's entire outfit of wagons and oxen was already on the road to Santa Fe, Russell at first declined to undertake the task, which would involve buying on credit about a quarter of a million dollars worth of wagons, oxen, and equipment. Quartermaster Brent, waving his objections aside, ordered him to assemble the necessary trains and be ready to start within sixty days. There being nothing else to do if the firm wished to remain eligible to receive government contracts, 11 trains, a total of 286 wagons, 3,432 oxen, and some 300 bull-whackers were ready when the time came for the army to march.[15]

The trains moved smoothly along, and reached the Green River Valley ahead of the army. Then disaster struck. The Mormons, who were in a mood to resist, captured and burned three entire trains, a total of seventy-eight wagons, containing three months' rations for the troops, and drove the oxen to Salt Lake City. Other oxen starved to death because the Mormons had burned the grass along the road, and still others died from over-work or froze to death in the frigid mountain weather. Nearly two-thirds of the animals with which the trains started were lost, as were 254 wagons.[16]

Meanwhile, a two-year contract to transport from 50,000 to 15,000,000 pounds of military supplies to Salt Lake City in 1858-59 was signed on January 16,[17] before news of the debacle in Utah reached Leavenworth. This time the contract was signed by Russell, Majors & Waddell. These supplies were for the troops already in Utah and for 3,000 reinforcements to be sent that spring. Ten days later two expressmen from Utah arrived with the bad news, and work at assembling an inventory of losses was begun immediately. When it was finished, a claim for $493,702.61 was presented to the government.[18] This huge claim remains entirely unpaid to this day. The same expressmen who brought the shattering news also bore the receipted bills of lading, which represented transportation charges of $323,201.64 against the War Department. When Russell presented these bills to the War Department, he was told that its appropriation had been exhausted and no money was available with which to meet them. Therefore, he would have to wait until Congress passed a deficiency bill.[19]

The situation, which involved both Secretary of War Floyd and the freighting firm, was now desperate. Supplies for troops already in Utah, as well as the 3,000 reinforcements, had to be transported, but neither the Secretary nor the contractors had any funds available for transporting them. The simple truth was that Russell,

Majors & Waddell was bankrupt, and most of the financial difficulties it encountered in the next two years were a direct result of
losses in Utah and the failure of the War Department to pay for
the transportation of supplies promptly.

Because Secretary Floyd had no money, and Russell, Majors
& Waddell had exhausted its credit in outfitting in 1857 for its regular business and the transportation of supplies to Utah, some new
expedient to relieve the ruinous situation had to be found.

The problem was solved by the issuance of "Russell, Majors &
Waddell acceptances," or drafts against anticipated receipts which
would be due the firm for transporting Army supplies in 1858.
These were endorsed by Secretary Floyd, who assisted in raising
money through their use. They were to be regarded solely as obligations upon the firm, and none were to be presented to the War
Department for payment. It was intended that Floyd's endorsement
should mean that the sum of money covered by them would be due
the freighting firm within the time specified.[20]

The motives and integrity of both Russell and Secretary Floyd
in issuing these acceptances have been widely and unjustly condemned. Quartermaster General Thomas Jesup seems to have been
the only official who objected to the acceptances at first, but he was
overruled. Between March 25 and December 28, Russell issued
$1,090,714 worth of the acceptances. By this method the problem in
1858 was solved, but that was all. Between January 4 and September
13, 1859, he issued $2,680,363[21] worth; these appear to have been
largely used to retire those issued in 1858.

The new system of issuing acceptances worked too well in the
end. Instead of adjusting his badly scrambled finances and pulling
the freighting firm out of debt, Russell, in the winter of 1858-59,
with John S. Jones as partner, organized the ambitious Leavenworth
& Pike's Peak Express Company to operate a line of stage coaches
between Leavenworth, Kansas, and Denver.[22] Though neither Majors
nor Waddell approved of the new company, they allowed the
freighting firm to cash a large amount of acceptances upon it.

Although the operation of the line was highly successful, as a
money maker it was a failure. By the latter part of October 1859,
it owed $525,532.[23] To protect the freighting firm and Russell's
personal credit, the partners organized and incorporated the Central
Overland California & Pike's Peak Express Company,[24] took over
the bankrupt concern, and assumed its indebtedness.

At this time, Russell conceived the idea of obtaining the major contract for transporting United States mail to the Pacific Coast, then held by the Butterfield Overland Mail Company over the southern, or oxbow, route. If successful in obtaining the contract, he meant to move the line to the central route. His first step in that direction was taken on May 11, 1859, when he bought the J. M. Hockaday & Company mail line between the Missouri River and Salt Lake City.[25] On the same day, the Post Office Department cancelled George Chorpenning's contract to carry the mail from that city to Sacramento, California, and awarded it to the Central Overland California & Pike's Peak Express Company.[26] This planted Russell firmly on the central route and in the position of a powerful competitor when the Overland Mail Company's contract expired in 1863, providing he could successfully manage his affairs until then.

Russell's next move was to clinch the argument that the central route was the best one for a mail line to the Pacific Coast. On January 27, 1860, he telegraphed his son John that he had determined to establish a Pony Express to run from St. Joseph, Missouri, to Sacramento, California.[27] This he did, not primarily to provide the swiftest possible transmission of mail, but as an advertising device to prove that the central route could be successfully traveled regularly the year round. This romantic institution, with its swift ponies and sturdy riders, operated with almost perfect regularity and efficiency from April 3, 1860, to October 26, 1861, when the completion of the transcontinental telegraph line put it out of business. Like the majority of Russell's enterprises, it made no money and cost the firm perhaps $500,000.

While Russell was putting the Pony Express into operation, his affairs drifted from bad to worse. By midsummer, acceptances for large sums were being protested almost every day, while bankers and other entrepreneurs refused to accept new ones as security for loans. What was worse, early in the year President Buchanan told Secretary Floyd that the acceptances were irregular and improper, and that the practice should be discontinued. Floyd agreed to sign no more of them, but did not keep his word.

When the contract for transporting supplies to the military posts in the Southwest in 1860-61[28] was signed, it was supposed that the supplies would be ordered out in May as usual, and financial affairs were adjusted accordingly. For some reason, however, the wagons were not loaded and dispatched until August and September. This meant that most of the payments for transportation would be received in the latter part of September, fully six months after obligations based upon the usual starting date had matured.

While this crisis was at its height in July 1860, Russell was introduced to one Godard Bailey, a relative of Secretary Floyd by marriage, and the custodian of the Indian Trust Fund in the Interior Department.[29] This fund consisted of bonds of various states representing unpaid annuities to Indian tribes. Bailey had heard that Floyd was in trouble because of his endorsements of Russell's acceptances, and asked Russell if it were true. When Russell replied that it was, Bailey said that he had control of certain bonds which he would lend to be used as collateral in obtaining loans, with the strict understanding that they be not sold, and returned to him. Russell agreed, and Bailey gave him $150,000 worth of bonds, without telling him to whom they belonged. As security, Bailey took Russell's note for that amount.

Because of the financial condition of the country in the middle and latter part of 1860, Russell was able to raise only about $97,000 on the bonds, a "drop in the bucket" in relation to his needs. Some of the bonds he had used as collateral were about to be sold, $300,-000 worth of acceptances were about to be protested, and he had no money to take care of the situation. Having no other recourse, he returned to Bailey, who informed him as to the ownership of the bonds. Russell was stunned. But, though he was already technically and unknowingly involved in embezzlement on a large scale, he persuaded Bailey to let him have $387,000 more from the Indian Trust Fund. When this amount failed to adjust his finances, in November he obtained $333,000 more, making a total of $870,000 worth of embezzled bonds.

Not long afterward, Bailey confessed what they had done and was imprisoned. Russell was arrested in his New York office on Christmas Day 1860 and taken to Washington. The ruin of Russell, Majors & Waddell was now complete, and its partners disgraced. Each made a series of deeds of trust for the benefit of creditors, covering everything they owned, which left them penniless.

In spite of the bond scandal, Russell might have won in his battle for the major mail contract had it been pushed to a conclusion, but it was not. While it hung in the balance, word reached Washington late in February 1861 that the Confederates had destroyed the Butterfield line in southern Missouri, Arkansas, and Texas.

The contest for the contract was ended when a bill providing for the relocation of the Butterfield Overland Mail line from the southern to the central route was enacted. Because that company was also in dire financial straits, its president, William B. Dinsmore, on March 16, 1861, sublet the eastern half of the line, from the

Missouri River to Salt Lake City, to the Central Overland California & Pike's Peak Express Company.[30] In a letter to Waddell on March 20, Russell expressed satisfaction with this arrangement, and believed it would enable Russell, Majors & Waddell to solve its financial problems. It turned out, however, that he was, as usual, overoptimistic. The company continued to operate on loans from Ben Holladay, who on March 15, 1862, foreclosed a mortgage he held on it, and bid it in at auction for $100,000. He said the company owed him $208,000. The firm of Russell, Majors & Waddell made a deed of trust to its creditors, and went out of business.

Why did the firm fail? The answer is bad luck, overconfidence, poor judgment, and reckless management. Another question is: What contribution did it make to the development of the West? The answer is that during the decade 1850-60 it developed freighting on the Great Plains to its highest degree of efficiency, and carried supplies to the forts and military posts in the West and Southwest that kept the wild Indians more or less in submission. The Pony Express, its best known and probably most valuable contribution, provided the swiftest possible means of communication between the East and West when a strong secession movement threatened to carry California into the Confederacy.

After failing in an attempt to stage a comeback in Colorado, from 1861 to 1865, Russell gave a deed of trust for the benefit of creditors in the amount of $136,903.43 and went back to New York. Day by day he sank deeper into poverty-stricken obscurity. Having no other means of support, he peddled "Tic Sano," a cure for neuralgia. On September 10, 1872, he died at the home of his son John in Palmyra, Missouri, some five months after Waddell's death in Lexington. Majors outlived his partners twenty-eight years, dying in Chicago on January 14, 1900.

The Burlington Railroad:

A Citizen of the West

RICHARD C. OVERTON
University of Western Ontario

The Burlington is, and long has been, a very big railroad and, for the West, a very old one. The original 12-mile segment that was chartered in 1849 by the turn of the century had grown to nearly 8,000 miles and today consists of approximately 11,000 miles in 14 states. At least twenty million documents pertinent to Burlington history are in existence. Because the company has never gone into receivership or lost its key records, the corporate minute books of more than 200 constituent companies are still carefully preserved in its vaults. So is the vast bulk of executive correspondence, though that for the nineteenth century is deposited in the Newberry Library. In addition, there are tons of reports, statistics, and artifacts of all sizes, shapes, and descriptions.

Thus, even though the Burlington is by no means the largest railroad system in the country, or even in the West, it has generated enough historical documents to keep not one but a team of historians busy for their whole professional careers. Because the company is history conscious, it is a meticulous record keeper and cooperative with historians. It is a responsible citizen of the West.

What are the origins of the Burlington? Actually, it began as a series of disconnected lines. The oldest segment is the Aurora Branch, chartered on February 12, 1849, to link the mill town of Aurora with the main line of the Galena & Chicago Union, twelve miles to the north. The first train, composed of a borrowed engine and borrowed car, made its run over this segment on September 2, 1850. The Burlington had three other small forerunners in Illinois: the unpronounceable Peoria & Oquawka hoped to run between Peoria and the Mississippi River; the Northern Cross sought to link Quincy with the western terminus of the Illinois-Michigan Canal; and the Central Military Tract planned to connect Galesburg with what later became the Rock Island Railroad.

The Burlington as a system really began when James F. Joy, John W. Brooks, and John Murray Forbes, all officials of the Michigan Central Railroad, began buying securities of the four unconnected forerunners with the idea of linking them together and providing a western feeder for the Michigan Central. They started to carry out this program in the winter of 1851-52, adopted the title Chicago, Burlington, and Quincy (CB&Q) in 1855, and on January 31, 1856, completed the construction of the railroad that exactly fitted its name. However, it was not until 1864 that the present corporation came into being. During the same year, incidentally, the company built a direct line between Chicago and Aurora, thus relegating the original segment to the minor branchline status it has held ever since.

Even before organization of the original CB&Q was completed, Forbes, Joy, and Brooks realized that feeders in Illinois alone would not be enough. Therefore, they obtained the funds and talent to acquire and complete the Hannibal & St. Joseph across northern Missouri by 1859, and the Burlington and Missouri River across Iowa a decade later. The pattern continued across the Missouri: between 1869 and 1872 the same triumvirate sponsored the Burlington & Missouri River Railroad in Nebraska and built it almost 200 miles west of the Missouri River to a junction with the Union Pacific at Kearney. Meanwhile, they had extended the Hannibal & St. Joseph into Kansas City, and linked Kansas City and Omaha along the east bank of the Missouri River. Thus, by 1872, the Burlington group of lines served a strategic swath of midwestern territory which extended from Chicago to the very edge of the farmers' frontier.

Forbes, Brooks, and Joy—what a combination! Forbes was the George Washington of the Burlington. Born a proper Bostonian in 1813, he made a fortune in China and, at the age of twenty-three, settled down as a capitalist in Boston. At this time he had no particular interest in railroads; perhaps he would have gravitated into them eventually, but Brooks and Joy influenced him to take the first plunge, in 1846. Brooks, born in 1819 and, like Forbes, a New Englander, was a professional engineer who was trained by the great Laommi Baldwin. In 1845, at the age of twenty-six, he was superintendent of the Auburn & Rochester and looking for bigger fields to conquer. In that respect he was like the third member of the triumvirate.

James F. Joy, born in New Hampshire in 1810, was a go-getter from the outset. Working his way through Dartmouth College and Harvard Law School, he early decided that only the West was large enough for his talents, and hung out his shingle as a lawyer in Detroit in 1836. The state of Michigan, at the time, had started to build the Detroit and St. Joseph to form part of a through route between Detroit and Chicago. But the state had neither the talent nor the funds nor the popular support for any such enterprise, and late in 1845 put the rickety 144-mile line on the auction block. To Brooks the engineer and to Joy the lawyer, this looked like a golden opportunity; they persuaded Forbes to mobilize the capital to buy, rebuild, and complete the Michigan Central.

The project prospered from the outset. By the time the rails reached Lake Michigan, the original idea of using a ferry from St. Joseph to Chicago was abandoned for an all-rail route. During the winter of 1851-52, as the rails were laid around the south end of the lake, Brooks and Joy persuaded Forbes to help them pick up and piece together the original components of the CB&Q.

The way these men worked together constituted a pattern of Burlington history for the first quarter century of its existence. Joy was invariably the advance agent, the promoter, the salesman, and the lobbyist. He studied local projects and plans, scrutinized charters, and dreamed up countless propositions whereby, in return for promised financial aid, local groups would alter their individual plans to suit his wide-ranging schemes and eventually yield financial control and management to the CB&Q. Once Joy had negotiated such an arrangement, Brooks would appear on the scene and take charge of such construction or rebuilding as was necessary, while Forbes would approach eastern capitalists to mobilize the necessary funds.

In brief, Joy was the spark plug, the planner, the strategist; Brooks the technician; and Forbes the financier. But Forbes was more than that: so well established was his reputation for integrity and balanced judgment that he was looked upon as the natural leader of what became known as "The Forbes Group." Modern business historians call this group an "entrepreneurial alliance." By the end of the Civil War the alliance was interested not only in the Michigan Central and Burlington group of lines, but also in the Mount Savage Iron Works—which later became the firm of Calumet & Hecla, Inc.—the St. Mary's Falls Ship Canal, and many lesser enterprises.

The alliance never had any formal structure. Although more of its members lived in Boston than anywhere else, they were spread from one end of the Northeast to the other and carried on their business by correspondence, not only among each other, but with a host of young and promising lieutenants that they sent into the field. One such lieutenant was Charles Elliott Perkins, son of an impecunious minister, but descended, through both his father and mother, from the best Boston families. As a lad he spent a summer with his eastern relatives and caught Forbes' eye. Thus, in 1859, Forbes offered him a clerkship on the Burlington and Missouri River of Iowa. At this time, that railroad was just completing its first seventy-five miles into Ottumwa, and Perkins' career developed along with it; by the year 1872 he was in charge of the railroad.

In that same year the Burlington and Missouri River Railroad in Nebraska arrived at Kearney, the point farthest west on the system. At this time, there was no reason to go any farther; the Union Pacific had been completed in 1869, and two side-by-side transcontinental railroads could not be justified. If the Burlington were to expand, the most promising direction seemed to be toward the Twin Cities. Joy discovered that two roads were projected from Dubuque on the west side of the Mississippi; another series of lines ran from Aurora westward. By building relatively short links, these various properties could be hitched together to form the greater part of a through route toward the Twin Cities.

This was the sort of challenge that Joy loved, and by 1872 he had twenty years of experience. His usual technique, when approaching a struggling independent local company, was to offer to market their bonds in exchange for a majority of stock. Furthermore, the CB&Q would usually agree to accept its share of joint revenues in the form of company bonds. The funds thus supplied would enable the local company to build or improve its road, the CB&Q obtaining control with a minimum outlay of money. It was actually a "pay-as-you-go" system, used by the Burlington a dozen times.

When it came to the proposed River Roads, as the two railroads north and south of Dubuque were called, Joy naturally attempted to make the same sort of deal. He found, however, that they had promised a majority of their stock to the construction companies involved. Hence, and probably not thinking much about it, he and five other CB&Q directors promptly bought control of the construction companies. Once this was done, he negotiated the necessary traffic contracts, and construction began on the River Roads.

This time everything seemed to go wrong. The contracts between the River Roads and the construction companies were so loosely drawn that, in effect, the construction companies were not obligated to finish the lines once they had used up the proceeds of the railroad company stocks and bonds. Because of the Panic of 1873, the two River Roads found it impossible to meet their interest payments. Joy arranged through the CB&Q board to have that company pay the interest due, but he failed to tell Forbes and Griswold, among others, that he and other members of the board had an interest in the construction companies which would be saved only if the River Roads themselves were kept from bankruptcy.

Wholly by chance Forbes found out about this dual relationship of Joy and several other directors. Joy stoutly maintained that, no matter how casual all these dealings had been, it was for the good of the Burlington as a whole and that no CB&Q stockholder, other than those who, like himself, had invested in the construction companies, had lost any money.

But to Forbes this was not good enough. He refused to accept the notion that a director with conflicting interests could properly serve the company. Determined that Joy should be ousted, he organized and waged a battle for proxies. The affair, known as "The Revolution of 1875," was treated in banner headlines across the nation. Of Joy's contributions to the system there could be no doubt; he had been bold, brilliant, and imaginative. But in the River Roads affair he was not only casual but brazen. Forbes could not compromise with single-minded fidelity, and a majority of the stockholders agreed with him. Thus Forbes won the day; more importantly, so did the Burlington. In a decade remembered in railroad history for the Credit Mobilier scandal, this was no mean accomplishment.

After Joy's departure, Forbes emerged as the system's strong man of the East, while the extraordinarily gifted Perkins forged to the front in the West. Named a director of the CB&Q in 1875, Perkins became president in 1881, and for the next twenty years ruled as well as reigned in a way that no other president of the system has before or since. By this time, both the Burlington and Missouri River of Iowa and the Burlington and Missouri River Railroad in Nebraska had been consolidated into the CB&Q, and in 1883 the company obtained permanent control of the Hannibal & St. Joseph.

Meanwhile, between 1875 and 1881, Perkins had his hands full in a prolonged battle with Jay Gould. When Gould failed to isolate the Burlington from its friendly connections, he proposed in 1877 to lease the Burlington and Missouri River Railroad in Nebraska as part of the Union Pacific. Some members of the CB&Q board, awed by the mighty Gould, were in favor of the proposition. Had it been approved, the history of the West would have been profoundly affected. But Perkins and Forbes stood firmly against it, and Gould had to be satisfied with a treaty by which each system agreed not to invade the territory of the other. Such an arrangement meant little to Gould. Quickly changing hats, he had his Missouri Pacific build into eastern Nebraska, whereupon Forbes and Perkins promptly extended the Burlington direct to Denver.

Meanwhile the company had gained access to St. Louis, and in 1886 sponsored a subsidiary which carried the system into the Twin Cities. With this accomplishment, the Burlington reached its "natural boundaries." It also served directly on its own lines Chicago, Omaha, Denver, St. Louis, and Kansas City; in between, the rich Granger country was laced by internal lines. The only other major building of the century was the line northwestward to Billings, completed in 1894 in order to provide an interchange with the Pacific Northwest.

The goal of the Forbes group was the permanent buildup of the Burlington; they had no notion whatever of building a "speculator's railroad" for quick sale to somebody else. From the very earliest day, the physical plant was built as solidly as possible, and according to the most advanced technical ideas. Just as quickly as possible timber trestles were replaced by stone or iron; stations and shops—such as those at Aurora—were built of massive stone and brick rather than timber. Great care was taken to keep equipment in top condition. As early as 1877, the company established a testing laboratory at Aurora—among the first established by any railroad.

The Boston group was devoted to the doctrine of *laissez faire*. The original Aurora Branch charter had given that company exclusive right to fix its own rates and fares. When the states started passing the so-called Granger laws in the early 1870's, the CB&Q tried its best to ward off such legislation, claiming that only the market place could fix prices and that it was in the interest of the railroad to charge the lowest possible rates so as to attract the most business.

But the Burlington was fighting a losing battle. This it found out when it decided to test a maximum rate law passed in the early seventies by Iowa. The case went all the way to the Supreme Court and was decided on the same day in 1877, and in precisely the same way, as the celebrated *Munn vs. Illinois*. In *CB&Q vs. Iowa*, the highest tribunal simply applied the doctrine that a business clothed with the public interest must submit to regulation to the extent of the interest thus created. Much as the Burlington disagreed in principle with state regulation, it insisted that the company obey meticulously whatever laws were on the books. This was not done for moral reasons; its conservative managers simply felt that in the long run they would lose less financially and gain more in public and government relations by obeying the law. In other words, from more than one standpoint, honesty was regarded as the soundest policy.

During the middle eighties, when federal legislation was under discussion, Perkins took a tremendously active part in trying to convince Congress, Senator Shelby M. Cullom in particular, that the railroads were their own best judges when it came to rate making. And he campaigned vigorously against the anti-pooling sentiment of the day, maintaining that stable and orderly rates arrived at through agreement were far more beneficial to shippers and railroads alike than cut-throat competition. But, as he ruefully said later, his ideas had no more effect than a "fly on a cartwheel."

The Interstate Commerce Act became law in 1887, and the Burlington obeyed it, though Richard Olney, a counsel and director of the company, strongly urged that it be violated as a test case. To this, Perkins firmly objected; he thought that, if the law did not work, the good sense of the people would cause Congress to amend it. In this, he was quite correct, although the amendments—notably the Hepburn Act—were hardly to his liking.

Basically, the nineteenth century attitude of the Burlington toward labor was consistent with the policies of *laissez faire*. Management had a lively sense of the dignity of the individual and earnestly tried to see that each man had proper working conditions, good tools, and every opportunity for advancement. But anything that smacked of paternalism was out of order. And only reluctantly did the company, by the middle eighties, consent to deal with system union officials; under no circumstances would they deal with national unions. The most serious strike on the system occurred in 1888, when, during Perkins' absence from Chicago, a subordinate officer refused to display a sufficiently conciliatory attitude toward a variety of alleged grievances.

As a result, most of the engineers on the system walked out, and they were later joined by the switchmen. The company won the struggle; within a matter of weeks it had hired enough men to keep the trains moving. But from then on the company relaxed many of its fixed ideas about paternalism, and among other things established, in 1889, a Relief Department that provided all employees, on a contributory basis, with life insurance and a measure of protection against illness and accidents.

Because of the basic fact that the men who had invested in the Burlington and were in charge of it intended to stay with it, the company consistently and instinctively identified itself closely with the communities it served. This was particularly notable in the land-grant areas of Iowa and Nebraska where, quite literally, the railroad established whole communities. It set up immigrant houses for prospective settlers; it transported their household and farm goods, either free or at reduced tariffs; it gave land buyers up to ten years to pay for their property and granted substantial discounts if the land were improved; and, when hard times came in the middle seventies, it granted countless extensions of time, the records revealing that not a single farmer who remained on his land was ever dispossessed. In a granted area, the company donated a lot to the first church established regardless of denomination, and helped establish a newspaper and a school. It was indefatigable in displaying the produce of its area; crop samples from Iowa and Nebraska were sent to fairs all over the world, and it was the Burlington that first introduced alfalfa in Nebraska.

This community identification and activity may not have been dictated purely by a high moral purpose. The point is that the railroad was in business to stay, and it was smart enough to know that it could never succeed unless it helped solve the problems of its own communities.

At the turn of the century, the Burlington, like England, resembled a "tight little island." Its lines totaled approximately 8,000 miles. It was one of the larger systems of the day, stretching from Chicago and St. Louis on the east to Kansas City, Omaha, Denver, Billings, and the Twin Cities. It had approximately 14,000 stockholders, many of whom had held their shares for a generation or more.

But bigger systems and consolidation were in the air. Both

Harriman, chairman of the Union Pacific, and Hill, president of the Great Northern and the controlling voice in the Northern Pacific, felt that the Burlington would be an essential complement to their systems. Once this fact became known, various Wall Street groups began scrambling for Burlington stock, and before long the price began skyrocketing. Because in Perkins' view it would be a calamity if the road were controlled by a shifting group of speculators, he determined that it would be far better to sell to either one of the large systems that sought to acquire it. Of the two, he strongly and consistently favored the Northern Lines. So it was that in 1901 the Burlington was sold jointly to the Great Northern and the Northern Pacific for $200 a share.

The combination was a natural one, for the Burlington not only supplied an essential link between the Twin Cities and Chicago, thus bringing both Northern Lines directly into Chicago, but its network dovetailed splendidly with that of the Northern properties. There was another equally compelling consideration: James J. Hill had proved himself one of the most capable railroad managers the nation had ever produced. He was not a New Englander; in fact, he was born on a farm in a tiny town in central Ontario. But he shared instinctively the ideas of Forbes and Perkins. Because he was well aware of the proven success of Burlington methods and administration, he was wise enough to make no changes in executives. No change of name was made, nor any change in administration that would not have taken place anyway. George B. Harris, long a trusted lieutenant of Perkins, took the latter's post as president.

Why was it that the Burlington did not build to the West Coast or to the Gulf of Mexico? During the 1880's and the 1890's, the company gave much consideration to expansion. George W. Holdrege, long-time manager of the Lines West, in particular, was an ardent expansionist. Surveys were made through the Rockies and along both the Colorado River and the Grand River; they were also made from central Wyoming west to Oregon and down to Salt Lake City. Time and again the company plotted out the country from Alliance through Billings on toward Great Falls. And, on at least two occasions, acquisition of the Katy was seriously considered.

None of these plans was carried out for two simple reasons. So long as the Burlington could keep open the gateways at its perimeter, it was assured of a steady flow of traffic with major connecting lines. Thus there never seemed to be any need to make the tremendous financial outlay for a major extension. The conservative executives of the Burlington were well aware that expansion had brought the Northern Pacific, the Union Pacific, and the Santa Fe into receivership. Furthermore, the Burlington always enjoyed a tremendous amount of traffic which either originated in or was destined for its own territory. Therefore, it seemed preferable to improve the property intensively and to make maximum use of it.

However, once the Burlington became affiliated with the Northern Lines, a short route between the Pacific Northwest and the Gulf seemed especially desirable. A logical solution seemed to be the acquisition of the Colorado and Southern and its wholly owned affiliate, the Fort Worth and Denver City. This system, acquired in 1908, connected with the Burlington in central Wyoming and gave the company access to the territory between there and Denver, and then through Colorado Springs, Pueblo, Trinidad, Amarillo, and on into Fort Worth. From that city, connections existed with the Gulf Coast, and eventually the Colorado and Southern obtained a half interest in the old Trinity and Brazos Valley, more recently known as the Burlington-Rock Island. This line provided access to both Houston and Galveston. In 1914, the Burlington completed a more direct link between Orin Junction and Billings.

Virtually all other construction during the twentieth century has been for purposes of improvement. Because of speed and low-grade requirements, the CB&Q built its Centennial Cutoff, completed in 1952, which greatly shortened the western end of the Chicago-Kansas City line.

About a generation ago, a spectacular change took place in motive power and equipment. From the beginning of 1932 until August 1949, the president of the railroad was Ralph Budd, an engineer by training, and a student of James J. Hill. Budd came to the Burlington at the depth of the Depression, but he had new ideas and a vigorous approach. He decreased the number of operating divisions, lent his support to the construction of the Dotsero Cutoff— thus leading to a quadrupling of business through the Denver gateway for the Burlington—and, in a mighty effort to recapture passenger business, introduced the first diesel-powered streamlined train, the Pioneer Zephyr.

The first run of this train, highlighted later by the dawn-to-dusk run from Denver to Chicago, on May 26, 1934, ushered in a new era in railroading. Within a few years, all the principal Burlington passenger trains were of the diesel streamlined type, and before long the steam engine was on its way out in freight service as well. Another "first" was Budd's introduction of the Vista Dome in 1945.

Since 1949 the president of the Burlington has been Harry C. Murphy, an engineer by profession, who started work with the company in 1914. The problems he has faced have been mainly those of technological change. Yet, like all railroads today, the Burlington is undergoing other critical changes. It must fight harder than ever for traffic, it must spend vast sums for technological improvement, it must somehow find a way to cut down on unneeded manpower without creating undue hardship for labor, and it must press for a more realistic rate regulatory structure.

Fortunately—and certainly this is one of the distinctive things about the Burlington—its financial house has always been kept in order. The Bostonians who dominated the railroad during the nineteenth century were not only honest but cautious. Early in the company's history they established sinking funds and kept a sharp eye on the relation of funded debt to earning capacity. These financial methods were continued under Hill and the men trained by him; during Ralph Budd's presidency funded debt was greatly simplified and reduced on the CB&Q; and the present administration has improved the finances of the Colorado and Southern and the Fort Worth and Denver. The CB&Q has regularly paid dividends since 1863. So far as the record shows, it has never, in its whole 113 years, defaulted on any obligation.

A formal proposal is now pending to merge the Great Northern, the Northern Pacific, and the Burlington. If the merger occurs, it will not mean any change of attitude whatever so far as the Burlington is concerned, any more than it did when the CB&Q was sold to the Northern Lines in 1901.

The Burlington has earned the title "Citizen of the West." It has been honest and reliable, assumed and discharged civic responsibility, and been imaginative and foresighted. Above all, it cast its lot with the West, and has played an important role in its development.

The Mining Engineer in the West

CLARK C. SPENCE
University of Illinois

In recent years, historians have devoted more attention to the development of the western mineral industry—an industry with its own problems of capital formation, labor-management relations, and technology. However, an important figure in the development of the industry, the trained mining engineer, has long been ignored. Not a pathfinder, not a pioneer in the traditional sense, he has been eclipsed by more colorful figures on the western scene. Few monuments, biographies, or place names on the map recall his contributions, yet he was instrumental in guiding the thorough and efficient exploitation of underground resources after the boom days had passed.

Prior to 1870, few formally educated mining engineers were employed in the West. The backbone of the mineral industry was, and would continue to be for some time, the practical man of experience, often with the title "Captain" before his name and a touch of Cornwall in his speech. Only gradually would mining school graduates come to replace these men in positions of importance.

At first—perhaps to about 1880—most engineers were educated in Europe: a handful at the *Ecole des Mines* in Paris, or at comparable institutions in Berlin or Madrid; a larger number at the Royal School of Mines, London; the majority at the *Königliche Sächsische Bergakademie* at Freiberg in Saxony, an institution which was to mining what Heidelberg and the Sorbonne were to arts and letters. American students at Freiberg included some who became the most prominent geologists and mining engineers of the nineteenth century: the soft-spoken Janin brothers of Louisiana; John H. Boalt, whose name would be perpetuated by the University of California law school; Raphael Pumpelly, the "American Humboldt"—engineer, geologist, archaeologist, and explorer; Rossiter W. Raymond, the most versatile of all, a founder and guiding light of the American Institute of Mining Engineers for more than forty years, "sailor, soldier, engineer, lawyer, orator, novelist, storyteller, poet, biblical critic, theologian, teacher, chess-player"; and, of course, the best known of all mining engineers except Herbert Hoover, that "Wizard of Modern Gold Mining," John Hays Hammond, reputed in his day "to have the most wonderful scent of the yellow metal of any living man."[1]

During the Civil War, the Columbia School of Mines had opened its doors and begun to train engineers. By 1890, competing with a score of other institutions, it was awarding about as many degrees in the mining field as all other American colleges combined. Among the others, California, Colorado Mines, the Massachusetts Institute of Technology, and the scientific schools of Yale and Harvard were outstanding, and would eventually train more men in the profession than the Columbia School of Mines.[2] Some engineers underwent apprenticeship training with British engineering firms, and a handful were privately trained by fathers who were practicing engineers. And one, at least, successfully entered the field after a full four-year course from the International Correspondence School at Scranton.[3]

There was no typical mining engineer in the West, either in education or background. Like bluff William Cowan Jackling, he might have worked his way up through mining school from poverty. He might be the son of financier William C. Ralston of California or of General O. O. Howard. He might be the father of future actor Basil Rathbone. Or he might have been born into an engineering family like the Rickards, which at one time had eight members in the American Institute of Mining Engineers.[4] If not native-born, the chances were good that he came from England or Germany.

The so-called "mining engineer" was sometimes trained in another engineering field. This occurred because it was not uncommon, for example, to employ a mechanical or civil engineer to design, erect, and repair machinery for hoisting, pumping, and milling, and then to place him in charge of mining operations as well.[5] Civil, mechanical, and even electrical engineers often made reputations as mining engineers. Hennen Jennings, for example, who grew to professional maturity as a mining engineer in the West and to international prominence in South Africa, was a trained civil engineer. So also was Arthur D. Foote, a visionary but an able man destined to live forever in the shadow of his wife, novelist Mary Hallack Foote.

Whatever his education, the professional engineer had to overcome an early prejudice of practical miners against "them d—— eddicated fellers." When young John Hays Hammond returned from Freiberg in 1879, he sought employment with George Hearst, a family friend and one of the most important mine owners in the West. Hearst, at first refusing him, stated: "The fact of the matter is, Jack, you've been to Freiberg and have learned a lot of damn geological theories and big names for little rocks. That don't go in this country." "Anything else?" asked Hammond. "No," said Hearst, "Freiberg is enough." "Well," said Hammond, "I'll make a confession to you if you won't tell my father. I *didn't* learn anything of importance at Freiberg." He got the job—at $50 a month.[6]

Part of the hostility on the part of the practical miners stemmed from the superior attitude frequently displayed by fledgling engineers, who sometimes made costly errors that practical miners never forgot. A standard witticism of the ordinary miner was: "How are things in Cripple Creek? . . . Oh, they are about the same as usual. The tenderfeet are taking the ore out where they find it, and the mining engineers are hunting for it where it ought to be." The hostility continued into the 1890's, though most western engineers had by then won acceptance and their services were strongly in demand.[7]

Their acceptance was indicated by their many imitators—the "local butchers, bakers and candlestick-makers, who put M. E. to their names" and posed as mining experts. In the Black Hills in the nineties these self-styled "engineers" and "professors" were "thicker than flies around the bunghole of an empty beer barrel in summer time."[8] Because the public often lumped together indiscriminately the bona fide engineer and his imitators, some of the opprobrium directed at the latter undoubtedly fell upon the shoulders of the former. In time, however, most of the imitators faded into the shadows.

Before settling into a mining career, a surprisingly large number of graduate mining engineers worked temporarily at other types of employment. Many did survey work for rivers, harbors, and railroads; one began his career as assistant engineer on the Brooklyn Bridge; another as chemist with the American Sugar Refinery; one taught school; James Douglas, who has been called the "Bryce of mining," for a time managed an insane asylum; and literally dozens, including John Hays Hammond, Herbert Hoover, and the Hague brothers, were employed by state and national geological surveys.[9]

Once established in the mining field, the professional engineer might turn his talents in any of several directions. But especially in demand were inspecting engineers, who examined and reported upon mining property offered for sale. In this kind of work, the engineer sampled and tested ores; carefully studied vein formations; and, if the mine was a producing one, examined the company books. Sometimes he carried with him an elaborate cipher, by which to convey information secretly to his employer or broker from the nearest telegraph station. One such cipher even included a few private code words, presumably for communication with a hearth-bound wife.[10]

Their professional reputation being at stake, many engineers made their inspections and prepared their reports with great trepidation. A California engineer, J. S. Phillips, considered the Blue Jacket mine to be the only one he ever inspected on the Pacific Coast which "fulfilled all the geological requirements of a perfect lode." Geologically perfect or not, it was a failure; and it was partially for this reason that he moved his offices to New York.[11]

Thomas A. Rickard left the profession to become an editor after the adverse publicity that occurred when he overestimated the ore reserves of the Camp Bird mine in Colorado. "So long as I examined relatively small mines for individuals," he wrote later, "my work as a consulting engineer was delightful. . . . But when I was called upon to report upon mines the purchase of which involved millions of dollars, I found that I had to be mixed up in a kind of business for which I had a decided distaste."[12]

Rickard's undoing in the Camp Bird episode was the result of relying upon information furnished by others, a not uncommon failing:

> The expert appears in the field, fills himself to bursting from the foreman, under-foreman, miners and everybody else about the place from whom he can pick up a few crumbs, down to the logger and the Chinaman. Then he gives it all off as his own, and to further enhance the importance of the production, it is padded out with a great many pages and columns of figures, copied from the company's books, as to the gross receipts and dividends referred to.[13]

An inspecting engineer always had to be alert against the danger of deception. Many ingenious "salting" schemes were attempted and a few succeeded. The best known instance, no doubt, occurred in 1872, when Henry Janin, a conservative engineer of skill and integrity, prepared an innocent and glowing report on diamond fields that had been "discovered" in northwestern Colo-

103

rado, only to have the fields exposed by Clarence King as a clever swindle.[14] On some occasions, a mine operator simply kept inspecting engineers so plied with liquor that they could neither properly sample ore nor conduct an inspection. More than once, inspecting engineers lost their own money in "salted" mines that seemed to offer great opportunities.[15]

Most examining engineers were trustworthy, but a few of them contributed to the following stereotype:

> With leather leggins and doe-skin suit he rides at a furious
> pace,
> And the anxious miner weighs every word and tries to read
> his face.
> He has few scruples but takes many drams, and he'll take a
> double fee
> From the man who buys and the man who sells, and serves
> them both loyally.[16]

This type of engineer made his inspection for a fee contingent upon sale of the property, a practice unacceptable to most mining engineers; or he guaranteed the owner a favorable report—for a price. Occasionally a mining engineer went to prison for chicanery of some sort, for, as one of the Rickards put it, "the moral code of some men is the penal code."[17]

Many inspection reports either displayed too much imagination or were totally noncommittal. Concerning the ultra-imaginative reports, one reader of the *Mining and Scientific Press* said: "A collection of mining romances in the shape of reports on mines, if published, would afford entertainment for readers of fiction unequaled by any modern publication."[18] Inspecting engineers, especially academicians, were sometimes guilty of overusing scientific terms and of "slinging solid chunks of geology around with an appalling looseness." "I have seen a report," said one of the profession, "which started with the nebular hypothesis, and traced the progress of the earth from its pulpy state right down through its various stages to oxidation of the outcrop of a particular vein in the year of grace in which the report was written."[19]

The noncommittal reports were usually the result of an inability of the inspecting engineer to foretell the future. Even conscientious engineers qualified their opinions and sought to protect themselves by hedging, though their employers were demanding clear-cut answers.[20]

In addition to their role as consultants when property changed hands, mining engineers often served as mine managers.[21] In this capacity, practical experience was obviously a great help. Ideally, the engineer-manager "should be able to run an engine, know how to run a mill in all its branches, know when each stamp is doing its duty, detect a loose mortar-hole, cut out any timber for a shaft or drive or elsewhere, sharpen a pick or drill; in fact he must be a miniature encyclopaedia."[22] Some engineers, without practical experience, did a creditable job because of their administrative and bookkeeping capability and because they had capable mine and mill foremen under them.[23] Yet, because of the tendency—especially in the 1860's[24]—toward the premature or needless construction of expensive milling equipment,[25] a practical background was highly desirable. A certain amount of integrity was also required, for equipment manufacturers frequently gave a kick-back to engineers recommending the purchase of their equipment.[26]

Engineers competed for inspection and managerial posts not only with practical miners, but also with men from all walks of life. As time went on, specialization occurred, more and more engineers confining their work either to consulting or managing. Frequently, though not always successfully, they worked for several mining companies at one time.[27]

The elite of the profession found testifying lucrative. They served as expert witnesses on one side or the other in the great tangle of litigation that was common in the mining world, particularly in the sideline boundary disputes arising under the controversial apex law. Such testimony was both costly and prodigious. For example, in a suit between two Montana companies, ten mining experts testified at a total cost of more than $100,000 to the litigants. The testimony of scientific witnesses in an 1877 Nevada case was expected to "make a book as large as any on geology yet published." And, one editor added, the opinions would be "more diversified than is usual in such cases, and some of the statements made are entirely original."[28]

A confusing complex of apex litigation in the two decades after 1890 brought a steady parade of leading engineers and geologists to Butte, some for Anaconda and some against. Among them was Clarence King. In the evening, he would join with such men as Louis Janin, Rossiter Raymond, or Nathan Shaler of Harvard in scintillating conversation.[29]

Masterminding the Anaconda cases was D. W. Brunton, a University of Michigan engineer who had specialized in apex questions in Colorado before Marc Daly brought him to Montana. He was responsible for the establishment of Anaconda's geological department, under Horace Winchell, which thoroughly mapped and surveyed the company's mines for purposes of the lawsuits. When consolidation ended most of the litigation, Winchell's staff then began to deal systematically with the Butte area on a district-wide basis, and soon the region became the classic example of mineral zoning; and Anaconda's mode of mine mapping, a by-product of the litigation, became recognized throughout the world.[30]

Lawyers and "honest partisans" like Janin and Raymond, the latter the nation's foremost authority on the law of the apex, recognized that expert witnesses were seldom objective. The courts acknowledged the shortcomings of such testimony, but admitted it as the best available. Yet the situation was manifestly absurd: leading scientific men propounded intricate and contradictory geological theories before juries and judges who knew nothing of science or of the technicalities of mining.

Despite suggestions that special boards of arbitration be established or that the courts select their own non-partisan witnesses, which elicited little response, the litigation went on as usual:[31]

> A dozen lawyers on a side,
> And eminent experts multiplied;
> Maps of the biggest and the best,
> And models till you couldn't rest;
> Samples of rock and vein formation,
> And assays showing "mineralization,"
> And theories of that or this,
> And revelation of "genesis,"
> And summings-up of sound and fury
> Poured out upon the judge and jury.
> No matter now which party lost—
> It took the mine to pay the cost;
> And all the famous fight who saw
> Beheld, with mingled pride and awe,
> What science breeds when crossed with law.[32]

Most mining engineers in the West became interested in mine speculation, promotion, and ownership. Not infrequently they accepted stock in exchange for their services.[33] Many speculated profitably in the stock of the companies employing them, despite the questionable ethics of the practice.[34] Some, like "Jack" Hammond, who moved his offices to New York in the 1880's to be near the sources of capital, or Hamilton Smith, Jr., co-organizer of the

Rothschild-backed Exploration Company, Ltd., at times in their careers concerned themselves almost exclusively with the promotional aspects of mining.[35]

· Hammond had an interest in the Bunker Hill & Sullivan Mining and Concentrating Company from its inception, as did also Frederick W. Bradley, another example of the engineer-promoter-owner. A graduate of the University of California School of Mines, Bradley was first resident manager of Bunker Hill & Sullivan, then president. In the early 1920's, he was an executive officer in sixteen mining and smelting companies.[36]

Income varied with prestige and experience. Few mining engineers were millionaires like Herbert Hoover, John Hays Hammond, Daniel Jackling, and a few others, but most enjoyed a comfortably high standard of living. A provincial definition of a mining engineer in 1899 was: "One who makes funny figures on blazed stumps and charges a big price."[37] Neophytes might expect a beginning salary of from $50 to $150 a month; more experienced men often commanded $5,000 to $10,000 a year as mine managers. Consulting fees ranged from a few hundred dollars upward, the elite frequently collecting from $2,000 to $10,000 for a single report. John Hays Hammond once, in 1900, received $50,000 from a Colorado firm for consultant services. He admitted that he charged "all the traffic would bear, or almost the limit" on the ground that his reputation was at stake.[38]

The life of the mining engineer in the West was a roving one. "The mining engineer is like a soldier or sailor," wrote Edward McCarthy, an Englishman. "He has to pack his traps and say good-bye to loved ones at a moment's notice, and when requested to do so."[39] T. A. Rickard estimated that from 1889 to 1902 he averaged 35,000 miles a year, including two voyages round the world. During the first year after his marriage, he was "at home only once for a whole week."[40]

Travel conditions left much to be desired. Raphael Pumpelly made a grueling trip from Missouri to Tucson by Overland Mail coach in 1860, then continued to the Santa Rita mines by wagon. Another engineer made horseback journeys in Colorado of thirty-five days duration, often spending ten or twelve hours a day in the saddle. Another traveled by canoe in the Northwest in a driving rain with nothing to eat but salted clams and stewed herring. Rickard made a number of professional trips in the San Juan Mountains on skis or snowshoes and was once swept off the trail by a snowslide. "It was a healthy and vigorous life," he commented later.[41]

Hays Hammond made a two-week inspection trip into Death Valley under scorching summer suns; a few years later, he and a fellow engineer traveled 200 miles from the railroad to examine a mine in eastern Nevada, the two of them taking turns running alongside their runner-equipped buckboard to keep from freezing. Once at the property, they inspected the water-filled mine at the twelfth level in a collapsible boat, the water being "over the head" of the diminutive Hammond. They stayed so long underground that word of disaster had been sent out by the time they finally reached the surface.[42]

Other physical hazards were encountered, such as loose timbers, rotten ladders, reptiles, and insects. An engineer examining an abandoned mine near Tombstone found a host of horned toads and rattlesnakes, about a thousand rats, and half a dozen fearsome Gila monsters. He stated: "I wouldn't give a cuss—for the mine—except as a side-show—or a menagerie. It's worth a hundred thousand dollars for that—a regular bonanza."[43]

The mining engineer was also exposed to the violence of the West. When Raphael Pumpelly arrived in Arizona in 1860 to re-open the Santa Rita mines, he first had to contend with a murderous blacksmith—an ex-convict from Australia; next, he was ambushed by Apaches, who stole his horse; then he was one of the party who found the remains of a German engineer, Frederick Brunckow, his body pierced with a rock drill and flung by Mexicans down a mine shaft. After eighteen months of such adventures, Pumpelly left the Southwest, marveling that he was the "only one of at least five successive managers of the Santa Rita who was not killed by Mexicans or Indians."[44]

Life in subsequent decades was less perilous, but mining and mining towns still provided excitement. When a company fell behind in meeting its payroll, sometimes irate miners made life miserable and even uncertain for the engineer-manager.[45] A graduate of Virginia Polytechnic Institute was actually stoned to death by miners in Mexico after his firm had defaulted on wage payments.[46] "Jack" Hammond witnessed a gun fight on his very first day in the town of Bodie in 1880; Herbert Hoover long remembered Steeple Rock, New Mexico, where he was assistant mine manager in the 1890's. The inhabitants "practiced a good deal of original sin," he said, and the manager, another engineer, also served as deputy sheriff, in the best tradition regularly incarcerating his prisoners in an unused mine shaft until the sheriff arrived.[47]

Living conditions in such towns were often crude and sometimes impossible for genteel families. However, bachelors and engineers without their wives seemed to have enjoyed themselves in early Leadville, for example; and Hammond, James Hague, and a friend made a congenial trio at Grass Valley in California. "We spent our time," said Hague, "with quartz by day and pints by night."[48]

The life of the engineer was by no means as risky as that of the common miner, who spent from eight to ten hours of each working day underground, yet accidents took their toll. Some engineers perished on the trail; others were killed during mine accidents. In California, one plunged 800 feet down the shaft of the Eagle Bird mine; and another at Leadville died a horrible accidental death by drinking water from a glass that had contained a few drops of potassium cyanide, used for testing ores.[49]

Most engineers shared the typical business views of the late nineteenth century.[50] They were firm believers in free enterprise, the open shop, and the cult of the self-made man. In a bitter struggle against organized labor, engineers used the blacklist, supported the anti-foreign, anti-Jewish American Protective Association, and took the lead in forming local "Citizens' Alliances" designed to block unionism. They viewed the Western Federation of Miners as a dictatorial and irresponsible body seeking to overthrow the capitalist system, and they compared the Butte Miners' Union— "a gang of Irish-Austrian-Italian anarchists"—to the dread Mafia. An attempt was made to murder Frederick Bradley in San Francisco because of his uncompromising stand against labor. In Colorado, in 1902, Arthur Collins, an engineer and indomitable foe of the unions, was fatally shot as he sat in the Smuggler-Union club room at Telluride.[51]

The mining engineer came to play a distinctive role in the development of the West. A skilled professional man of better-than-average education, he came to be highly respected. His opinion, even on non-mining matters, carried considerable weight. Possibly because of the roving nature of his work or because he sometimes resided in the East, his influence was not as great in civic and political affairs as it might have been.

A few mining engineers held various local offices: ward leaderships, mayoralties, lesser territorial posts, and seats in state legislatures. Several, including James B. Grant and Jesse McDonald of Colorado, and Emmet D. Boyle of Nevada, served as governors of their respective states, but no professional mining engineer served in Congress until William F. Englebright of California was seated in 1907.[52] Herbert Hoover's political bent occurred after he retired as an active engineer. John Hays Hammond, who was personally acquainted with every President from Grant through Hoover, except Arthur, "enjoyed a flutter in the direction of the vice-presidency" with Taft in 1908. He later became so close to Taft as an unofficial adviser that Colonel Edward House was subsequently referred to as "the John Hays Hammond of the Wilson Administration."[53]

In their own way, mining engineers did much to popularize and advertise the West. They wrote widely for the press and displayed cabinets of minerals at national and international expositions. They discussed mining before such groups as the Bullion Club of New York. Especially after 1880, they brought the West and its resources to the forefront at professional meetings of the American Institute of Mining Engineers.[54]

Many of them wrote skillfully on both technical and non-technical subjects. James D. Hague, for example, is best remembered for his contribution to the mining volumes published in connection with Clarence King's survey of the Fortieth Parallel and in connection with the census of 1880. *The Explorers', Miners', and Metallurgists' Companion*, written by J. S. Phillips, became the Bible of many self-educated mining men in the quarter of a century following its initial publication in 1871. Augustus Bowie's *Hydraulic Mining in California* (1876) had gone into eleven editions by 1910. Hoover, Hammond, Rickard, and a few others published memoirs which are more interesting than modest. T. A. Rickard, the author of at least twenty-five books, wrote one of the first histories of American mining.[55]

Because of the nature of their work and interests, mining engineers were among the early organizers and supporters of technical and scientific societies in the West.[56] Some divided their lives between engineering work in the field and in the classroom, although the exodus from responsible academic posts—even presidencies—to consulting offices was more noticeable than the flow from the great outdoors into the Halls of Ivy. A few became university presidents and served on boards of regents.[57]

But the most important contribution of the mining engineer to the West was in helping the mineral industry advance through better management methods and improvements in mining practices. He sponsored better planning and greater preliminary development; the increased use of power, especially electrical; the development of advanced engineering and equipment for tunnelling, boring, hoisting, draining, and ventilating; and the establishment of countless innovations for working all types of ore. When improved technology was employed and as production increased per unit of capital and manpower—all possible because of the mining engineer—mining became a modern industry.

The West served for all the world as a kind of gigantic postgraduate school of mines. It was a major crossroads for mining engineers of all nations, where ideas were exchanged, tested against the western environment, sometimes discarded, but often adapted and even exported in modified form.[58] The American mining engineer was a member of an international fraternity, and in the 1890's he began to displace the long-established British engineer abroad. Dozens of men who gained their experience in California, Colorado, and Nevada, who represented the elite of American mining engineering, traveled to western Australia, South Africa, and other parts of the world, where they played key roles in mineral exploitation.[59] Through them, the West indirectly made its imprint on the world mineral industry.

THE MISSOURI FUR TRADE—

GROWTH AND DECLINE

Manuel Lisa and the Opening
of the Missouri Fur Trade

RICHARD E. OGLESBY
Eastern Illinois University

The main topic of discussion in St. Louis the first week of August 1808, whether over rum at Yosti's or Landreville's, or over after-dinner wine at the stately mansion of Auguste Chouteau, was the impending trial of George Drouillard for the murder of Antoine Bissonette. As a conversation piece it was not new, for Bissonette's death had taken place nearly fifteen months before and the town had been well apprised of the circumstances at that time. However, the principals, George Drouillard and his employer, Manuel Lisa, had just arrived from the headwaters of the Missouri. The town constable had them in detention while one of the attorneys for the defense, Edward Hempstead, was appealing for their release on a writ of *habeas corpus*.

Despite the widespread speculation regarding the alleged murder, few thought the government had much of a case against Drouillard, the half-breed hunter-trapper-interpreter who had served with such distinction on the Lewis and Clark expedition. Of more serious consequence, at least to the leading businessmen of the city, was Manuel Lisa's arrival back in town after an absence of eighteen months—back from the Rocky Mountains and the sources of the Missouri. Moreover, he had returned "indemnified . . . by considerable benefits."

Here was a point to be pondered by the closed group of French merchants, led by Auguste Chouteau and his half-brother Pierre, who, until that time, had held the economic destiny of St. Louis in their cautious hands. For the first time, their status was challenged by a man who, if he continued his profitable course, bade fair to surpass them all. They could not afford to let Lisa's newly won monopoly of the Northwest trade go unchallenged.

In the eyes of St. Louis residents, who had long braved the uncertainties of life in the dirty frontier town on the west bank of the Mississippi, Manuel Lisa was an upstart and a troublemaker. His arrival in 1798 had been accompanied by a violent disruption of the status quo, for which he had been mainly responsible. First, he had acrimoniously petitioned for the institution of free trading privileges in Missouri; he had gone over the head of the lieutenant governor in St. Louis directly to New Orleans in an attempt to procure a share of the tightly controlled trade in the Spanish province. Failing in this, he had managed, by dint of a generous "gift" to the royal treasury, to wrest the valuable trade monopoly with the Osage Indians from the brothers Chouteau. The bitter fight engendered on that occasion caused Lisa to be jailed for a short period.

The purchase of Louisiana by the United States ended all special trading rights, and Lisa had then joined with the adventurer Jacque Clamorgan in an attempt to promote trade in the direction of Santa Fe. This project brought him into conflict with the American government in the person of Gen. James Wilkinson, governor of Louisiana, who was sending Lt. Zebulon M. Pike, fresh from his failure to find the source of the Mississippi, into the same area, ostensibly to explore the headwaters of the Arkansas. After causing the lieutenant some difficulty by having Baroney Vasquez, his interpreter, arrested for debt, Lisa had disavowed any interest in the Southwest and turned his attention northward to the Missouri, perhaps to establish himself there before Wilkinson could send the wandering Pike to seek out the sources of that river.

In any case, Lisa had moved into the Missouri country, entirely ignoring his neighbors and fellow citizens of St. Louis. He had formed a partnership with Pierre Menard and William Morrison of Kaskaskia, Illinois Territory, purchasing the major portion of his goods, $12,649 of a total reputed to be $16,000, from G. Gillespie and Company of Michilimackinack, through the Jewish trader, Myers Michaels. He had then embarked, in the spring of 1807, for the Rocky Mountains.

Now he was back in St. Louis from an adventure many had called impossible and more had called foolhardy, his pockets jingling with profits. So optimistic were the three partners that they proceeded to reorganize, giving Drouillard equal status as a partner, and began preparations for a second voyage.

The St. Louis merchants realized that to enter into competition with Lisa at that time was dangerous at best. Having been the first trader into the great Northwest, and having treated the Indians fairly in his dealings with them, Lisa would have first claim to their allegiance and the pick of their pelts. His men were even then searching for the best beaver waters and would have a distinct advantage over competitors. To break such a hold would be a long and costly operation. Thus, if the St. Louis group was to share in the upper Missouri trade, some sort of combination with Lisa and his partners was necessary.

The partners, particularly Lisa, were definitely interested. Not only had Manuel seen for himself the boundless possibilities of the Northwest, but he had also seen that a handful of men and a $16,000 outfit would never be able to take proper advantage of it. Therefore, when a large organization was proposed, with the promise of greater capitalization, it was fully in accord with his thinking.

During the many meetings and discussions over the winter of 1808-1809, from which emerged the St. Louis Missouri Fur Company, the full and fantastic story of the first commercial voyage to the mountains was related. Recruiting from fifty to sixty men, including several who had been members of the Lewis and Clark expedition, to man two sturdy keelboats, Lisa had set out for the headwaters of the Missouri in April 1807. After departure, he had had to return to St. Charles to bring back forcibly one of his *engagés*, Jean Baptiste Bouché, who had imbibed a bit too freely and gotten into debt.

It was common practice when signing up an *engagé* to contract to advance him a small portion of his wages, ideally to allow him to clear up his debts and purchase whatever personal articles he wanted to take along, but practically so that he could have one last spree before setting out for the mountains, where hardship was severe and alcohol dear. Tavern owners were free with credit to such men, knowing their employers would pay up all bills rather than have the creditor lawfully detain the *engagé* for debt and hold up an entire party. A similar scene was played with monotonous regularity every time a group left for the mountains.

In this case, Lisa would have saved himself much grief and money had he left Bouché to the tender mercies of the barkeep. But, as Bouché had been paid for his services, Manuel had felt bound to try to extract his money's worth of labor from the fellow, so he took him along with the expedition after settling his debts.

Aside from the normal difficulties encountered in attempting to propel a clumsy keelboat against the four-mile-per-hour current

117

of the mighty Missouri, whose turbid waters held all sorts of snares for the unwary steersman, the Lisa party had experienced little trouble until it arrived at the mouth of the Osage River, 120 miles upstream. There Bissonette deserted, and Drouillard was dispatched to bring him back "dead or alive." Drouillard, a skilled tracker, complied with his instructions, bringing in his prisoner hovering somewhere between the two states stipulated by Lisa. In the course of the capture, he had shot and seriously wounded the fugitive. After questioning Bissonette as to his motives, Lisa loaded him into a canoe to return to St. Charles for medical treatment. The next day, before reaching aid, Bissonette died, causing the government to lodge the murder charge against Drouillard.

At the mouth of the Kansas, Francois LeCompt, a half-breed trader of renown who had spent much time with the Kansa Indians, hailed the passing boats. He was promptly engaged to accompany the party, thus adding another to the impressive array of men already well acquainted with the north country. These experienced hands—John Potts, Peter Wiser, Edward Robinson, and the others who had been with Lewis and Clark—provided seasoned leadership for the greenhorns and were able to impart to them the knowledge necessary to survive in the wilderness as well as how to catch a beaver or "lift" a scalp.

While struggling through the vicious eddies and numerous sand bars which marked the mouth of the Platte River—considered the far boundary of civilization and the gateway to the prairies—the group received a stroke of good fortune in the person of John Colter, who was canoeing his solitary way downriver toward the settlements. This intrepid Virginian had already traversed the continent with Lewis and Clark, and was no doubt delighted to see some of his old comrades among Lisa's men. He had received an early discharge from the Lewis and Clark expedition at Fort Mandan to join Forrest Handcock and Joseph Dixon, two independent trappers, in a partnership to hunt and trap in the vicinity of the Rocky Mountains, through which he had just recently come.

There he had trapped out the winter with Handcock and Dixon, but in the spring of 1807 the association dissolved, and Colter departed for the civilization from which he had so long been absent. Lisa would not allow so valuable an asset to slip through his fingers. His entreaties, the presence of Colter's friends, and a good offer, probably including the status of free trapper, served to turn Colter's eyes once more toward the mountains.

Difficulties began to mount shortly after Colter joined the party. The party apparently carried only enough food to reach the vicinity of the Platte, this being the practice of later expeditions, and had the misfortune to find only a small amount of game. The land of the Sioux, in which they found themselves after passing the Platte, was poor country for hunting, though not usually because of any lack of wildlife. Wandering bands of Indians liked nothing better than to fall upon a lone forager and take home his scalp as a trophy.

Even with such expert hunters as Colter and Drouillard scouring the countryside, the party by July 12 was reduced to one quarter pound of meat per day per man. Here it was that Bouché, having already caused a delay in embarkation, and more trouble by refusing to obey orders after the crew had got under way, was accused of stealing meat from the larder with the intention of causing the expedition to fail. The charge may well have been true judging from that *engagé's* later activities, for he continued to be a troublemaker for the rest of his stay in the mountains. Little could be done with the man short of shooting him, and no one wanted that responsibility.

Sioux country was passed without meeting any of the tribe, although Bouché did his best to make this possible by absenting himself on an unauthorized hunting trip for four days while the party waited for him. Lisa preferred to keep him under surveillance in camp rather than have him wandering by himself in the wilderness. The peaceful passage through the Sioux country was a bit of good luck few later expeditions would share. However, by the time a real crisis was met, what had been a green and unseasoned group of men in April had become a hardened and veteran crew of boatmen and hunters capable of meeting and handling any difficulty.

Their first encounter with hostile Indians came at the Arikara village. This tribe, an offshoot of Caddoan stock, had originally migrated northward with the Pawnees from the Red River of the South. They had split from the Pawnees and settled in villages, living a semi-sedentary life, and being visited by many of the nomadic tribes of the West. Of volatile and unpredictable temper, the Rees, as they were known to the traders, became the most dangerous and treacherous Indians on the Missouri.

The Lisa party, on their arrival, found 200 to 300 warriors drawn up along the bank. The Indians fired on the vessels when they came into range and ordered them to land. Lisa complied, but upon touching shore summarily commanded the natives not to set foot on his boats, which order they respected. As the Indian women began to appear, carrying sacks of grain with which to trade, a warrior dashed among them, slashed the bags with his knife, and spilled the contents on the ground. Taking this as a hostile sign, Lisa ordered the men to arms and had the boat-mounted swivel guns leveled at the crowd.

The Indians, startled by the sudden action, fell back in confusion, but soon came forward with pipes of peace and bade Lisa to council with them. He agreed to meet the chiefs, smoked and talked with them, and distributed the usual presents before leaving the village. He was then, and continued to be, a believer in giving substantial and desirable gifts to the many tribes with which he came in contact. This partly accounted for the great success he enjoyed as a trader and helped give him considerable influence over the tribes. The Arikaras apparently were undecided themselves as to a course of action against the white men, and the disciplined movement of the crew convinced them that a battle was not in their best interest. Lisa always seemed to know when a show of force would be most effective.

The Mandan, next tribe above the Rees, and thereafter, in contrast to their neighbors, the most consistently friendly of the Missouri tribes, provided the company with several anxious moments before it was safely passed. After the experience with the Rees, Lisa wisely decided to proceed alone and on foot through the three villages while the boats remained offshore, ready on a moment's notice either to fight or to run. All went well until Manuel reached the uppermost of the towns.

There the chief refused the presents brought to council and demanded a quantity of powder. The situation was tense, but Lisa was its equal. He knew that "his life was in no danger while his death could not procure them his goods, and resisted their repeated solicitations in a bold and firm manner." Again resolution accomplished his purpose, for the chief capitulated, accepted the presents, and permitted the party to pass in peace. The men were learning an invaluable lesson in Indian diplomacy, and the wiser saw that the red man always respected the strong and the brave, and the man who kept his word. Possibly Lisa left a small outfit with this sedentary branch of the Sioux, but if he did his limited resources were taxed to the utmost.

120

A few days later the expedition was confronted by a huge war party of Assiniboins massed on the bank of the river. There were so many of them that, as Lisa himself put it, "The whole prairie was red with them." Again taking the initiative, he directed the boats straight toward the waiting horde. He then ordered all the small arms and swivel guns discharged into the air. "This was intended to strike them with terror; the effect was ludicrous, they fell back, tumbled over each other, and fled to the hills with precipitation." Only a few chiefs approached to smoke the pipes and receive the presents which Lisa offered.

By a thorough knowledge of the Indian character gained from his long experience in the field, and the ability to play a bold hand in the face of great odds, Manuel Lisa had carried his men through three potentially dangerous situations. The other parties on the river that year did not fare so well; Ensign Pryor's party was defeated by the Rees; and the news of that debacle caused Ramsay Crooks and Robert McClellan to turn back before reaching the upper river.

The Lisa party, unaware of the activity below them, continued toward the mountains. They left the Missouri at the mouth of the Yellowstone and turned up the latter stream to its confluence with the Big Horn, where, on the wooded point between the two rivers just above their junction, they erected temporary shelters and began constructing Fort Raymond.

It was very late in the season, sometime in early November 1807, and the men, with the exception of the slacker Bouché, who refused to make wooden pins to fasten a roof, worked quickly to complete the shelter before the snows arrived. They lost no time reconnoitering the surrounding country, both for buffalo and other game animals and for likely beaver waters. They found the Yellowstone and the Big Horn, together with their numerous tributaries, teeming with the flat-tailed furry creatures whose skins satisfied the demands of London society by furnishing the raw material for their tall hats. The prospects justified a good deal of optimism on the part of all hands.

Lisa attributed to Bouché the delays in transit which had caused the company to arrive so late in the year, blaming him for missing the valuable fall hunt. To mitigate this loss, Lisa decided to notify the Indians of his arrival and to ask them to come to the post to trade. To accomplish this mission, he sent John Colter on one of the most grueling winter odysseys ever accomplished by man. Carrying a pack weighing thirty pounds which contained a few supplies and presents for the Indians, his rifle and ammunition, Colter set out to find as many tribes as he could and send them to Fort Raymond. He found the Crows at the upper end of the Wind River Valley, then struck west, across the massive Wind River Range—a difficult climb in the best of weather.

Continuing into Jackson's Hole, a lovely valley entirely surrounded by tall mountains, he noted the sublime peaks of *Les Trois Tetons,* points which became the most important landmarks for trappers in the area. Crossing the Tetons into Pierre's Hole, he began a large circle north and east, back to the fort. On the return trip he viewed some thermal activity on the upper Shoshone, his description of which caused the skeptical trappers to dub it derisively "Colter's Hell." Arriving back at the fort, Colter joined the rest of the hunters in making short forays for food and beaver pelts.

In the spring of 1808, he was again sent out to call on the Indians. While in company with a band of Crows, he was forced, in order to "keep his hair," to join his hosts in resisting a Blackfeet attack. He so distinguished himself in action that many attributed the subsequent hostility of the Blackfeet toward the whites to that incident. The event certainly did not help relations, but the Blackfeet had other, deeper causes for their implacable hatred.

Many historians have assumed that the original destination of the Lisa expedition was the Three Forks of the Missouri and that the purpose of the expedition was to establish relations with the Blackfeet, nominal possessors of the area. This is a logical assumption because the company was headed for the "headwaters of the Missouri," and, in the opinion of the former members of the Lewis and Clark company, the Three Forks country was the richest in furs of any section of the Northwest. Other historians have assumed, no doubt correctly, that Drouillard and the other former members of the Lewis and Clark company advised against going into Blackfeet country for fear of reprisals by that tribe for the incident in which Meriwether Lewis had killed two members of their confederation.

John Colter may have added an even stronger argument. He had probably discovered the previous winter that the Crows, into whose lands the expedition would penetrate if it chose to ascend the Yellowstone, were a trading people who were already apprised of the white man's avid interest in beaver skins. Moreover, the Crows were adept at the trapping and preserving of skins in the white man's way, having been instructed in the art by Antoine Larocque, a French member of the British Northwest Company who had traveled among them several years before on a trading and exploring mission.

It is a tribute to Lisa's sagacity that he took the advice of his subordinates, read well the signs of approaching winter—which might have made it impossible to reach the Three Forks—and decided to operate in Crow country. This decision was basic to the success of the expedition. The Blackfeet were not then, nor did they ever become, trappers of beaver and traders of skins for the white man, British or American. They were true plains Indians—strong, warlike, and self-sufficient. They roamed a vast hunting ground stretching northward from Three Forks to beyond the Saskatchewan River, followed the migrations of the buffalo, upon whom they were dependent for all the necessities of life. So, while neighboring tribes took to trapping and trading skins to the British for blankets, guns, cloth, and other supplies, the Blackfeet remained disdainfully aloof. What need had a Blackfoot, wrapped in a buffalo robe, for a Hudson's Bay blanket; what need had he for a gun when he was more than a match for his enemies without one?

Relations of the white men with the Blackfeet were friendly, if not profitable for the British, until about 1806-07. By that time, British trade with the foes of the Blackfeet had increased to the point where the foes were well enough supplied with weapons to stand up to the haughty Blackfeet and even defeat them in battle. Then, the Blackfeet became hostile to all whites, British and American alike, and jealously guarded their frontiers against any intrusion. When they learned that American trappers were operating in their lands to the south, they drove the trappers out and captured a rich booty of furs and equipment which they traded with the British for the now-needed guns and ammunition. If Lisa had chosen to move into the Three Forks country in 1807, his expedition might well have met the same fate which befell that of the St. Louis Missouri Fur Company two years later.

Colter's aid to the Crows had only added fuel to an already burning fire, the flames of which would scorch the next party to violate Blackfeet boundaries.

Life went on in a normal manner during the long winter months at Fort Raymond. The hunters roamed the vicinity, bringing their kill to a scaffold which had been erected about a mile from

123

the fort. From there it was carried to camp by the *engagés*. The irrepressible Bouché refused to bring in the meat on November 29, and a great feast was held at the scaffold by grizzly bears and wolves. This could have been a serious loss had game become scarce, and Lisa later placed an excessive valuation of $1,000 on the destroyed meat.

Etienne Brandt, one of the more trusted *engagés*, being privileged to distribute goods along with Lisa, Drouillard, and Benito Vasquez, Lisa's second in command, took his cue from Bouché and began to steal from the storeroom. He was caught and chastised by Lisa, who also threatened him with a knife. Brandt deserted shortly thereafter and went to live with the Indians. He turned up in St. Louis in 1809 and sued Lisa for what amounted to defamation of character. Lisa and Drouillard countersued to collect damages and won, though Brandt took refuge in the law for the benefit of insolvent debtors.

By the time spring came, the trappers had their traps and guns well oiled and were anxious to break the confines of the garrison and get to the business at hand. They were not a gregarious lot, and long confinement with a number of people always made them restless for open spaces—that is, except for Bouché. On the first of May, Vasquez finally had to order him to lay his traps. Predictably, he refused and never trapped a beaver while he was in the mountains.

He even tried to foment a mutiny by spreading the rumor that Lisa had given the men poor powder, but the cooler heads realized that that would be the last device of an entrepreneur. Except for Bouché, the men were well satisfied with their lot. Beaver were plentiful and chances of making a profit were excellent.

George Drouillard, as Colter had done, conducted an exploratory trip into the wilderness, in part retracing Colter's steps the previous winter, but keeping more to the south—always on the lookout for Spaniards, who were reputed to have a mine in the vicinity. The establishment of trade relations with the Spanish, his former countrymen, was never far from Lisa's thoughts, and he would make efforts in the future to open trade to Santa Fe from the upper Missouri. The Crows undoubtedly told him of the Snake Indians, across the Divide, who traded directly with the Spanish and may even have had Spanish articles to show him. This undoubtedly further stimulated his already active imagination.

The information brought back to St. Louis by Colter and Drouillard was incorporated into the maps which William Clark was preparing for the government and became the basis for the geographical knowledge of the area for many years.

The short period of the spring hunt was spent in the immediate vicinity of Fort Raymond, though plans were made for small groups to follow Colter, Potts, and the rest of the Lewis and Clark men to the Three Forks area in the fall. All the men were anxious to tap the rich beaver resources of that area. One of the groups would eventually cross the Divide and invade what was nominally a British preserve. Another small party of three men was sent south to trap "the River of the Spaniards," and perhaps meet representatives of that nation to begin negotiations for opening trade to Santa Fe.

On June 4, Baptiste Tibeau departed, likely to trade with the Crows, with $1,922.05 of equipment and Indian trade goods. He probably planned to acquire pelts from the Crows' spring hunt. With Baptiste Marie, he borrowed $51.00 from Lisa on the same date, indicating that Marie was going along and that the two would do a little trading for themselves. So sanguine of the expedition's success was Lisa that the debt was payable in seventeen beaver skins, or three dollars a pelt. This was an unbelievable price for skins in the mountains, for they often did not bring that much in the St. Louis market. Thus, it is not strange that a majority of the men stayed at Fort Raymond while Lisa returned to St. Louis; it was entirely conceivable that each of them would make his fortune. Lisa's fair treatment of his men also accounts for the recurrence of many names on his list of *engagés* from year to year.

Only one incident marred the accomplishments of the spring. Edward Rose, the mulatto trapper-interpreter who had lived for some years with the Osages, had been sent to the Crows for the winter to trade for beaver and horses shortly after Colter had discovered their whereabouts. Later to become one of the most notorious of the mountain men, Rose fancied himself an Indian and dedicated his life to proving it to Indian and white alike. Perceiving that the Indian custom was to respect the man most who gave away all of his possessions, by spring he had become well respected, having given away all his trade goods.

Returning to the fort sometime after the weather broke, and being unable to account for the loss of the goods, he got into a bitter argument with Lisa and leaped upon him. Lisa would probably have been killed had not John Potts happened on the scene and pulled off the struggling Rose. Lisa, whose boat was waiting to take him to St. Louis, left the two men grappling, climbed aboard the boat, and headed out into the current.

Rose, when he finally freed himself from his assailant, was infuriated when he saw the departing boat. He ran to a swivel gun and fired a shot at the boat. The shot hit the cargo box and would have hit the crew had they not been on their benches.

Fortunately, Rose was restrained from reloading and firing another shot. A few days later, he left the fort with all the goods he could beg, borrow, or coerce from the men, and headed back to the Crows.

Despite this incident, Rose was destined to turn up again and again in Lisa's employ; Lisa forgave him and used him on several occasions as a trader and interpreter. Evidently Rose's worth was such that Lisa could afford the loss of goods his employment usually entailed. This is quite a tribute to Rose, for Lisa was not one to give up a penny if there was a way to avoid it. Because Rose's name is conspicuously absent from the long list of debtors at Lisa's death, Rose either made good the losses or Lisa wrote them off as a business expense.

Had it not been for the murder trial that Lisa and Drouillard had to face in St. Louis, their return would have been a complete triumph. Carrying the proceeds of the winter and spring hunts at Fort Raymond, Lisa could well have been proud of the results of his first expedition. Not only were his profits handsome, but they represented only two-thirds of a hunting season. Even as he returned, most of the men were preparing for the fall hunt at Three Forks and the "River of the Spaniards" and were operating from a substantial fort in excellent beaver country. Contact had already been established with the Crows and could be expected with the other tribes in the vicinity. Lisa's crew was entering most of the good beaver country of the Rockies.

In his dealings with the St. Louis merchants on his return, Lisa not only provided for the creation of the St. Louis Missouri Fur Company, a relatively large-scale venture, but clearly demonstrated his grasp of the potentialities of the fur trade of the northern Rockies.

After all, it was he who, on his first expedition, had set down the principles by which that trade could be prosecuted successfully. The first principle was the establishment of several posts along the Missouri for trade with the local natives; this insured their continuing friendship, a small profit, and the guarantee that the great Missouri highway would always be open. The second was the building of posts in the mountains to be stocked for trade, but more particularly to be used as outfitting posts for bands of trappers who would comb the mountains for beaver pelts, where lay the big profits.

Lisa spent the rest of his life in a vain attempt to put these principles into operation, but circumstances and a lack of capital doomed him to disappointment. Indeed, not until the days of Kenneth McKenzie, who had the backing of the Astor fortune, were these principles carried to their final and successful conclusion.

McKenzie could then adopt the title which more properly belonged to his predecessor and mentor, Manuel Lisa, "King of the Missouri."

127

The Decline of the Fur Trade on the Upper Missouri, 1840-1865

JOHN E. SUNDER
University of Texas

The fur trade of the Missouri Valley originated in the eighteenth-century advance of France and Spain across the plains of North America. By the 1830's the fur trade of the upper Valley—long nurtured by Manuel Lisa and his predecessors and successors—had become the preserve of John Jacob Astor's American Fur Company. The Astor men, a potent force on the Missouri, built permanent river posts and established a water transportation system to tie the upriver posts to St. Louis.

Although the trade grew during the years between 1820 and 1840, it was not as glamorous as the mountain trade to the southwest of the river. The mountain rendezvous, symbolic of the trade, amid towering peaks and isolated parks, was an eye-catching spectacle. When the rendezvous system—hard hit by problems of supply, demand, and organization—ended in small, poorly attended meetings in the valley of the Green River, the upper Missouri reassumed the important trade position it had held earlier in the century.

Remnants of the mountain trade remained, particularly the posts along the south fork of the Platte and the wandering free trappers who saw little future in the organized fur trade. But new settlement and large-scale overland migration ended the promise of the mountain trade.

The scepter of the mountain trade passed to the region of the upper Missouri. This region may be defined conveniently for historical study as the curving waterway extending from Sioux City, Iowa, to Fort Benton, Montana. Because large population movements bypassed the region until the sixties, the trade in furs and buffalo robes was carried on in near isolation from the flow of men hungry for land and gold. For twenty-five years, between 1840 and 1865, the upper Missouri and its tributaries dominated the western trade.

Several decades ago Hiram M. Chittenden, in his work on the

fur trade, outlined briefly the upper Missouri trade after 1840. His outline remains valid. He noted that, following the retirement of Astor in 1834, the Western Department, essentially the so-called "Upper Missouri Outfit" of the American Fur Company, was transferred to Pratte, Chouteau, and Company of St. Louis. In 1838, when Bernard Pratte entered politics, the company was re-organized under Pierre Chouteau, Jr., who held a twenty-percent stake in the business.

Death, retirement, and quarrels among the leading investors resulted in frequent stock shuffling. With each new shuffling, the Chouteau interest remained constant or increased until, by the late fifties, Pierre Chouteau, Jr., and his son, Charles Pierre, held more than sixty percent of the stock. The upper Missouri agents, in charge of the major company fur posts, held minor shares in the business, but policy was set by Pierre and Charles Chouteau.

The small opposition fur companies operating on the upper river referred to Pierre Chouteau, Jr., and Company as the "American Fur Company" because Pierre Chouteau was Astor's successor on the upper Missouri. The Chouteaus were part of the small group of wealthy Americans who, before the Civil War, when millionaires were rare, invested substantial capital in western business. The total Chouteau family investment in the upper Missouri fur trade approximated one-half million dollars per year. The St. Louis office of the company was impressive, newly built, and fireproof. The upper Missouri posts, notably Benton, Union, and Pierre, were outstanding manmade landmarks on the plains.

As long as the Missouri Valley fur trade remained profitable and capital was available, small fur companies willingly competed with Pierre Chouteau. Anti-Chouteau investors in St. Louis and in New York City provided a reservoir of capital for the small companies. Robert Campbell of St. Louis was an outstanding example of an investor who always opposed the Chouteaus. For more than thirty years his fortune and his business and political alliances were available to those who competed with the American Fur Company and its heirs.

John A. N. Ebbetts of New York was one of the first traders to oppose Chouteau in the decade of the forties. Ebbetts, having $5,700 in capital and the backing of two prominent St. Louisans, concentrated his trade near Fort Pierre during 1840-41, sold liquor to the Indians, and thoroughly irritated Chouteau. In 1842, he obtained additional support from several New York friends, received additional capital, doubled his trading force, and spread his trade west into Montana. The future looked extremely promising for Ebbetts' group, known professionally as the Union Fur Company, but the liquor trade brought trouble from the Federal Government and Ebbetts' employees were a quarrelsome, irresponsible lot. By 1845, the company, because of its own business mistakes and Chouteau's power, gave up and sold out to the Chouteau company.

While Chouteau's agents inventoried the goods of the Union Fur Company, Alexander Harvey, Charles Primeau, Joseph Picotte, and A. R. Bouis, all former Chouteau men, announced that they were ready to battle the powerful company. Supported by $50,000 in capital and dependable commercial connections, Harvey, Primeau, and Company took to the upper river in 1846 and engaged in a profitable trade for several years. Pierre Chouteau, Jr., was not surprised to see the new opposition on the river and, as Harvey and his experienced associates persisted in the trade, made at least one offer to unite the two companies. This offer was rejected by Harvey, who continued his staunch opposition. In July 1854, however, Harvey died aboard a Mackinaw boat on his way to St. Louis. His partners—Picotte, Bouis, and Primeau—continued the business in desultory fashion until 1857, when Chouteau prevailed.

As had happened when the Ebbetts company had failed a dozen years earlier, a new company—Frost, Todd, and Atkinson—stepped in immediately to oppose Chouteau. Daniel M. Frost, John B. S. Todd, and A. G. Atkinson, supplied by Robert Campbell and advised by Picotte and Chouteau's old agent Malcolm Clark, obtained an upper Missouri trading license and moved into the field. For approximately two years this company contested the upper river with Chouteau. It then decided that Dakota land speculation was more lucrative and surrendered its river fur trade. Malcolm Clark and Primeau, with Campbell's blessing, then hastily organized a new upriver opposition company, but soon stepped aside and left Chouteau in control of the river throughout the uncertain years of the Civil War.

Other opposition fur companies, partnerships, and loose associations were active on the Missouri between 1840 and 1865, including LaBarge, Roy, and Shaw in the early forties; Larpenteur, Smith, Lemon, and Boller in the early sixties; and LaBarge, Harkness, and Company in the mid-sixties. However, none of these small fur companies wrested control of the Valley fur trade from the Chouteau company.

During the 1830's, 1840's, and 1850's, the fur companies active in the upper Valley perfected the structure and conduct of the river fur trade. Permanent trading posts were built in strategic locations, and with them were associated many small and scattered satellite posts. All posts were surrounded by resident or transient Indians. The larger posts not only supported grazing, crop raising, and boat building activities, but they also flourished as social centers. Busy fur posts—which were established for political and business motives—resembled active church missions; in power and prestige they were the counterpart of Spain's southwestern missions, established for political and religious motives.

The architecture of the upriver posts reached a peak of elaborateness and grandeur in the 1830-1860 period, when trade was declining. The leading posts—about which a great deal more is now known, thanks to the recent excavations of the Missouri River Basin Survey—were stocked in great variety, furnished fairly comfortably, and provided a relatively high standard of living for upper echelon employees. However, some of the smaller and badly managed posts were "vile and filthy," as one candid traveler noted.

Post supplies and trade goods were transported upriver from St. Louis in steamboats owned or chartered by the companies. The boats normally made annual trips, leaving St. Louis between mid-April and early June and returning, loaded with robes and furs, later in the summer. Steamer traffic as far as Fort Union developed before 1840, and by 1860 improved light-draught steamboats opened traffic to Fort Benton.

River boats were built, or rebuilt, to conform to the erratic demands of the upper Missouri, which had many snags and bars and dangerously low water. Steamers were constructed to draw less than four feet of water, were designed for maximum freight space, and were built in a manner that made them extremely maneuverable. The boilers were capable of utilizing every bit of power from wood—laboriously cut, sometimes with great danger, along the river. The fur company vessels early set records in river navigation and left a lasting mark on steamboat design.

Keelboats were used when necessary on the Yellowstone, and fifty- to sixty-foot Mackinaw boats, built on the upper Missouri, regularly conveyed loads of robes and furs downriver all the way to St. Louis or to points between Weston and Sioux City, where the Mackinaw cargoes were transferred to river packets.

The Chouteaus led the way in improved fur company organization during the years of decline in the trade. Salary scales were perfected; employee responsibilities were better defined; greater care was given inventories; a system of express messengers was developed to bring the upriver posts closer to each other and to St. Louis, even during the winter months; and a fairly dependable chain of command was established.

Because all the companies carefully watched the St. Louis, New York, and European fur markets, the international character of the fur industry was strengthened. If the St. Louis market reported, as it did throughout much of 1850, an "active demand" for furs, sooner or later the New York and London markets would be affected. Because marketing was a constant gamble, the St. Louis companies vied with each other for the latest auction reports and fur catalogs from C. M. Lampson of London and the fur houses of New York City.

Although the average value of a beaver skin brought to St. Louis in 1850 was worth only one-half to two-thirds of what it had been twenty-five years before, the value of buffalo robes had increased; and many lesser furs, especially muskrat, were in demand. The fur companies not only sold abroad, but they also purchased an amazing variety of goods from foreign and domestic manufacturers—everything from beads to fireworks—for shipment up the Missouri. They were interested in tariffs, shipping charges, and in a favorable balance of trade.

Fur trade statistics are scattered and contradictory; no thorough, overall study is available on this aspect of the trade. The elusive statistics suggest that the furs and robes brought into St. Louis were worth, on an average, one-quarter to one-half a million dollars annually between 1840 and 1865. In 1820, the fur trade accounted for twenty-five percent of the city's commerce; in 1860, less than one percent. The latter figure, interestingly enough, is approximately the same as the percentage figure accounted for by furs and skins in the annual total U.S. merchandise exports at that time. Even in the "big" trade years of the 1820's and 1830's the total U. S. export of furs and skins did not exceed one or two percent of the total merchandise exported.

Facts dealing with the structure of business and business statistics may give historians an outline of the organization of the fur trade, but they do not answer fully the question of how the upper Missouri trade adjusted to the changes occurring in Montana and the Dakotas. Did the fur men realize that the trade was past its prime? Were they hostile to the agents of change—the missionaries, Army men, artists, and scientists—who brought outside influences to the upper Missouri? The average trapper, likely illiterate, left few records that answer the question. However, the literate fur company owners and managers made no great effort to resist change. On the contrary, they accepted it and even assisted to bring a new era to the upper Missouri.

For example, a close relationship existed between the Federal Government and the upper Missouri fur trade in the period 1840 to 1865. For years, even before 1840, the traders had been in constant association by letter and personal contact with national political leaders. The Chouteaus and Robert Campbell supported the Democratic Party; other traders backed the Whig-Republican party. At times, Missourians in Congress, including Senator Thomas Hart Benton, served as spokesmen for the fur trade interests.

Federal patronage was important to the fur men because the Commissioner of Indian Affairs in Washington, the Superintendent of the St. Louis Indian office, and all Missouri River Indian agents, as political appointees, were potential threats, if unfriendly, to the power of the great fur traders. As a result, most members of the St. Louis Indian service and the service on the upper Missouri were hand picked by the fur companies—in most instances by Pierre and Charles Chouteau.

A few Indian agents opposed the Chouteaus or the fur trade in general and lodged complaints with their superiors in Washington. However, except during the liquor suits of the mid-forties—and they were finally settled out of court—the agents opposed to Chouteau and the trade received little attention from the Federal Government.

The power of the companies was no less real on the state level, where the Chouteaus and the opposition companies commanded spokesmen in the Missouri legislature. Yet, in 1841, after a bitter legislative battle, Pierre Chouteau failed in an attempt to incorporate his company formally by state law because of the charge that his company would become an even more formidable giant and would stifle all upriver competition.

In the forties and fifties, the upper Missouri traders had many opportunities to serve the Federal Government. The fur companies actually became an ex-officio arm of government—an arm which Washington needed in a part of the United States where its power was weak. The fur companies were delighted to be of assistance. If they convinced the Indians that the fur trade was favored by the Great White Father, fur company power would be greater, to say nothing of the profit which the traders derived from doing government work under contract.

The companies carried government messages to and from the upper Missouri; guarded and delivered official documents; transported Indians to and from eastern pow-wows and moved groups of them, bag and baggage, to locations designated by the government; provided steamboats to help the government prove the navigability of the upper Missouri; and, during the fifties and sixties, carried military supplies and troops engaged in the northwestern Indian campaigns.

The fur traders also cooperated with military surveyors of wagon and railroad routes. For cash and praise, they carried messages for the surveyors and provided supplies, transportation, guides, and interpreters. Isaac Stevens commented in 1853: "Both the fur companies zealously co-operated, placing at my disposal not only all the animals they could spare, but guides, hunters, and their information." And G. K. Warren added in 1855: "For information about portions of the country I had not visited, I had the benefit of frequent consultations with the fur men."

Army officers and most other visitors to the upper Missouri were welcomed at the trading posts, where daily life tended to be monotonous. In the late forties a French visitor to Fort Pierre was served "a most excellent dinner [of] buffalo tongues, pemmican . . . and . . . corn bread," followed by a "ball" and a brawl. Such visitors commented sympathetically on the fur companies, which over the years created a good public image. Even though on occasion the companies denounced one another bitterly, they were interested in public relations and cultivated a "good press."

Nowhere were the fur traders of the upper Missouri praised more consistently or completely than in missionary circles. Most missionaries who visited the area between 1840 and 1865 were convinced that the fur traders relished the northwestward spread of the gospel. Of course, most fur traders knew that the trade might operate as it pleased on the Missouri if it was publicly praised by the missionaries. The traders also realized that the missionaries might bring peace to the warring river tribes, which would result in more stability for the fur trade.

Before 1865, most of the missionaries on the upper Missouri were Roman Catholics associated with the Rocky Mountain efforts of Father De Smet or the Minnesota efforts of Fathers Ravoux and Belcourt. They were cordially received at the fur posts, transported on fur steamers—on which Pierre Chouteau gave them space for small altars and religious services—and supplied by the posts. Because the Chouteaus and many of their employees were Roman Catholics, the Catholic Church received strong support on the upper Missouri and gained an initial advantage in missionary endeavors on the High Plains.

Protestant missionaries, though less active than the Catholics, were also welcomed by the traders. Stephen Riggs preached at Fort Pierre in 1840, being given "all the assistance" possible. The Reverend and Mrs. Elkanah Mackey—upon the invitation of Alexander Culbertson, who was high in the councils of the Chouteau company—visited the upper Missouri in 1856. Two years later, two Lutheran missionaries, Jacob Schmidt and Moritz Braeuninger, traveled along the Yellowstone. Finding living conditions intolerable, they sounded one of the few discordant notes in the missionary hymm of praise to the fur traders.

Itinerant artists early learned that the upper Missouri was a painter's paradise. Before 1840 the first artists in a long procession journeyed along the river and captured on canvas—with varying degrees of talent—the Indians, the land, and the fur trade. By the sixties, greater numbers of artists traveled up and down the river on fur company steamboats, moved overland with surveying parties, and filled sketchbooks with life along the high Missouri. Isaac Sprague, the landscape artist, was on the river with Audubon in 1843. Carl Wimar saw the Missouri in 1858 and 1859, painting it with a vigor contradicting the painstaking technique he had learned at Dusseldorf. William Jacob Hays visited the upper river in 1860. William Cary, always keenly aware of the picturesque and the striking, wandered about the fur country the following year. The artists reported that the fur men welcomed them and facilitated their work. Few trappers or traders—with the possible exception of Rudolph F. Kurz—knew much about oils and watercolors, but they respected creative talent and welcomed the artists to the upper Missouri.

Historians have too long ignored the scientists who visited the upper Missouri before the Civil War. These scientists were encouraged by the fur traders. Any visiting scientist, amateur or professional, whether backed by public or private funds, could expect fur company cooperation and was free to undertake field work along the river. Geologists, zoologists, and botanists found sympathetic fur company employees stationed on the upper river—employees who were willing to assemble specimens of animals, plants, and minerals for scientifically minded visitors. Because many of the fur traders were experienced amateur physicians and hospital corpsmen to the Indian tribes, they considered visiting scientists as professional colleagues.

Outstanding examples of cooperation between the fur men and the scientists occurred in the field of paleontology. Rickard, in his classic history of American mining, stated that "men of education" first recognized the Dakotas in the period 1830 to 1850 because the fur traders sent fossils downriver from the Dakota fur posts. Alexander Culbertson was one of the fur traders who collected and shipped fossil remains to the outside world.

His brother, Thaddeus Culbertson, a scientist, visited the upper Missouri, as did the geologists and botanists John Evans, Benjamin F. Shumard, Ferdinand V. Hayden, and F. B. Meek. Between 1849 and 1856, these men studied the magnificent fossil remains in the Badlands and the plants and animals along the river. Their outstanding discoveries were published in the leading scientific journals of the day.

Charles Chouteau was one of the founders of the Academy of Science of St. Louis. With the assistance of his principal upper Missouri fur agents, at least five of whom were corresponding members of the Academy of Science, he presented many choice fossils, Indian artifacts, and even a meteorite from Fort Pierre to the Academy museum. Also, on at least two occasions, he paid the expenses of a taxidermist for a trip to the upper Missouri. On another occasion he paid the expenses of a fellow member of the Academy for a similar trip. Chouteau's steamers and the boats operated by other fur companies not only carried scientists, but they also transported downriver to St. Louis scientific specimens, crates of stuffed animals, and live animals destined for private collections, museums, and menageries.

Alexander Culbertson and Edwin T. Denig, both leading upper Missouri fur agents, were highly respected for their knowledge of Indian affairs and ethnology. Culbertson advised the government on Indian policy and, anticipating the future, favored the education of the upper Missouri Indians in agricultural and mechanical subjects. Denig sent the government thorough written accounts of the vocabularies and customs of the upriver tribes.

In 1865, Pierre Chouteau, Jr., and Company sold most of its upper Missouri properties to a group of investors from St. Paul, Chicago, and New York City. The sale marked the end of dominance of the upper Missouri fur trade by St. Louis merchants. Three years after the sale, the *St. Louis Journal of Commerce* editorialized: "The time when large fortunes were made [in the fur trade] has long since passed." Though the newspaper's statement was accurate, it did not warrant permanent pessimism. At the end of the nineteenth century the fur trade to St. Louis revived considerably, and as the new century began a renaissance occurred in the industry.

Any study of the fur trade on the upper Missouri in the quarter century between 1840 and 1865 is the study of what Howard Lamar, in his volume on Dakota, calls a half-breed society of trappers and traders in transition to a new era of grazing, farming, and mining. The leaders of the old fur trade welcomed the missionaries, Army surveyors, artists, and scientists, who were harbingers of change.

They recognized that the golden age of the trade was over and that resistance to change was useless. Despite their successful steps in perfecting the structure and conduct of the trade, volume and profits had gradually fallen. The history of the upper Missouri fur trade calls to mind the controversial perfection and decline theories of Spengler, Toynbee, and even Parkinson. Between 1840 and 1865 perfection and decline commanded the fur posts on the upper Missouri and manned the oars of the robe-laden Mackinaw boats.

THE SPANISH INFLUENCE—

ON LAND AND SEA

The Second Frontier: The Spanish

DONALD J. LEHMER
Dana College

Everyone who has even a nodding acquaintance with the study of American history has heard of Frederick Jackson Turner and his frontier hypothesis. In the years since Turner first presented the hypothesis, it has been extensively elaborated upon, criticized, and defended. Strangely enough, most of those who have dealt with the frontier have treated it as an Anglo-American phenomenon. They have usually ignored the fact that a second frontier also engulfed vast areas in the New World.

That second frontier was the outrider of Spanish settlement in North America—a frontier which began its growth in the islands of the Caribbean, moved westward with Cortez' fleet, and pushed out from Mexico City to cover the southern half of the continent. It is certainly an important frontier in the overall story of American history—important both as a historical episode and as a factor in understanding the frontier as a social process.

In his original presentation, Turner said: "Stand at Cumberland Gap and watch the procession of civilization, marching single file—the buffalo following the trail to the salt springs, the Indian, the fur trader and hunter, the cattle-raiser, the pioneer farmer—and the frontier has passed by. Stand at South Pass in the Rockies a century later and see the same procession with wider intervals between." The watcher at Cumberland Gap and at South Pass would see that procession.

But what of a watcher somewhere between Mexico City and Zacatecas, or at El Paso del Norte on the Rio Grande? He, too, would see the Indian and the cattle-raiser, but the other familiar figures of the Anglo-American frontier would be missing. In their place, he would see the conquistador in half-armor, the long-robed friar, and the *encomiendero* and his retinue of Indian serfs.

The Spanish frontier had a different cast of characters from the Anglo-American, and that difference is a significant one. The two frontier expansions proceeded by entirely different sets of cultural processes—processes which are symbolized by the typical frontiersmen of Spain and Anglo-America.

The Anglo-American frontier movement was typically a gradual westward trickle of individuals in the sequence of fur trader, cattle herder, pioneer farmer, equipped farmer, and city developer. It was only the miners who poured into new mineral areas in a sudden flood. Both sequence and rate of movement were different on the Spanish frontier. There, the initial movement was made by organized and disciplined parties which went forward with a swashbuckling rush—the *entradas* of soldiers, a few priests, and their Indian allies and porters. Sometimes, as in the case of Coronado and De Soto, those *entradas* were relatively ineffectual.

More often they effected a military conquest of a native population which laid the foundation for the second stage of the Spanish frontier's advance. That stage might well be called the "triumvirate of settlement." Mining, ranching, and farming were initiated by the Spaniards almost before the dust of conquest had settled; their mines, ranches, and plantations stabilized Spain's hold on the newly won ground.

Throughout most of Anglo-America, the growth of cities was slow because of a gradually evolving and stabilizing agricultural economy. It was only on the miners' frontier that boom towns mushroomed. Thanks to a richer and more varied frontier economy, New Spain's cities developed more rapidly; cathedrals, public buildings, libraries, and palatial homes were constructed within a few short years after the initial conquest.

The Anglo-American pioneer depended on his own backbreaking labor to establish himself in his new home. On the other hand, the Spaniard built his New World empires with Indian labor. Newly conquered tribes were put to work for Spanish masters. It was the Indians who drove the mine shafts, planted the fields, and did the other heavy work which established Spain's "triumvirate of settlement." It was also the Indians who built the cities of Spain's urban frontier.

Except in New England and in the Mormon settlement in Utah, the organized church was relatively unimportant on the Anglo-American frontier. In Spanish America, the cross and the sword moved forward together as partners in the frontier advance. The church helped Spain establish her hold on her conquered Indian populations, and did much to train the Indians in the ways of their new European masters. In the end, it was the church which carried the Spanish frontier to its ultimate limits by the development of the mission establishments, which spread far to the north of Spain's true colonial empire.

Government-making was a favorite occupation of the Anglo-American frontiersman. In Spanish America, representatives of the Crown moved forward with the frontier, taking along the bureaucratic sutures which bound each forward step to the vice-regal and the royal courts. Royal control weakened as Spain's frontier moved farther and farther from the centers of government, but it was an ever-present factor which, even at a distance, deprived the Spanish frontiersman of the political freedom of his Anglo-American counterpart.

On the Anglo-American frontier, land was typically held in small tracts, by individuals. In striking contrast, most land grants on the Spanish frontier were enormous by American standards. Hence, on the Spanish frontier no great area of free land was open for settlement by individuals as in Anglo-America.

In Anglo-America, the frontier was typically a social leveling agent. On the Spanish frontier, thanks to Spanish tradition and the presence of a variety of racial elements, class-caste stratification moved forward with the frontier itself. During the *entrada*, the Spaniard ranked above the Indian ally, who in turn ranked above the newly conquered native. As frontier settlement developed, the characteristic levels of Spanish colonial society emerged—the descending order of European-born Spaniard, American-born Spaniard, mestizo, Indian, and Negro.

Such differences between the Spanish and Anglo-American frontier institutions are facts—dry bones of history which can be articulated into a skeleton. The skeleton can also be covered with a musculature of interpretation. Such an interpretation must take into account both physical environments and a variety of cultural factors.

Significant differences exist between the environments in which the Anglo-American and Spanish frontiers originated. The Anglo-American frontier spread westward from the Atlantic through the well-watered forest lands of the eastern United States. Those lands originally teemed with the animals which made the fur trade possible; when cleared, they made good farms. But they lacked the mineral resources for the large-scale development of mining. They lacked, too, the open pastures which would have made possible the development of ranching in the same manner as in the Spanish colonies.

In contrast, Spain's frontier moved north across an arid region rich in precious metals and bearing enough grass to support herds of cattle. Farming was possible in the Spanish lands, too, but there the basic tool was the irrigation ditch rather than the clearing axe of the American pioneer.

Such environmental differences were directly responsible for many of the differences between the frontier institutions of eastern Anglo-America and those of the Spanish frontier. Environmental factors made the log cabin, the birchbark canoe, and the long rifle the trademarks of the Anglo-American frontiersman. Different environmental factors made the horse, the mine shaft, and the adobe house the trademarks of the Spanish frontier.

The importance of climate, vegetation, topography, and mineral resources becomes apparent when one notes the changes in the American frontiersman's techniques in the arid lands west of the Missouri River. Many of his methods there were borrowed from the Spanish, who had already adapted to the new and strange environment. This is certainly true of the ranching complex which grew up in the American West. Methods, equipment, and details of costume were all taken over from the Spaniard. Irrigation practices and associated laws were also borrowed from the Spaniard and the Mexican. Mexican mining laws were taken over by the Americans when they acquired the southwestern quarter of the United States. These are things which are rooted in the land and the nature of the land. Beyond them, other and more significant differences derived from differences between the cultures.

Culture has been cynically defined as "the part of history which the historian takes for granted." Here, the historian cannot afford to take culture for granted. Cultural factors were fundamental in determining the divergent patterns of the two frontiers. Many of the differences between the Anglo-American and Spanish frontiers were reflections of cultural differences between England and Spain. Many more derived from differences between the cultures of the Indian populations encountered by Anglo-Americans and Spaniards in the New World.

England and Spain were far different sources of colonial expansion. Seventeenth-century England was basically an agricultural nation, though a small-scale manufacturing establishment was emerging and mercantilism was on the rise. English society had a well-defined class structure, but not necessarily a rigid one. The base was the working class, both on the farms and in the cities. The English middle class had grown in both size and importance since the days of the Tudors. The nobility and gentry stood at the top of the class hierarchy, but the military and economic power of the old feudal aristocracy had long since been destroyed. Parliament provided a strong check on the Crown, both by tradition and through its control of the nation's purse strings. The English church stood apart from Rome, and had been divided and redivided to the point that no one faith was dominant in the country's affairs.

In colonial government and administration, England was usually permissive. Because of its large surplus population, it was glad to see emigrants move westward across the Atlantic to build up the overseas empire, particularly during the period when England and France struggled for the mastery of America north of Mexico. England was also glad to see settlers from other countries in northern Europe move to her American colonies. The Englishman who moved across the Atlantic carried with him the attitudes of his homeland. He also took with him the growing mercantile traditions of the day, a sturdy independence, and a strong preference for democratic government.

Spain was a far different fountainhead of colonial enterprise. The Spain from which Columbus sailed was just emerging from nearly eight centuries of warfare against the Moors. In fifteenth-century Spain had risen the prejudices which led to the expulsion of the Jews and the expulsion or Christianization of the Moors. These events were reflected in the social and economic structures of the sixteenth century. The country had a polyglot working class before the expulsion; those who remained afterward were Spaniards, and most of them were averse to working either as agriculturists or craftsmen. The expulsion of the Jews excised much of Spain's commercial class, leaving a preponderantly working class-upper class social structure.

Spanish rulers in the late fifteenth century had begun to whittle away the strength of the old feudal nobility. Under Charles I and Philip II, Spain came close to absolute monarchy. The powers of the nobility and the cities were progressively curtailed, government being centered more and more in the hands of the king through a growing bureaucracy. The Catholic Church was the only accepted church in sixteenth-century Spain, heresy was hunted out by the Inquisition, and the church was a vital and active factor in the national life.

When Spain came to build its empire in America, it was conditioned by the situation at home. The colonies were regarded as royal provinces. Every detail of civil and religious administration was regulated from Spain. Because emigration to the colonies from Spain was rigidly controlled and foreigners were excluded from Spanish America both for economic reasons and to prevent the taint of heresy, Spain's colonies received only a trickle of European settlers by contrast with Anglo-America.

Such were the major differences between England and Spain. Those differences were inevitably reflected in the Spanish and English colonial developments in the New World, and they were in part responsible for the differences between the Spanish and Anglo-American frontiers. However, another source of those differences is found in the native cultures of North America.

One of the most important differences between the Indians of Spanish- and Anglo-America was that of population density. In central Mexico, pre-conquest population has been estimated at about 300 per hundred square kilometers. In the United States east of the Mississippi, it ranged from two to thirty per hundred square kilometers. Thus, Spain colonized an area of dense native settlement, and the Anglo-American frontier moved across an area of sparse native population.

The Anglo-American pattern of Indian-white contacts was established by the first colonists along the Atlantic seaboard. The native economies there were based on gardening and hunting; each tribe required control of an extensive territory for its game preserve. The tribes lived in relatively small, semi-permanent villages; they practiced a fairly simple Stone Age technology; there was little craft specialization; and inter-tribal trade was minimal. Political organization was, with a few exceptions, rudimentary, and provided little basis for a concerted resistance to the intrusions of the white settlers.

During the first phase of contact, the Anglo-American settlers depended heavily on the Indians. They learned from them how to cope with the new land in which they lived. The early fur trade was, in most areas, a matter of cooperation between Indian and white.

Later, as the whites expanded their agricultural activities, they needed more and more land. This was taken from the Indians by a series of sales and treaties or by warfare which displaced the native population. At the same time, the native culture was weakened as it became more and more dependent upon white trade goods. Rum and the whites' epidemic diseases made inroads into the Indian population. Eventually the Indians rebelled against what was for them an intolerable situation.

Time and again as the frontier moved west a nativistic revival occurred among the Indians—one last convulsive outbreak of hostilities. These outbreaks can be followed from the wars of Opechancanough and King Philip through Tecumseh and Pontiac to the Ghost Dance of the late 1800's. But invariably they were too late. After their final defeat, the Indians were either driven westward or confined to reservations, and what remained of their lands were left open for white settlement. Thus, the pattern of Indian-white relations on the Anglo-American frontier was a replacement of the native peoples by the white settler.

A far different situation existed in Spanish America. An accident of history directed Spain's colonists to the one real center of native civilization in North America. In Mexico, they discovered the Aztec Empire, a true empire by European standards. Recently established by a military conquest of surrounding tribes, the Aztecs dominated a complex of vassal states which had reached a high degree of cultural development. The economy which supported the dense native population was based on intensive agriculture. Interregional trade was well developed, and markets were regularly held in the cities.

The cities themselves were true urban centers, having avenues, temples, libraries, and aqueducts. In them dwelt a collection of specialists—potters, weavers, metal workers, scribes, priests, warriors, and government officials. Because of the recent military conquests, the Aztec socio-political organization bordered on a feudal aristocracy. The religion was a vigorous one, which involved the worship of a variety of gods and the use of temples, monasteries, tributes, and human sacrifices.

Cortez and his followers set the pattern for the Spanish frontier expansion when they moved against the Aztec capital of Tenochtitlan. They moved with Indian porters carrying their supplies and baggage, with Indian allies fighting alongside them in battle. It was this sort of exploitation of the native peoples which established Spain on the American mainland. The Spaniards already had a model in the practices followed at home in dealing with provinces reconquered from the Moors; it was easily transposed to the New World.

As the Spanish frontier expanded, no displacement of the native population occurred as in Anglo-America. Instead, Spaniards took the places of defeated native rulers, and Catholic priests were substituted for the proponents of the native religions. The bulk of the Indians were left on their ancestral lands to provide the labor force which built an overseas empire for Spain. The native cultures were

147

exposed to new products and ideas brought from the Old World by the Spaniards.

The process of exposure was far different than on the Anglo-American frontier. There, the European guns, steel knives, and brass kettles were trade items, and they remained trade items. The Indians of Anglo-America grafted these items onto their own culture as displacements for the native counterparts. However, they did not learn the techniques which would have enabled them to produce the new items. The technologies of mining and smelting, blacksmithing, even such rudimentary ones as gun repair, were not acquired by the Indians as the Anglo-American frontier advanced. For this reason, the native cultures were weakened rather than strengthened by borrowing from the whites.

In contrast, the Spanish settler brought both traits and technologies to his Indian wards. Indian laborers were taught to use Spanish tools, and Indian craftsmen were taught to fashion the implements of Spain. Religious instruction included the language of the conquerors and many of the characteristics of Spanish society. Thus, the expansion of the Spanish frontier left behind a culture which was neither Spanish nor Indian, but a vigorous hybrid which has lasted down to the present day.

During the years which followed Cortez' conquest, the *entradas* and the "triumvirate of settlement" pushed out from Mexico City. The Spanish frontier moved down through the tangled mountains of southern Mexico, into Central America and Yucatan, west to the Pacific Coast, and northward across the high plateaus above Mexico City.

Gold and silver were the primary concern of the first Spaniards who moved north, sword in hand, from Mexico City. The *entrada* swept up whatever precious metals the natives had on hand; then the search for mines began. The great mineral deposits were discovered one by one, and exploited by Indian labor. The miners needed food, and fields were planted and herds of cattle brought in to provide meat. After a few years it became apparent that wealth could be had from the fields and ranches as well as the mines; the Spanish "triumvirate of settlement" was well established. Settlement moved erratically from one mineral-rich area to another, fields and ranches gradually filling up the intervening regions. Episodes such as the Mixton War caused temporary checks in the frontier development, but a far more serious problem occurred because of a shortage of native labor.

Beyond the boundaries of the advanced native cultures of Mexico, the Indian population was not only far less dense, but it was not nearly so amenable to working for Spanish masters. Lacking Anglo-America's steady flood of immigrants to provide a labor supply, the Spaniards were faced with an acute labor shortage. Slave-hunting expeditions in the northern hills and the emigration of civilized groups from the south helped some. In 1598 the Spanish frontier made a long jump to the north when Juan de Oñate established an island of settlement in the Rio Grande Valley of New Mexico, where the dense population of the Rio Grande pueblos provided a new labor supply. Elsewhere, the labor shortage greatly reduced the momentum of Spain's frontier advance before 1600.

Because the progressive absorption of the available supply of native labor was a major check to the Spanish frontier advance, Spain created another unique institution which carried its frontier northward to its ultimate limits. That institution was the mission, developed as one of the manifold activities of the Spanish Church. Bolton has long since pointed out the vital role which the mission played in the ultimate advance of the Spanish frontier. The missions, together with the presidios, flung a protective fringe far beyond the heartland of Spain's colonial empire.

But even the extent of the mission frontier was determined in part by Indian culture. The mission establishments were based on farming. So long as Spain encountered tribes like the Pima and Papago and some of the southeasterners who were already agriculturalists, the missions could be established without too much difficulty. The same was true among native peoples like the California tribes and those of east Texas who had lived by gathering wild food plants. In other cultural settings, the mission was a failure. Spanish friars had as little success in attracting hunting peoples like the Apache and Comanche to agriculture as did the United States Indian agents two centuries later.

In broad terms, then, the two frontiers were contrasts between cultures. The Anglo-American was rooted in the English way of life, and it represented an adaptation of that way of life to the environment of northern North America. Ever-growing numbers of Europeans flowed westward across the continent, carrying their democratic traditions, building their economy themselves, and pushing the sparse, unexploitable native population aside.

The Spanish frontier had its roots in sixteenth-century Spain, and it adapted to the environment of Mexico and the Southwest.

149

Relatively small numbers of Europeans, constrained by Spanish absolutism, developed the techniques of using the native population to exploit their segment of the New World. The Anglo-American frontier used its constellation of traits to engulf a continent; the Spanish frontier used its approach to engulf both a continent and its population. Between them, the two frontiers gave North America its European heritage.

Spanish Scientific Exploration Along the Pacific Coast

DONALD C. CUTTER
University of New Mexico

Possessing claim to a large share of the earth's surface because of the explorations of Columbus, Balboa, and others, Spain was early interested in the uniqueness evident in the New World. Indeed, the acknowledged father of natural scientific inquiry in the New World is the oft-quoted, highly respected author of *Historia General y Natural de las Indias, Islas y Tierra Firme del Mar Oceano*, Gonzalo Fernández de Oviedo y Valdés, whose multi-volume work was written between 1535 and 1557, though his experience in the Americas dated back to his first visit there in 1514. Oviedo, however, was more of a chronicler than a naturalist.

More in the spirit of true scientific inquiry was the activity of Dr. Francisco Hernández. Virtually a contemporary of Oviedo, he and his young son Juan traveled in New Spain from 1570 to 1576. A true naturalist, he dedicated himself to a study of the botanical, animal, and mineral kingdoms of the extended viceroyalty. So avid was his research that his health failed and he returned to Spain in 1577, though his enlightened monarch, Phillip II, had desired that he continue his labors in the South American viceroyalty of Peru.[1]

Hernández prepared for publication sixteen volumes of materials concerning his findings in New Spain, but like many other Spanish projects of a worthy nature they were left unprinted, in the archives of *El Escorial*, near Madrid, only to gather dust and finally be destroyed by fire in 1671. Fortunately, in the late eighteenth century, the prominent historian Juan Bautista Muñoz discovered copies of the first six volumes. He set the leading Spanish botanist of the period, Casimiro Gómez Ortega, director of the *Real Jardín Botánico* (Royal Botanical Garden) to work on publishing them, especially the botanical material.[2]

At this propitious point, the first Spanish scientific group to be interested in the Pacific Coast was organized. Probably oblivious of the work that Ortega was doing, an Aragonese physician residing in Havana, Dr. Martin Sessé, a graduate of the University of Zaragoza, suggested in a letter to him his willingness to direct a full-scale scientific expedition in New Spain which would complete the work of Dr. Hernández.[3]

As a result, Sessé was soon in the field in Mexico with three other scientists. The expedition, known as the *Botánica Mexicana,* was really interested in all aspects of natural history. It also became interested to some degree in the Pacific Coast from San José del Cabo to Nootka Sound and beyond.

A second important scientific exploring expedition of the late eighteenth century which explored the Pacific Coast was the Malaspina group, a naval contingent headed by the Italian-born Spanish naval career officer, Alejandro Malaspina, who was ably seconded by Captain José Bustamante y Guerra.[4] This expedition had the same objectives as those of the ill-fated Captain James Cook of the Royal Navy and of the French Count of La Pérouse, whose disappearance was still a mystery to the world at the time of Malaspina's departure from Cádiz in late July of 1789. By May 1791, the two-vessel Spanish naval task group was on the west coast of Mexico, poised for a trip to California and the Pacific Northwest coast.

The expedition had strong political overtones. A major objective was to seek the fabled, elusive, and strategic Strait of Ferrer Maldonado, a sort of reverse Northwest Passage leading to the Atlantic.[5] If such a strait existed, the Spanish proposed to claim it. Despite the prevailing doubts about the existence of the strait, the Malaspina group was confident of success, for it issued orders to some detached personnel indicating that the vessels would next be at Veracruz, after having made the passage.

A second objective of the expedition was even more politically opportunistic, concerning as it did investigation of the Spanish claim and military posture in the Nootka Sound area of the west coast of Vancouver Island, at 49° 30′ N. latitude. The situation at this focal point of international rivalry had been magnified to undue proportions by the reports of an untrustworthy British captain, and by the acts of a stubborn and opinionated Spanish junior officer.[6] Both courts had become embroiled; war seemed possible.

Additional Spanish naval scientific activity had preceded and would follow the Malaspina group, but the outstanding personnel and organization of this group enhance its importance. However, it should be noted that an earlier Spanish naval expedition had visited Baja California in 1769 for astronomical observations. Led by the Tarragonese officer, Vicente Doz, and accompanied by the French Abbé Chappé and Lieutenant Medina, this expedition sought to obtain an accurate observation of the transit of Venus and to correlate this with other sights in the interest of a more accurate geographical determination of west coast points, long a subject of some controversy. Failure of this earlier expedition resulted from the death of all the prominent members except Vicente Doz.[7] Any significant result was soon more than overshadowed by the multiple methods of longitudinal observations employed by Malaspina's group.

A third naval scientific voyage was an offshoot of the Malaspina exploration. After their visit to the Northwest coast, the Spanish naval scientists of the Malaspina expedition were not yet convinced that they had determined one way or the other the existence of Ferrer Maldonado's strait. Though Malaspina was convinced that he had not missed the strait north of Nootka, he was uncertain about the area around 48 to 50° N., in which existed the strait known as Juan de Fuca, named for a fictitious Greek pilot of a much earlier period. The relatively deep drafts of the *Descubierta* and *Atrevida* had made Malaspina cautious about any attempt at the close inspection of inland waterways. But the Nootka Sound dispute with England demanded a thorough inspection. The area in question was the tangled skein of waterways and canals that stretch inland both north and south of the Strait of Juan de Fuca, the northern outlet of which is Queen Charlotte Strait.

Therefore, when Malaspina reached Acapulco after the Northwest coast phase of his expedition, in cooperation with the viceroy of New Spain, the Conde de Revilla Gigedo, he sent two small, forty-six ton sailing vessels, the *goletas Sutil* and *Mexicana*, constructed at the Spanish Naval Department of San Blas for the purpose of detailed coastal exploration.[8] They were commanded by four of Malaspina's top officers, Dionisio Alcalá Galiano, Cayetano Valdés, Juan Vernacci, and Secundino Salamanca, and manned by a mixed crew of Malaspina veterans and San Blas personnel. The activities in 1792 of these men, all later to become prominent Spanish senior officers, are related in some detail in *Relación del viage de las goletas Sutil y Mexicana*, probably written by their scribe, artist, mapmaker, pilot, and jack-of-all-trades, José Cardero.[9]

The group followed approximately the same operational procedures as the Malaspina expedition. It cooperated with British Captain George Vancouver and his men, who were on a similar expedition but had other political motives. Artist Cardero drew an unusually interesting series of illustrations during the reconnaissance of the Strait of Juan de Fuca. A set of good maps was prepared, as well as a lengthy description of operations. The expedition named various places for Spanish naval figures, particularly members of the Malaspina group.[10] Though an abbreviated version of the final report of this expedition has been published several times,[11] the original and complete version still awaits publication.[12]

Of special anthropological note is the word list and extensive catechism of the Rumsen and Esselen Indians of Mission Carmel, prepared by the expedition toward the end of its reconnaissance, after it had traced the coast southward from Nootka to Monterey in the fall of the year. An abridged version of the word list was published with the *Relación del viage.*

Another scientific exploration of two sorties was made along the Pacific Coast in 1791 and 1792 by several members associated with the *Botánica Mexicana* expedition. The first of these sorties— made by José Longinos Martínez, a native of Logroño, accompanied part of the way by his associate, Jayme Senseve—was a brief study of the area from the tip of Baja California to as far north as Monterey, and perhaps beyond. The emphasis was on botany and certain physical phenomena.[13]

The second sortie—and the final effort by Spain in exploring the Pacific Northwest—was led by José Mariano Moziño, accompanied by botanical illustrator Atanasio Echeverría and natural scientist José Maldonado, all three of whom were attached to the more politically oriented expedition "Of the Limits to the North of California."[14] Headed by the San Blas commandant and leading Pacific Coast naval figure, Juan Francisco de la Bodega y Quadra, this expedition had been sent to reconcile the differences between England and Spain at Nootka, and to ascertain Spain's ability to maintain its interests in the northern area. The prominent Creole doctor-naturalist Moziño, a well-trained Mexican-born botanist, conducted some notable studies at Nootka, where he was located for nine months, from April 1792 to February 1793. After learning the language of the Nootkans, he compiled a comprehensive linguistic study and dictionary.[15] In conjunction with the dictionary, he prepared an interesting ethnological, geographical, and zoological work entitled *Noticias de Nutka,* which was scheduled to be published in the Universal History of North America.[16]

Except for the two expeditions to Baja California, all of them had a common denominator. To each was assigned one or more sketch artists, whose function was somewhat analogous to the photographer of today. Though occasionally one of them might employ artistic license, for the most part they illustrated with fidelity to detail the items deemed of interest by their superiors. Their wealthy pictorial record speaks well for the thoroughness of the eighteenth century scientific expeditions. The artists played a key role in the attainment of scientific objectives.

Though some of them specialized in one type of drawing, their range of abilities had to be extensive. Sometimes they paid special attention to fauna and flora, strictly from the botanical and zoological standpoint, but at other times as part of a more general scene. Their sketches of native Indian types and their unique customs have enhanced the ethnological record.

Coastal profiles, some much like modern hydrographic office charts, were drawn as aids to future navigation and as proof of the thoroughness of exploratory endeavor.[17] Numerous sketches were made of the Spanish settlements visited on the Pacific Coast—Nootka and Monterey.

The most comprehensive Spanish exploring expedition of the period was that of Captain Malaspina.[18] Organized in Spain with the strong support of the Minister of Marine, Antonio Valdés, the expedition set sail in 1789, staying abroad until 1794, a total of 62 months. Every effort was exerted to recruit well-qualified personnel and obtain the best equipment. Originals or copies of pertinent documents at various archives were abstracted. Seamen were recruited from the areas of Vizcaya, Asturias, and Santander, where they were presumed to be hardier.[19]

Malaspina, who was permitted to select his officers from among the active list of the navy, picked those having the requisite qualifications and experience. Felipe Bauzá, Chief of Charts and Maps, had been engaged in a general mapping of Spain under Vicente Tofiño; Alcalá Galiano, under the command of Captain Antonio de Córdova Lazo in a 1785 study of the Strait of Magellan, "had busied himself with observations on the soil, climate, aspect and composition of the land, animal and vegetable products, and human races"; Secundino Salamanca was considered to have ability in history; Vernacci in astronomy; Ceballos in cartography; and Hurtado in art. Surgeon Pedro María González assisted in astronomy and natural history, and some of the men doubled as scribes. Perhaps not insignificantly, Cayetano Valdés was the Minister of Marine's nephew.[20]

The two vessels used by the expedition, the *Descubierta* and *Atrevida*, which combined security, comfort, and economy, were constructed in an identical manner. Each was 120 feet in length and displaced 306 tons, having a loaded draft of approximately 14 feet. All personnel were Spanish naval officers and men, except for Chief of Natural History Antonio Pineda, an army colonel; the natural scientists, Botanist Luis Neé and Naturalist Tadeo Haenke; and the original artists. All except Haenke, who was Bohemian, were Spanish subjects.[21]

Before departure, the Spanish archives were combed for materials that would shed light on the objectives of the expedition; and subsequently, at each major stop, officers obtained all available source materials from local archives. In this manner, Malaspina obtained considerable information about the Pacific Northwest coast as a basis for further inquiry. In the Mexican viceregal archives, Lieutenants José Espinosa and Ciriaco Ceballos hopefully sought: 1) maps of Guadalajara and California prepared by Jesuit Father Consag; 2) "memorials of Alarcón, perhaps an ex-Jesuit who left important notices about the geography and civil history of the nations of the Río Colorado"; 3) the printed account of Sebastián Vizcaíno; 4) maps made by Kino of California, Sonora, Pimería, and the Río Colorado; 5) papers or old Mexican volumes of Boturini; and 6) "a dictionary and grammar of each of the languages known on the north coasts of Mexico."[22]

Though not all of these documents were found, other worthwhile ones were, such as the many journals of the San Blas naval officers, who since 1769 had been making regular supply runs and periodic exploratory trips along the Pacific Coast. The Minister of Marine, Antonio Valdés, produced some unexpected aid when he forwarded to Malaspina seven maps that had been sent in by Brigadier of the Navy Josef Bermúdez, commander of the Cavite Arsenal in the Philippine Islands, some of which concerned the coasts of America along what was then considered to be California.[23]

Other documents obtained for use by the expedition included Palóu's biography of Junípero Serra, Miguel Costansó's diary of the Sacred Expedition, some of Anza's journals, diaries of both Bruno de Hezeta and Juan de la Bodega, and many other documents concerned more with the *Provincias Internas* than with the coastal region itself.

Some half dozen or more separate accounts were kept by expedition members, not to mention the guard books of each of the two vessels, maintained only while in port. Special reports on various topics were compiled with regularity by the more competent members.

Three stops were made by the *Descubierta* and *Atrevida* along the Pacific Coast. The first, and northernmost, was a nine-day stop at Mulgrave Sound, Lituya Bay, Alaska, at approximately 59° 30′ N. and 140° W., or 133° 45′ West of Cádiz, the prime meridian for Hispanic explorations. Among the Tlinget Indians, whose friendship was soon temporarily won, Malaspina and his men carried out extensive observations. The nearby glacier, now called Malaspina Glacier, was studied; the height of Mt. St. Elias was calculated;[24] and the bays in the area were explored. An observatory, in the form of a tent, was established for scientific headquarters. In the tent, experiments were conducted with the simple pendulum for gravitational calculations in cooperation with the French, who were attempting to establish an international standard of weights and measures.[25]

Though many "lunar distances" were shot and geographical positions were calculated using marine chronometers, poor weather hampered astronomical and meteorological observations. A lumber summary was compiled,[26] birds were described scientifically,[27] and colored zoological plates were drawn. The artists sketched several curiosities, including sea-otter kidneys, and the local Indians.

The initial friendship with the natives and with their chief, Anaku, was temporarily destroyed by an incident ashore. However, because of the chief's interest in peace and trade, harmony was soon restored. Trade with the Indians was controlled, the Spaniards seeking mainly artifacts, such as native arms, articles of dress, and manufactures. Whenever possible, for security's sake, negotiations were conducted on land rather than on board ship. Severe punishment was prescribed for any men who violated trading regulations. In attempting to learn the native language, the officers were "to pay special attention to those words which have the most direct connection with our needs and with all the objects of good management."[28] A word list which was compiled was shipped back to Spain, along with some artifacts, for purposes of later classification and correlation. Other artifacts were similarly shipped from Nootka and Monterey.[29] Ballast, wood, and water were taken aboard at Mulgrave Sound to replenish the depleted stores on the twin vessels.

Upon departure from Mulgrave Sound, the expedition moved southward, inspecting the shoreline, making geographical observations, drawing profiles of the promontories, and to a great extent proving the lack of existence of any strait leading to Hudson's Bay. Stopping at Nootka Sound on the large offshore land mass now known as Vancouver Island, Malaspina was at a site of diplomatic controversy between England and Spain.

He inspected the physical location of the Spanish settlement and fortifications at Yoquot and Hog Island and sought any other information that might be helpful to the viceroy, Conde de Revilla Gigedo, or to his representatives at Nootka.

To this end, and to strengthen the Spanish hand, Malaspina and his men won the confidence of the vacillating chief of the Nootkans, Maquinna, by treating him with great respect. This important chieftain, who held a potential high card in the Nootka controversy, was a willing informant for anthropological purposes[30] and was a testator to the validity of Spanish claim to the area based on priority of discovery and legality of purchase of land from the natives.[31]

The sketch artists were particularly active at Friendly Cove, Nootka. They made many drawings of local Indians and of their cultural activities. Tomás Suria, artist-engraver on loan to the expedition from the Mexican mint and disciple of the prominent Gerónimo Antonio Gil, composed several classic representations of Nootka chiefs and kept a journal of his activities.[32] The drawings of young José (Pepe) Cardero, formerly cabin boy of Lt. Cayetano Valdés, were becoming increasingly skilled. This skill, combined with bravery and application, would win him an assignment as artist with the *Sutil* and *Mexicana* in the same area the following year and subsequently a commission as a Lieutenant in the Naval Supply Corps.[33]

At Nootka a series of good maps were either drawn or collected. The observatory was again established, this time on shore near the headquarters of the military commandant, and the customary series of calculations, annotations, and observations were effected. Felipe Bauzá spent considerable time in drafting appropriate maps, establishing ranges therefor ashore, and taking bearings of all significant landmarks. Naturalist Tadeo Haenke observed the natural phenomena of the area; and a small group, led by José Espinosa, explored in detail the labyrinth of canals that led inland from

Friendly Cove in the direction of Tasis Mountain and Maquinna's interior village site.[34] This group in 1791 explored Nootka Sound, circumnavigating Nootka Island, which lay offshore from Vancouver Island.[35] In 1792, Galiano and Valdés, in the *Sutil* and *Mexicana*, circumnavigated Vancouver Island, which at that time was being called "Vancouver and Quadra's" Island, for both the Nootka commissioners. Later this was shortened to Vancouver Island.

After a two-week stay among the Nootkans, Malaspina and party again moved southward, planning to follow the coastline as closely as possible. Unfortunately, foggy weather and an imperfectly known coastline forced them somewhat farther out to sea than anticipated until about 41°, from which point southward to Monterey a fairly close inspection of the coast was possible.

In California, which Spain had settled in 1769, twenty-two years prior to Malaspina's visit, the expedition made primary observations and obtained useful second-hand information. Some of the founding fathers were still available to act as informants, and a number of "firsts" in California history were established. Haenke became the botanical discoverer of the *Sequoia sempervirens;*[36] several species of oak were subsequently discovered and botanically described for the first time by Botanist Luis Neé, from samples brought from California by the paymaster of the expedition;[37] and the first California original pieces of art still extant were drawn by artists José Cardero and Tomás Suria. Four of the pieces of art were California birds in color and three were coastal profiles.[38]

California was primarily of interest to the expedition because of its frontier character. One of the leading Hispanic frontier institutions, the mission, was studied by the visitors. Despite the reputed liberal tendencies of the Italian-born commander, the mission system was not only given a clean bill of health, but it was also eulogized—especially the self-sacrifice of the Franciscans led by the well-known Father Fermin Francisco de Lasuén.[39] Lasuén was particularly helpful to the scientific ends of the expedition, especially in providing guides for field trips and obtaining artifacts.[40]

No less helpful, in his own way, was the commandant of the local presidio of Monterey. In an effort to meet the secondary purpose of Malaspina's visit, that of the three R's of navigation (rest, recreation, and relaxation), Lt. José Darío Arguello provided mounts, daily *novilladas* in the courtyard of the presidio, and liberal quantities of fresh provisions, including milk.[41] So helpful were the Californians that the explorers were able to complete their observations—botanical, mineralogical, and general—within a two-week period, and sail southward to rejoin those members who for several months had been carrying out commissions in Mexico proper.

The *Relación del viage*, expurgated of all mention of the expedition commanded by Malaspina, and with the commander's name deleted, is about all that saw light of any of the Malaspina ventures for almost a full century. According to Baron Alexander von Humboldt, Malaspina was "more famous for his misfortunes than for his discoveries."[42] A plan which allegedly would have supplanted Spanish Chief of State Manuel Godoy as Queen María Luisa's lover and confidant with Malaspina apparently backfired to the suave round-the-world explorer's disadvantage.[43]

Because of the decline of its sea power in the Pacific, its abandonment of the centuries-old claim to exclusive sovereignty there, and increasing commitments in Europe, Spain reaped little or no advantage from the numerous well-equipped and well-staffed scientific expeditions it dispatched to the Pacific Coast. However, the westerner of today can at least appreciate the notable efforts of these eighteenth-century Iberian men of science.

THE TERRITORIES—

POLITICS AND INDIANS

The Reluctant Admission: The Struggle To Admit Arizona and New Mexico to the Union

HOWARD R. LAMAR
Yale University

Fifty-one years ago last August, as President William Howard Taft signed the statehood bills which admitted Arizona and New Mexico into the Union, he remarked: "Well, it is all over. I am glad to give you life." Though this may sound like the classic statement of a political obstetrician happily officiating at the birth of new states, Taft and his predecessor, Theodore Roosevelt, were probably the most reluctant executive midwives ever to sit in the White House. Neither had ever been enthusiastic over the entrance of Arizona or New Mexico. What was "all over" in the way of a statehood movement had been going on sporadically since the 1870's, had been intensified between 1891 and 1900, and had become an all-engrossing struggle between 1901 and 1910. Claude Bowers has called it "one of the most stubborn and historic contests over the conversion of Territories into States in the history of the Union."[1]

On the occasion of the fiftieth anniversary of statehood for Arizona and New Mexico, it seems worthwhile to review the admission efforts, not so much to relay new historical information, for the late Marion Dargan at the University of New Mexico and his students have studied some aspects thoroughly; nor is it for sentimental reminiscence.[2] The review is desirable because the history of these statehood movements tells us much about the way the East, the nation, and Congress viewed this part of the Southwest and how such an image, however incorrect, can affect history and policy.

Secondly, the history of these movements demonstrates rather dramatically how national fads, issues, and unrelated crusades can interfere with local wishes and hopes. Much of American history is built around the interplay of region or state with the nation or the Federal Government. Arizona and New Mexico are no exceptions to this time-honored process, but during their drive for statehood the interplay seemed remarkably complex and highlighted the dif-

163

ferences and lack of understanding between region and nation. Finally, the statehood drive of Arizona and New Mexico echoes the struggles of other territories to gain admission in that it began as a politicians' idea and ended as a people's movement.

Statehood would not have been achieved when it was had it not been for the presence of three unusual territorial delegates and a Rough Rider governor in the Southwest. It took a southerner, an Irishman, a Pennsylvanian, and a frontier sheriff to do the trick. The southerner was the slight, keen-eyed Marcus Aurelius Smith, a Kentucky lawyer who arrived in Tombstone, Arizona, in 1881 to hang out his shingle. As much as any single person this little man from Cynthiana guided to success the statehood movements of Arizona, New Mexico, and even that of Oklahoma. Possessed of a southern accent, an unlimited fund of humorous stories, and an indomitable will, he was one of the shrewdest judges of men ever to come into the Southwest. Within months of his arrival in Arizona, he was a noted territorial figure. Outspoken, acid in debate, and absolutely fearless, he marched through a series of local offices to become territorial delegate in 1886, and was returned to that office between then and 1912 some seven more times. An almost legendary political figure, he was to serve as one of Arizona's first senators in 1912.[3]

His secret was always to work within the political and economic framework which he found in Arizona. He joined his constituents in a dislike of the wild Indians; and he knew that Arizona's future lay in large-scale mining, cheap transportation, and irrigation. While pleasing the older merchant-ranchers and the small miner oligarchy in Tucson, he also cultivated the copper executives of Bisbee and those of the Santa Fe and Southern Pacific Railroads, for all of whom he was occasionally legal counsel. To the silver miners, he represented a stalwart defender of "free coinage" and "bimetallism." He pleased the saloon element, yet he never crusaded on an anti-Mormon ticket. He was a Democrat with supporters from all ranks and every political persuasion.

It was during his first term in Congress that the statehood issue came up, for in 1888 the original Omnibus Bill, which eventually admitted the Dakotas, Montana, and Washington, at first also included Arizona and New Mexico. This fact and the attempts of neighboring Utah and New Mexico to gain admission between 1888 and 1891 whetted the appetites of Smith and other Arizona politicians to do the same. Because New Mexico was Republican and

Arizona Democratic, it was thought that Congress might be receptive: the admission of both would not disturb the party balance in the United States Senate. In 1891, twenty-one of Arizona's leading men met informally in Phoenix to write a constitution and petition for admission. Though the convention was Democratic in its makeup, it had the cooperation of popular Republicans like N. O. Murphy.[4]

The constitution which it prepared revealed much about the nature of the statehood advocates in 1891. Basically it was a Jeffersonian document tinged with the ideas of Populism and free silver. But its clauses concerning land, water rights, and corporation policies were so ambiguous that people wondered if it was not a "water and land grab" document.[5] Yet one fact was clear: the statehood movement of 1891 in Arizona was more a creature of professional politicians and interested economic groups than it was a people's crusade.

Meanwhile, a less subtle document had been written by a constitutional convention in New Mexico, which had met in 1889 and reconvened in 1890. The document it produced was soon to be called "a land grant constitution," the "Santa Fe rag baby," and the "Tom-Cat Constitution," the latter in reference to Thomas B. Catron's role in writing it. It, too, was hardly a product of a people's crusade, for the New Mexican Delegate Antonio Joseph, nearly all the Spanish-American voters, and many Democrats opposed both the constitution and the idea of statehood.[6] Nor was the fact lost upon Congress that two silver-producing territories were anxious to come into the Union. Although the people of Arizona voted in favor of their constitution and an Arizona Enabling Act passed the House in 1892, the Senate rejected the Act on the grounds that it seemed to repudiate certain contracts and set up a double monetary standard.[7] The New Mexican constitution was destined for defeat not only at the hands of Congress but from the voters as well. As for Congress' reluctance to admit, President Harrison put the reason bluntly to Delegate Smith: Congress was "opposed to the free coinage of Western Senators."[8]

Congressional rebuff only temporarily blunted the enthusiasm of Arizona Democrats for statehood. Cleveland's election in 1892 led them to introduce no less than five bills to Congress. The following year the statehood forces themselves met in Phoenix at the Opera House to petition Congress anew, to organize a permanent statehood committee in each county, and to send a delegation to Wash-

165

ington to lobby for admission. Cleveland proved hostile, however, because Smith and stand-pat Democrats had not voted for him but had voted for Hill at the 1892 National Convention. Indeed, Cleveland took revenge on Smith's group by appointing Louis C. Hughes, a temperance editor and opponent of Smith, as territorial governor.[9]

A Smith-Hughes feud, a split over free silver, and the rising Populist party all diverted Arizonans from the statehood cause until 1900. When the Populist fervor subsided after 1896, however, Smith had consolidated his supporters into such a strong organization that it was not surprising the territory returned him as delegate for eight out of the next twelve years.[10] By 1900 it was also true that Arizona's population was well over 100,000, its Indians were under control, its industries were booming, and it even boasted such evidences of advanced civilization as labor unions and strikes. The territory had contributed men like Bucky O'Neill to the Spanish-American War, and not the least of their services had been to give the region a good name. Smith was also aware that by 1900 even the Spanish-American population of New Mexico was willing to support statehood, while groups in Oklahoma were also agitating for statehood. Always one to see the question in a larger perspective, Smith knew that the three territories should pool resources and talents to fight for admission. For Arizona, the new campaign for admission formally began in 1901, when a new convention was held and a constitution adopted.[11]

Smith's statehood activities were more than matched by an exuberant Irish-born politician in New Mexico, Bernard S. Rodey. Despite Governor Otero's dislike for statehood, Rodey ran for delegate on a statehood platform in 1900. Many of the old leaders of the 1890-91 movement, such as L. Bradford Prince and Thomas B. Catron, were still ardent advocates, but Rodey gave the cause new life. He turned the Territorial Fair into an informal statehood convention in 1901. He tried to relate statehood to all public issues, such as the Elephant Butte Dam project and a cattlemen's lease law. He influenced Dennis T. Flynn, the Oklahoma delegate, to join forces with him. Every letter he sent out bore the stamp "Work for Statehood for New Mexico." Opponents were called Tories, Texans, and predatory birds of passage in such a way that most vocal opposition was silenced.[12] Rodey even gave cab drivers lectures on statehood. His witty nature and his ability to fire an audience with his enthusiasm earned him the nickname of "Statehood Rodey." The movement so captured New Mexican voters that Rodey was to be re-elected in 1902 with the largest majority in the history of the territory.[13]

When Rodey and Smith departed for Washington in 1901 they had ample cause for optimism. Both the national and local press seemed favorable to statehood. The Republicans did not seem hostile, and Smith had rounded up most southern senators as well as Teller of Colorado and Clark of Montana. New Mexican politicians persuaded Matt Quay of Pennsylvania to carry the fight in the Senate. In cooperation with Oklahoma's zealous statehood delegate, Dennis T. Flynn, the three men pushed an Omnibus Bill, to admit their territories, safely through the House in May 1902. Hopes rose as an estimated vote of the senators suggested that success was within reach.[14]

What the three delegates did not know at first was that the Chairman of the Senate Committee on Territories, Albert Beveridge of Indiana, was extremely hostile to the idea of statehood for the Spanish Southwest.[15] His attitudes toward the region deserve some consideration, for they were fairly representative of a large heritage of beliefs and images which were instilled in the American people— beliefs and images which were unexpectedly reinforced by the Spanish-American War, by the flirtation with imperialism at the turn of the century, and finally by a concern about the "new immigration" from Southern and Mediterranean Europe. What is equally important is that men like Theodore Roosevelt and Henry Cabot Lodge were in complete agreement with Beveridge's views. Then, too, many people believed that the West was somehow not quite as civilized as the more settled East. A combination of these beliefs and Beveridge's actions were to hold up the admission of Arizona and New Mexico for ten years.

The first of these beliefs involved the long-standing impression that the Spanish-speaking residents of the Southwest were at best second-class citizens—passive, pliant, and uneducated. It was argued they were not at home with United States law, the court and school systems, and the English language. To Senator Beveridge, in fact, the refusal to learn English was tantamount to a mild form of treason. Just as these beliefs were dying out, the Cuban troubles, the Spanish-American War, and the acquisition of Puerto Rico and the Philippines unfortunately revived the old myths of a backward Latin culture and people.

This belief in ethnic and cultural incompatibility was further reinforced by the impression that the Southwest was some sort of modern day "great American desert" that lacked enough water, good soil, adequate population, and the general wherewithal to support civilized man. Arizona is just "a mining camp," wrote Beveridge in 1902.[16] The westerners themselves had contributed to this belief because of their demands for new land and water laws ever since the 1870's. Then, too, many in the East felt that the Southwest was a colonial appendage of vested interests and big business. It was common rumor that the two territories were dominated by the Santa Fe and the Southern Pacific Railroads and a few large absentee-controlled mining corporations. Finally, eastern conservationists believed that the West wanted to grab timber and land for senseless exploitation.

No one was more taken with these beliefs and images than Senator Beveridge. In a swift trip to the Philippines soon after the Spanish-American War he had formed a very bad impression of the inhabitants and the culture.[17] The extension of his prejudice to the Southwest became apparent when he made a whirlwind trip through Oklahoma, New Mexico, and Arizona in the fall of 1902 to investigate their readiness for statehood. Though he liked the so-called "American" qualities of Oklahoma, he harped on a lack of English spoken, lack of schools, and the high degree of illiteracy in the other two states. As a highly moral Progressive much affected by muckraker literature, Beveridge, upon learning that Boies Penrose and Matt Quay of Pennsylvania and Senator Clark of Montana had mining and railroad interests in the two territories, began to feel that statehood was really a scheme to benefit these men. Later when a business associate of Matt Quay's, William H. "Bull" Andrews, ran for the New Mexican delegateship in 1904, Beveridge was certain that his suspicions were correct, for Andrews was involved in a railroad bond scheme relating to the Santa Fe Central.[18]

Beveridge had apparently reached these conclusions quite early, for his private correspondence with Albert Shaw reveals several efforts to round up eastern witnesses hostile to statehood even before he made his whirlwind tour.[19] Indeed the Senator and his committee moved with such speed on the tour that Mark Smith acidly commented to a House Committee in 1903:

> I met the committee—I could never have overtaken it—at Phoenix and it remained one day, the longest stop in all its record, so far as I know, and "investigated" a police judge and some census enumerators, and had an interpreter with them scouring the town to see whether some Mexican could not be

found who could not speak English and prove valuable witnesses for the purpose of investigation. " . . . it was a secret star-chamber proceeding from first to last."[20]

The result was that Beveridge reported a bill for the admission of Oklahoma in 1902 which made no mention of Arizona and New Mexico. To qualify for statehood, he explained, the population must be sufficient in number; the territories "must be on an equality with the remainder of the people of the Nation in all that constitutes effective citizenship; they must have developed the resources of the land they occupy; and finally have further resources susceptible of like development to bring their proposed new state up to the average of the remainder of the Nation." Future senators, he concluded, " 'should stand for a quantity of people and not a quantity of land.' "[21] His attitude was typical of that of Roosevelt, Lodge, and others who felt that the old Anglo-Saxon American was being threatened by other ethnic groups at the turn of the century.

At the same time, Beveridge's friends in the publishing world were attacking statehood as a scheme of business interests. Beveridge also received unexpected support from Senator Thomas R. Bard of California, who said bluntly that Arizona and New Mexico were not intelligent enough to be states. Ex-Governor N. O. Murphy was so incensed at this slander that he attacked Bard in speeches as did many southern Californians who, for business reasons, hoped Arizona would be admitted.[22]

Even so, the pro-statehood forces were not worried, for Senator Quay submitted separate reports in favor of the Omnibus Bill of 1902, while Senator W. R. Hearst and the Democrats turned in pro-statehood reports. But Beveridge was not to be defeated. After mobilizing many other senators and using filibuster techniques, he resorted to an unexpected device. For reasons of courtesy no vote could take place without his presence as chairman of the Territorial Committee; so at the crucial moment he hid on the third floor of Gifford Pinchot's home for a week. Thus no vote took place in the Fifty-seventh Congress.[23] Beveridge's use of Pinchot's home is not merely coincidental, for Roosevelt's chief of the Forestry Service had also become convinced that nearly everyone in New Mexico had a greedy eye fastened upon federal forest reserves there. His convictions had some basis in fact because various New Mexican interests were opposing the repeal of the Desert Land Law, had objected to Pinchot's creation of the San Mateo Forest Reserve, and had turned an 1898 grant of educational lands into a speculation scheme.

Roosevelt himself, though more in sympathy with the West, appears to have agreed with Beveridge and Pinchot. Indeed, he kept appointive federal officials in Arizona and New Mexico under such suspicious scrutiny between 1901 and 1909 that many persons began to long for statehood just to escape the vigorous presidential eye.[24] Through most of his second term, in fact, two special investigators, Ormsby and McHarg, kept the wires to Washington hot with charges of land schemes.[25]

Beveridge, Roosevelt, and the eastern wing of the Republican party were increasingly aware, nevertheless, that the statehood question for the territories within the continental United States was now a fairly prominent public issue. As a compromise, Mark Hanna and others suggested the solution of "Joint Statehood" in April 1904; New Mexico and Arizona, which had once been a single territory, would come into the Union as a huge Texas-like single state.[26] Under a bill introduced by Congressman Hamilton of Michigan, "jointure," as the single state idea was soon dubbed, seemed a reasonable way to cut down the number of senators while admitting the region to Congress. Echos of the old Federalist fear of the West could be seen in the measure. It also recalled a Democratic effort during the 1880's to make North and South Dakota a single state.

As was expected, the news of the Hamilton bill caused a storm of disapproval in the Southwest. When the city council of Phoenix learned that Roosevelt himself preferred a single state, they changed the name of Roosevelt Street to Cleveland Street. Arizonans declared that their business connections were with California, and those of New Mexico were with the East. Nor did they want to be thrown together with a large Spanish-American population. On the other hand, the Spanish-speaking natives of New Mexico had no desire to become a minority in a new political creation which, incidentally, was to be called Arizona. Yet when Solomon Luna and Governor Miguel A. Otero joined Delegate Wilson in remonstrating to the President, Otero disgustedly reported that their arguments did not impress Roosevelt "in the slightest degree."[27] Once again, however, luck was on the side of the territories, for Senator Bard of California, in continuing to oppose any form of statehood, helped defeat the Hamilton bill in the spring of 1905. Arizonans were so pleased that they held celebrations.

The escape appeared to be temporary, however, for in December 1905 Hamilton and Beveridge, with Roosevelt's support, reintroduced a jointure bill. Roosevelt not only advocated the measure in his annual message but began to put pressure on his governors in Arizona and New Mexico as well. Then the political fireworks really began. Despite orders from Washington, Governor J. K. Kibbey refused to support jointure, his position being seconded by an anti-jointure convention which met in Phoenix. In New Mexico, however, the traditional factionalism within the Republican ranks and the extraordinary anxiety of the latest Santa Fe ring to gain statehood led to all kinds of compromises.[28] "Statehood Rodey," who had become friendly with Beveridge, was persuaded to declare for jointure, while Governor Otero and a newcomer politician from Matt Quay's Pennsylvania, "Bull" Andrews, declared for single statehood.[29] The disagreement caused a split in Republican ranks and Andrews emerged as delegate, while Mark Smith was re-elected in Arizona.

Still it looked as if jointure would prevail, for under pressure the House approved such a bill and sent it to the Senate, where an enthusiastic Beveridge reported it within four days. A rider granting Oklahoma statehood was also attached. This time, however, Mark Smith laid several traps for the measure. First, he persuaded Senator Joseph Benson Foraker to propose an amendment, which Smith himself had drafted, to allow the two territories to hold a referendum on jointure. The combination of Foraker's old-fashioned eloquence and the Progressive love of referendum got the amendment adopted by a vote of forty-two to twenty-nine.[30] This was followed by a sudden move to strike out the name of Arizona and New Mexico and leave Oklahoma. Citizens of Tucson, upon hearing of this, were so happy that they poured into the streets, bands played, and a parade formed.

It remained for Arizona and New Mexico to vote on jointure. It was clear that Arizona would vote it down, and it did, 16,265 declaring against and 3,141 for. In New Mexico, however, the referendum produced a fascinating game of politics. Ex-governor Otero, backed by Thomas B. Catron, was an outright single stater and refused to cooperate with Roosevelt in any way. Roosevelt's young governor, Hagerman, agreed to jointure but was at loggerheads with the regular party leadership of H. O. Bursum. Bursum, Solomon Luna, Max Frost, and regular Republicans also cared little for joint statehood but were willing to bargain with Washington if Roosevelt would throw out Hagerman and let the conservative Republican machine in New Mexico continue undisturbed. Just what arrangements were made are not known, but in New Mexico a giant press and political campaign for joint statehood was inaugurated.[31] In a controversial election, Delegate Andrews squeaked in with a majority of only 370 votes, but the public endorsed jointure by a vote of 26,195 for and 14,735 against.[32] The election also marked the triumph of Bursum's control over the local Republican party. Ironically, Roosevelt and Beveridge had helped the very group they wished to destroy. And Beveridge failed to dislodge the established order in Arizona. Finally, it now appears that Bursum had hoped all along that, by being loyal and voting jointure, New Mexico would be rewarded with single statehood.[33]

Up to this point, Roosevelt appears to have endorsed Beveridge's anti-statehood policy. At the same time he could see that relations had become terribly strained with the Southwest. In a shrewd move, he replaced the controversial Hagerman with a former sheriff, Rough Rider, and Philippine police commissioner, George Curry. As the new governor, Curry managed to convert himself to Pinchot's forestry program, persuaded Roosevelt that statehood must come, quelled his personal dislike of Delegate Andrews in order to cooperate to obtain admission, and carefully reassured everyone that "a constitution will be drawn up by conservative businessmen and will be in striking contrast to that adopted by Oklahoma. Instead of driving away capital we will invite it."[34]

The general accounts of New Mexico's statehood struggle have suggested that Andrews was to be praised for carrying on Rodey's statehood crusade even though it was associated with many economic and political schemes. Yet Governor Curry's official papers are full of appeals for help sent by Andrews. Time and time again he wired Curry to "come on here without a crowd" and lobby for admission. Curry traveled to Washington so many times that it became a territorial joke and the subject of a reprimand from the Secretary of the Interior.

Andrews was lining up support everywhere, even to the point of obtaining summer jobs in New Mexico for the sons and relatives of congressmen. But it was Curry's task to persuade Roosevelt to influence Beveridge to relent, for as Andrews observed, ". . . there is no power on earth that will move Beveridge except the president."[35] Together, Andrews, Curry, and Mark Smith helped to obtain a separate statehood plank in both 1908 national party platforms. Further, Roosevelt is supposed to have asked Taft to pursue an admission policy. But Andrews correctly predicted that an enabling bill would fail to pass in the spring of 1909, when he wrote pessimistically in December 1908: "The incoming big chief [Taft]

is against statehood for this session [and] has written a letter to
that effect. . . . If the incoming chief had of helped as the outgoing
chief requested it would have been a sure thing."[36]

Taft refused to help Beveridge keep the territories out of the
Union indefinitely and is supposed to have concluded after a trip
through the Southwest that "even Arizona babies cry for admission."[37] Because of Taft's reluctant consent, it was merely a matter
of time before enabling acts were passed and final statehood bills
submitted. Before that could happen, however, all kinds of minor
difficulties harassed the statehood advocates.

Taft's Secretary of the Interior, Hitchcock, apparently tried to
bulldoze Arizona into the Republican column. Meanwhile a wing
of the Arizona Democratic party led by George W. P. Hunt had
embraced the principles of Progressivism so completely that Mark
Smith found himself in opposition.[38] Then, on the eve of the congressional vote for statehood bills, New Mexico was startled by a Texan
demand for three miles of New Mexican territory along her eastern
border in return for a favorable vote by Texas congressmen. Democrats in New Mexico were not only split into conservative and progressive wings, but they feared that statehood meant political control by Spanish-Americans.

Nor were the troubles all at home. In Washington, Beveridge
tried to insert a clause requiring state legislators to speak only
English.[39] Embarrassed local officials like Curry finally forced the
exclusion of that clause, but Beveridge did obtain amendments which
might disqualify Spanish-American voters and which did reduce public land acreage granted, refused to pay certain territorial debts, protected school lands, and required that the state constitution be approved both by the President and Congress.[40]

Still another skirmish came when New Mexico adopted such a
conservative constitution and made the document so difficult to
amend that Taft refused to consider it until the amending clause
was modified. Arizona, on the other hand, had gone the other way
and was exhibiting a wonderful affection for Progressivism. Future
Governor George W. P. Hunt captured the new mood with the
slogan: "Start in With a Clean Slate for a Clean State." The Arizona constitution was written in the full glare of an open, non-
caucusing convention in Phoenix and contained so many advanced
ideas—among them the initiative, the referendum, and the recall—
that it was called a labor union document, a socialist creation, and
even a clever device of mining and railroad companies. Some of the

constitutional convention's atmosphere and certainly its attitude was typified by a "Battle Hymn for Arizona," which ran:

> Don't let Federal Sucklings school you,
> Don't let Mercenaries fool you,
> Don't let Corporations fool you,
> Our Cause is marching on.[41]

Indeed, the document so alienated Mark Smith that he refused to speak in its behalf and darkly predicted that its radical clauses would lead to its defeat in Washington. Even the appearance of William Jennings Bryan in Arizona to campaign for ratification did not move Smith to make more than a perfunctory platform appearance. Here was a curious situation, for Republican Taft and Democrat Smith now found themselves on the same side, while Beveridge must have found it hard to believe that men like George W. P. Hunt of Arizona and Harvey Fergusson of New Mexico could be southwesterners. But even they were distrusted by Beveridge, for they were Democrats.

A further confusion was that, where New Mexico had been too conservative, Arizona was now too radical. As Mark Smith had predicted, Taft refused to approve the constitution until a provision allowing the recall of judges had been removed. After this was removed and Arizona was safely in the Union, the offending clause was put back into the constitution. It was not without some genuine glee that the *Arizona Gazette* headlined news of the constitution's ratification with the words: "Popular Government Succeeds Old Regime: Special Interest Dethroned."[42]

The Arizona-New Mexico admission fight demonstrated the classic struggle of a region acting to resist outside authority which attempted to standardize and force conformity. Though the Federal Government, by trying to make the two territories into one, was trying to be fair and achieve proportional representation in the national sense, it violated local political habits and customs in a fairly obtuse way. On the other hand, indignation over jointure helped make statehood a popular rather than a politicians' cause.

The struggle for statehood also illustrates another classic pattern in American political history—how national issues and fads can so vitally affect local causes. Not only did admission skirt the prohibition issue and involve the debating of women's rights and new ideas like the initiative and the referendum, but it was clouded by the silver issue, war, conservation and land policies, feelings about the new immigration, and anti-southwestern attitudes. The regional struggle between East and West, and the political struggle between conservative and insurgent Republicans in the 1910 Congress, both also played a vital role. All in all, then, the admission debate mirrored American prejudices and preoccupations at the turn of the century.

But to Beveridge, Roosevelt, Taft, fads, and crusades cannot be attributed all the blame. Many Arizonans and New Mexicans at first openly and later secretly supported continued territorial status. More than once the influential New Mexican banker, Jefferson Raynolds, dashed off to Washington to oppose statehood. Thus Washington officials had some reason to think that statehood was an artificially inspired goal. Furthermore, neither state changed its traditional frontier attitudes toward land policy, conservation, lax elections, and public education enough to impress Congress. Then, too, there was Delegate Andrews' close relation to Matt Quay, who was an arch symbol of corruption to muckrakers. And, at a crucial moment in 1909, Mark Smith did not hesitate to hold up the statehood bill for two weeks until Arizona got a 600,000-acre grant of land.[43] It is not surprising that Congress was so distrustful of statehood.

What Congress, Roosevelt, and Taft did not realize, however, was that a large number of citizens in the Southwest had come to believe sincerely that territorial status was a terrible stigma, an insufferable mark of inferiority. They agreed with a remark made by Governor Prince in 1902 that "a Territory with bad officials is a despotism, and not a republic; it is ruled by men named by an authority 2,000 miles away, who are not responsible to any local instrument of power." Such men, he said, should be compared to Butcher Weyler in Cuba or the territory to "an East Indian State under Hastings."[44]

It was such sentiments, reminiscent of the assertions of local liberty in the thirteen colonies, that led the Arizona and New Mexico citizens to campaign for their own independence fifty years ago. In so doing, they eventually forced Congress to observe the spirit of the Ordinance of 1787 rather than to pursue the imperial implications of Beveridge's New Nationalism. The nation had finally followed the flag into the Southwest.

Brigham Young and the Indians

GUSTIVE O. LARSON
Brigham Young University

The Act creating Utah Territory in September 1850 provided that the governor should also be *ex-officio* Superintendent of Indian Affairs. Brigham Young, the governor and the Mormon president, learned of his appointment in January 1851. The Mormons had entered the Great Basin in 1847, and, during the three years of un-official contact with his Indian neighbors before his appointment to the superintendency, Young had ample opportunity to familiarize himself with their characteristics and culture and measure them in terms of Mormon-Indian philosophy.

The redskins crept into Mormon philosophy through the Book of Mormon, in which they were known as Lamanites. They were presented as fallen remnants of a once mighty Israelitish people upon this continent who fell from grace through transgression, but who were promised regeneration when the Gospel of Christ would be brought to them. Upon acceptance of that Gospel, they would be restored to divine favor and assume leadership in the building of God's kingdom upon the American continent. It was to be the privilege and responsibility of the Latter-day Saints to bring the Mormon Gospel to the Indians and labor with them in the ful-fillment of its prophecies.

The natives of the Great Basin presented themselves early to test these Mormon claims of brotherhood, and they came first in their lowest form—the Diggers. Two bands of these, Utes and Sho-shones, competed for Mormon attention. The Shoshones claimed the land, which they wanted to trade for powder and lead. Speaking for Brigham Young, who was ill, Heber C. Kimball "discouraged the idea of paying the Indians for their lands, for if the Shoshones were to be thus considered, the Utes and other tribes would claim pay also. The land," he continued, "belongs to our Father in Heaven and we calculate to plow and plant it; and no man shall have the power to sell his inheritance for he cannot remove it; it belongs to the Lord."[1]

Their first Indian problem thus simply resolved, the Mormons proceeded to dispossess the Indians of their homelands for two decades before the United States Congress finally extinguished their title by treaty and made Mormon ownership possible. In the meantime, Mormon-Indian relations and Brigham Young's policy in dealing with them were vitally influenced by this unusual situation.

Their lands being pre-empted, the natives soon sought compensation by stealing Mormon livestock. The thieves were surrounded and slain by Mormon militia at Battle Creek in March 1849, a preliminary to a larger punitive expedition which was launched from Fort Utah in the winter of 1850. Captain Howard Stansbury, who was conducting a Federal Government survey in the area, recorded Young's attitude toward what threatened to become a recurring problem: "The President was at first extremely averse to adoption of harsh measures; but after several conciliatory overtures had been resorted to in vain, he very properly determined to put a stop, by force, to further aggressions, which if not resisted, could only end in the total destruction of the colony."[2]

In June 1849, Young sent two emissaries to confer with the Utes in Utah Valley, who were stirred up over the establishment of Fort Utah. In response to Young's message of friendship, Chief Walkara [anglicized "Walker"] returned a message: "The waters are mine; the Mormons may use them. We want to trade. Brigham is our white father. Bridger wants to trade but we wait for you. You do not come so we come to you in Salt Lake." This was the beginning of Young's association with the war chief, which alternately warmed and cooled during the next four years. The opportunist chief was baptized a member of the Mormon Church on March 13, 1850, two weeks before the assembly of the State of Deseret, on Young's advice, passed an ordinance prohibiting trade in arms, ammunition, and alcoholic beverages with the Indians. Though the chief was disappointed when he learned about the ordinance in May, he remained loyal until a band of Shoshones stole Ute horses and Brigham refused to join with him in revengeful pursuit. "Stay home and stop fighting" seemed strange advice to Walkara from a newly won ally. But it was advice which, oft repeated, was to gradually make its mark on the Utah Indians.

During their three years of unofficial relations with their Indian neighbors, Young and his associates further developed their Lamanite philosophy and practice. Said one of their spokesmen:

> The door has been unlocked to the Lamanites in these mountains and they will begin to embrace the Gospel and the records of their fathers, and their chiefs will be filled with the spirit and power of God, and they will rise up in their strength, and a nation will be born in a day because they are the seed of Abraham.[3]

Though President Young accepted this doctrine, his own pronouncements were increasingly directed toward the development of practical relations:

> We are here in these mountains with these Lamanites for our neighbors, and I hesitate not to say, if this people possessed the faith they ought to have the Lord Almighty would never suffer any of the sons of Jacob to injure them in the least . . . . But lest you should not have faith, we have caused to be done that which has been done in having this people prepared for any emergency that should arise. My advice is to *be on the watch all the time.*[4]

Beyond self-defense, the president sought friendly relations. He acknowledged the white man's trespass upon the homeland of the natives. "We are now their neighbors," he said; "we are on their land, for it belongs to them as much as any land ever belonged to any man on earth; we are drinking their water, using their fuel and timber and raising our food from their ground."[5] Making allowances for native customs, he said:

> Why should men have a disposition to kill a destitute naked Indian, who may steal a shirt or a horse and think it no harm when they never think of meting out a like retribution to a white man who steals, although he has been taught better from infancy.[6]

Young sought to develop in the natives a sense of individual moral responsibility. Speaking of the native custom of seeking indiscriminate and even mass revenge for a single death, he said:

> They do not care whom they kill if they can kill any of the [enemy] tribe. This has been taught them from age to age. The inhabitants of the United States have treated the Indians in like manner. If but one person or only a few were guilty of committing a depredation upon a white settlement they have chastised the whole tribe for the crime . . . . I will not consent to your killing one Indian for the sin of another. If any of them commit a depredation, tell the tribe to which they belong that they may deliver up the man or men to be tried according to the law, and you will make friends of the whole tribe.[7]

In 1852, he advised the settlers in the town of Fillmore:

> Never turn them away hungry from your door, teach them in the arts of husbandry, bear with them in all patience and long suffering and never consider their lives equivalent for petty stealing.[8]

On the other hand, sympathetic cooperation should not give way to familiarity:

> Let any man or company of men be familiar with the Indians, and they will be more familiar, and the more familiar you will find the less influence you will have over them. If you would have dominion over them, for their good, which is the duty of the Elders, you must not treat them as your equals. . . .
>
> You have been too familiar with them. Your children have mixed promiscuously with them, they have been free in your homes, and some of the brethren have spent too much time in smoking and chatting with them, and instead of teaching them to labor, such a course has encouraged them in idleness and ignorance, the effects of which you begin to feel . . . .[9]

Mormon missionary work among the Indians developed slowly and was initially limited to local contacts. However, in 1854, a large number of men were sent on a "Southern Indian Mission" into the Virgin River Valley. Young gave them the following instructions:

> You are sent not to farm, build nice houses, and fence fine fields, not to help white men, but to save red ones, learn their language, and this you can do more effectively by living among them as well as writing out a list of words. Go with them where they go, live with them . . . .[10]

In the following year, several large companies of missionaries departed for Las Vegas Springs in Nevada, the Elk Mountains in southeastern Utah, the Salmon River in Idaho, and Oklahoma. The purpose of these missions, of which only the Southern Indian Mission proved really successful, was to promote friendly relations with the Indians and lift their living standards by teaching them to farm and adopt some of the arts of civilized life.

Brigham Young apparently had little hope of seeing the Indians become in his time the "white and delightsome" people referred to in the Book of Mormon prophecies.[11] According to an account of his statement before the Legislative Council in Salt Lake City on May 12, 1849, he "did not feel as some of the Brethren do; he does not want to live among them and take them in his arms until the curse is removed off them. . . . This present race of Indians will never be

converted. It mattereth not whether they kill one another off or
Somebody else do it and as for our sending missionaries among them
to convert them it is of no use. But we will take their children and
school them and teach them to be clenly [sic] and to love morality
and then raise up seed amoung them and in this way they will be
brought back into the presance [sic] and knowledge of God."[12]

Because Young believed that the only hope of Indian regeneration was through the youth, he early sought to liberate them from
the chains of their environment. Speaking of a practice already in
vogue in some Mormon colonies, he recorded on May 13, 1851: "I
spoke upon the importance of the Iron Country Mission . . . advised
them to buy up the Lamanite children as fast as they could, and
educate them and teach them the gospel, so that many generations
would not pass away ere they should become a white and delightsome people, and said that the Lord could not have devised a better
plan than to have put us where we were in order to accomplish that
thing."[13]

The purchase of Indian children for the purpose of raising them
in Mormon homes appeared quite different to Young than the
slavery so prevalent among the Indian tribes. The Mexicans, on
their trading expeditions between New Mexico and California or
on slaving excursions into the Great Basin were carrying off large
numbers of Indian boys and girls to be sold in Mexico as slaves. It
was one of these expeditions that brought the slave issue to a head
in November of 1851. One Pedro Leon, who led a trading party,
carried a license to traffic in Indian slaves which was signed by
the governor of New Mexico. Brigham Young, while on one of his
tours of the settlements, challenged the legality of the license in
Utah Territory. Because of the defiance of Leon, he was brought into
court, his slaves were set free, and he was ordered to cease operations
in Utah. During their exodus, the Mexicans stirred up the Indians
against the Mormons.

On Young's recommendation, the legislature, on March 7, 1852,
legalized Indian slavery—a form of indenture—so that Mormons
might purchase Indian children and rear them under civilizing influences. As the governor said in recommending the measure:

> Under the present low and degraded situation of the Indian
> race, so long as the practice of gambling away, selling, or other-
> wise disposing of their children; as also sacrificing prisoners
> obtains among them it seems indeed that any transfer would be
> to them a relief and a benefit . . . . This may be said to present

a new feature in the traffic of human beings; it is essentially purchasing them into freedom instead of slavery. . . .[14]

The Act defined the procedures for purchasing Indian children and stipulated a limit of twenty years apprenticeship, during which period the master had to provide schooling, food, and clothing according to his own condition in life.

On April 23, because of the further invasion of slaving parties, Young issued a proclamation against all Indian slave traffic in Utah.[15] This interference with slave traffic, in which Chief Walkara had been active by raiding weaker bands and selling their children to the Mexicans, strained Mormon-Indian relations and resulted in the "Walker War" in the summer of 1853. Raiding continued and deaths mounted until October 14, by which time the Mormons were safe behind the walls of their forts.

Though a shudder passed through the Mormon communities, the war chief did not excite as much fear as pity in Young. The same day that he issued military orders on conduct of the war, on July 25, Young wrote the following letter to Walkara:

> I send you some tobacco for you to smoke in the mountains when you get lonesome. You are a fool for fighting your best friends and the only friends that you have in this world. Everybody else would kill you if they could get a chance. If you get hungry send some friendly Indian down to the settlements and we will give you some beef cattle and flour. If you are afraid of the tobacco I send you, you can let some of your prisoners try it and then you will know that it is good. When you get good natured again I would like to see you. Don't you think you should be ashamed? You know that I have always been your best friend.[16]

Chief Walkara returned warily to Utah in the spring of 1854, he and Young meeting in his tent at Chicken Creek for peace negotiations. It was an occasion charged with deep emotion, but in the end the firm magnanimity of Young prevailed. At Parowan some days later, he announced at a church service that the war was over.[17] A year later, when Walkara died, Brigham Young felt himself sufficiently identified with the tribe to write to the chief's half brother, Arrapeen: "I propose that the Utah's all get together and elect another chief, one that they will listen to as they did to Walker, and make him their captain, and if it suits them I should like for them to elect Arrapeen in his place."[18] Arrapeen was elected chief, and Mormon-Indian relations were good until he died in 1860.

When Congress extended the Intercourse Act of 1834 over

Utah Territory in 1851, Jacob H. Holeman was appointed Indian
Agent. Stephen B. Rose and Henry R. Day were appointed as sub-
agents to serve under Young, the new Superintendent of Indian
Affairs. This marked the beginning of a complicated seven-year
period of Indian administration that was characterized by a conflicting discharge of responsibility. The Gentile agents, Holeman
and Day, following long-established federal procedures, failed to
grasp the Indian problem in relation to a community struggling to
survive and expand on the frontier. Because they were Gentiles,
misunderstandings and suspicions were also bound to occur.

Young divided the territory into three districts. When sub-
agent Day became involved in the initial territorial political clash,
he joined the "run-away officials," and no successor was appointed.
Rose, being a Mormon, worked in harmony with Young; Holeman
was the lone Gentile officer in the Indian superintendency. During
his stay, until October 1853, he clashed more and more with his
superior. The Commissioner of Indian Affairs in Washington was
well supplied with letters from both—each defending his position.[19]

A major charge brought by Holeman was that the Mormon
colonists, in their rapid expansion, were stirring Indian unrest by
appropriating the best Indian lands and that Governor Young was
using his office of Superintendent in the interest of his people.
Holeman further charged that, because the Mormons were buying
Indian good-will by the liberal distribution of gifts at government
expense, other Americans appeared in an unfavorable light. "Therefore," wrote Holeman on November 28, 1851, "it seems to me officially that no Mormon should have anything to do with the Indians."[20] A month later he strengthened his recommendation for
Young's dismissal by asserting that "with the Governor at the head
of the Indian department in this territory it cannot be conducted
in such a manner as to meet the views of or do justice to the government. He has been so long in the habit of exercising his will
which is supreme here that no one dares oppose anything he may
say or do."[21]

When one of Holeman's letters came to Young's attention in
the Commissioner of Indian Affairs' annual report for the year, he
suddenly withdrew whatever support he had given the agent, who
thereupon launched another attack upon Young on February 29,
1852. "You would greatly oblige me," he wrote the Commissioner,
"by giving me some instructions in regard to my duties here. . . .
The superintendent and sub-agent Rose seem disposed to conceal

their movements from me—they never consult with me or pay any attention to my opinions."[22]

Replying to the agent's charges, Young informed the Commissioner on May 28, 1852, that though Holeman was reporting that the Mormons were stirring up the Indians by settling on their lands he had not even seen an Indian upon whose lands the Mormons had settled. The Shoshones and Uintahs, whom Holeman had seen, had been clamoring *for* settlement on their lands. The Utes, among whom the Mormons *had* settled, were south of the Oregon Trail and enemies of the Shoshones, and hence were no threat to the westward migration.[23]

Young sought to persuade Holeman to his view, but the agent continued indifferent to the interests of the community of which he was not a part. His responsibility, he felt, was to the Indians and their welfare, and to this end he labored zealously. On the other hand, *Superintendent* Young was also *Governor* Young in an expanding frontier community and *President* Young of a religious body which had a peculiar sense of mission with reference to their redskin neighbors. The contrasting points of view have been well stated by Dale Morgan:

> The question was not what was best for the Indians living in a political vacuum or cultural void, but how Indian interests could best be reconciled with the expansive forces of white colonization. Young foresaw that the Indians must suffer, in the loss of their historic folkways and culture patterns, but he saw also that their individual good would best be served by changing the character of their life and providing them with a new economic base. Mormon colonization was a more efficient utilization of the land and if by precept and example the Indians could be persuaded to change the pattern of their lives, settling down to an agricultural life, in the long run the Indians would gain more than they would lose from Mormon occupation of their lands. At best theirs was a sub-standard level of existence, attended by poverty and more than occasional starvation. Young's thinking about the Indians was thus discerning and farsighted, looking beyond the possible immediate injustices which aroused the zealot in Holeman.[24]

To Holeman's discomfort, his letters seemed not to be read in Washington. Because Superintendent Young's course was apparently approved, Holeman was not surprised when he was replaced on October 17, 1853. Agent Garland Hurt, who followed him, after an interval, also soon came into conflict with Young and the Mormons. Although he professed to harbor no bias against the Utah religionists when he arrived in Utah in the summer of 1854, he was prepared by May 2, 1855, to relate in a letter to Commissioner Mix the Gentile version of the Mormon-held concept of Indian destiny:

> These saints have either accidentally or purposely created a distinction in the minds of the Indian tribes of this territory between the Mormons and the people of the United States that cannot be otherwise than prejudicial to the interest of the latter and, what sir, may we expect of these missionaries? . . . I suspect their final object will be to teach these wretched savages that they are the rightful owners of the American soil and that it has been wrongfully taken from them by the whites, and that the Great Spirit has sent the Mormons among them to help them recover their rights.[25]

He had apparently been listening to some of the Mormon sermons.[26] He concluded his letter by recommending that the congressional act to regulate trade and intercourse with the Indians be invoked against the Mormon missionaries.

On one point Mormons and Gentiles were agreed. Young and his agents repeatedly urged upon Congress the desirability of abolishing the Indian land titles and locating the natives on a reservation. Young pressed vigorously for such action throughout his superintendency. Urging the Legislative Assembly to memorialize Congress in the matter, he said in December of 1853:

> Should Congress take steps to extinguish the Indian title in Utah and locate the tribes by themselves leaving a strip of well defined neutral ground between them and the white settlements it would nearly if not quite prevent such trouble and immense losses which our citizens have been compelled to wade through during the past season . . . ."[27]

Abolishment of Indian title to the land was doubly important to the Mormons, for not only would it solve the Indian problem but they would become owners instead of settlers. Recognizing this situation, Agent Hurt stated in his official report for 1855:

> I would take occasion to suggest here that treaties ought to be negotiated with these tribes as early as possible, for the title to their lands which are now held and occupied by the whites. It is a thing almost unprecedented in the history of our Indian policy to go into any state or Territory and make extensive or permanent improvements upon the soil claimed by the Indians without extinguishing these claims by treaty. The delay is not only unjust to the Indians . . . but it is equally so to the

pioneer who is forced to pay a constant tribute to these worthless creatures . . . .[28]

Because Congress took no action to establish reservations, Young began experimenting in 1851 with a "Farmers for the Indians" program in strategic locations. This program appealed to Agent Hurt, who soon after his arrival promoted a program in which Indians were taught to farm. Young sent him on November 23, 1855, recommendations for increased activities:

> I think there should be a small reservation in each of the following counties, to wit: Utah, Juab, San Pete, Millard, and Iron. The reason is obvious why each of these counties should furnish a reservation for the natives. . . . There should be a farmer at each of these points whose business should be not to farm for the Indians at the expense of the government, as is too often the case, but to teach them to farm, raise grain, cattle, etc., and to keep and preserve property.[29]

Although Hurt had obtained tacit sanction of his farm program, he involved the superintendency in serious financial difficulties by ignoring appropriation limits.[30] When called to account by the Washington office, he defended his program on the ground that it counteracted the Mormon influence exercised over the natives by the distribution of gifts. Also, he reminded his superior that Young favored the farming program. Young was indeed encouraged with the early results, as he indicated in his quarterly report to the Commissioner.[31]

Unfortunately, personal relations worsened between Young and Hurt, the latter complaining that assignments from the Superintendent not only interfered with the farm program but took him outside his district. Convinced that concert between himself and Young was impossible, he expressed a willingness on March 30, 1857, to resign.[32]

Relations between Young and the Indian Office in Washington, as well as with other government agencies, were also deteriorating. Commissioner Manypenny did not have the confidence in him that Lea had. Because federal appointees in Utah were regularly sending into Washington reports about Mormon irregularities, President Buchanan ordered troops to Utah to install new federal officers. Agent Hurt was among the last of the old officers to leave the territory; he fled by way of Uintah Valley to meet the oncoming army.

Young himself was relieved of his superintendency on March

3, 1857, as a result of congressional action separating the office from that of territorial governor. Jacob Forney was appointed his successor on August 27. However, because Forney could not assume his duties until the following spring, Young continued to serve until June 30, 1858, when he forwarded his final report to Washington.

Mormon interference with the Indians was named by Secretary Floyd as one of the reasons for dispatching troops during the "Utah War."[33] Young replied to the charge of interference with the Indians from the pulpit:

> There has been much prejudice raised against us on account of Indian depredations, notwithstanding the great trouble and and expense to which we have been subjected in preventing them and without which no person could have traveled across these mountains and plains. Why is the reason the Indians have acted so badly? Because of the practice with many emigrants of killing Indians wherever they could find them.

On another occasion he said:

> It has cost the government hundreds of thousands of dollars more for Indians in other territories than it has in this; and I have saved the government hundreds of thousands of dollars by helping keep Indians peaceful in Utah. . . . I have always told them to hold on, to stop shedding blood, and to live in peace.[34]

This statement was echoed in another he made during the Civil War:

> When President Lincoln wrote me requesting me to fit out one hundred men to guard the mail route, we at once enlisted the one hundred for ninety days. . . . We do not need any soldiers here from other states or territories to perform that service, neither does the government, as it would know if they were wise. I will, comparatively speaking, take one plug of tobacco, a shirt and three cents worth of paint, and save more life and hinder more Indian depredations than they can by expending millions of dollars vested in army to fight and kill the Indians. Feed and clothe them a little and you will save life; fight them and you pave the way for the destruction of the innocent.[35]

Certainly Young's "better to feed them than fight them" policy contributed much toward the amelioration of Indian suffering and improved the living standards of some of them. Though the burden rested somewhat heavily on Mormon households, the reward was an above-average record of peaceful relations with the Indians, whose lands were being occupied. The farm program, which was adopted in lieu of the desired reservations, promised success until it was interrupted by the "Utah War" and then disintegrated.

Had the United States Government responded in measure to the local efforts of the Utah superintendency, the Indian situation in Utah could have been brighter. But prejudice and misunderstanding, as always, claimed its victims, who in this case were the Indians. What might have been the results had a fraction of the millions expended to send an army to Utah been constructively used in support of Young's Indian program?

That Young's influence among the natives continued beyond his official relations with them was clear when a treaty was finally consummated with the Utah tribal chieftains at Spanish Fork on June 8, 1865. There, on the site of one of his unrealized Indian farm projects, having been invited by Superintendent O. H. Irish to do so, he participated in the treaty-making that extinguished title to all Utah Indian lands except for a reservation in Uinta Valley.[36] Throughout the proceedings, Young's influence was apparent as the chiefs repeatedly deferred to the counsel of "our oldest brother."

Young's contribution toward consummation of the treaty won an expression of gratitude in the Superintendent's report to the Commissioner: "The fact exists, however some might prefer it should be otherwise, that [Young] has pursued so kind and conciliatory a policy with the Indians that it has given him great influence over them. It was my duty and policy under your instructions to make use of his influence for the accomplishment of the purposes of government."[37]

THE WRITING OF WESTERN

HISTORY—POPULAR AND PROFESSIONAL

Owen Wister—The "Real Incident"
and the "Thrilling Story"

NEAL LAMBERT
University of Utah

In the summer of 1893, a prominent and unemployed Philadelphia citizen, "who sometimes wrote about what he had seen in his
hours of idleness,"[1] suddenly became an author of considerable responsibility. It is difficult to imagine that this very proper gentle-
man of Victorian Philadelphia was the same man who loved the
violent and uncivilized West so deeply, but Owen Wister was a complex and paradoxical figure, a man whose complexities made him
more interesting by far than any character that he himself created.

He was a connoisseur of French wines who could share a hip
flask with a rough stage driver and thoroughly enjoy it. He could
take great pleasure in playing poker with swearing cowboys or
piano for Franz Liszt. He was raised and trained in the center of
Victorian propriety, yet he could still maintain an honest commitment to the uncivilized West. After a few months of eastern life
he wrote to an army captain in Arizona, "I've had just enough
white-cravat and terrapin to do me for another year, & am ready
to be perfectly happy on bacon, coffee & condensed milk."[2]

Three years before, while still fresh from his fifth summer in
search of health and big game in Wyoming, Owen Wister had
written two western stories, "Hank's Woman" and "How Lin Mc-
Lean Went East." Henry Mills Alden, the editor of *Harper's Magazine,* accepted the stories, which met with such success that he
was prompted to accept two more in the spring of 1893. Shortly
thereafter, Alden began talking to Wister about doing a series of
western stories for the magazine. That summer a letter which
finally clinched matters came to Wister's Wyoming hunting camp.

The Messrs. Harper instructed Wister that "Each must be a
thrilling story having its ground in a *real incident,* though you are
left free scope for imaginative treatment. . . . You may, and we
hope you will, find several subjects, especially in connection with

191

Indian fighting, where actual facts will suffice for the framework of the stories."[3] By October of that year, Wister had put his affairs in order and was on a train heading west in search of those real incidents and actual facts which were to serve as the framework for almost all his subsequent thrilling stories about the West.

It is indeed remarkable how many actual facts, how many real incidents, and how many real people Wister put into his thrilling stories. A lady telegraph operator whom he met and an ex-convict cowpuncher who died on the bed in which Wister later slept appear prominently in "Separ's Vigilante." Dean Duke, the experienced and entertaining foreman of the Haggin, Hearst, and Tevis cattle concern, became foreman Dean Drake in Wister's story "The Jimmy John Boss." Wister's ride across the Arizona desert became an important part of "La Tinaja Bonita." A story that he heard about a half-breed renegade became a "Kinsman of Red Cloud," and so on, for almost all of Wister's stories.

Wister says in the preface to his first volume of western stories, "They are about Indians and soldiers and events west of the Missouri. . . . The visit of Young-man-afraid-of-his-horses to the Little Big Horn and the rise and fall of the young Crow imposter . . . and many other occurrences, noble and ignoble, *are told as they were told to me by those who saw them.*"[4]

This statement might be enticing to the reader in a preface, but it certainly does not describe how Wister turned the real incidents of history into thrilling stories for fiction. It does not suggest the many touches which he, as an imaginative writer, necessarily added to real incidents. Nor does it suggest that, in rendering thrilling stories, Wister failed to touch on the great human problems that were presented in the real incidents of the West.

Historians may well try to get a real incident down on paper just as it is told by those who saw it, but the man of imagination concerns himself with something more than this. Because he can bring his imagination to bear on the real incidents, he is able to add the immediacy of local color, both of language and landscape. The imaginative writer can give history a point of view by seeing it through the consciousness of one of the participants or as an omniscient observer. He can add a touch of sentimentality, or melodrama. He can render the real incident in terms of comedy or tragedy.

But, most important of all, he can probe beyond the incidents themselves; he can examine history in terms of its fundamental and ultimate meanings, not only to the people involved but to man in general. Wister himself said in his last journal: "It is imagination that takes the load of fact, supplied by experience and lifts it into universal truth."[5] That a writer uses real incidents in his stories is in itself insignificant. It is how the writer's imagination renders those real incidents that is important. This was the challenge that Wister faced. He met the challenge successfully in giving history immediacy and point of view, but he failed in the challenge to look beyond the thrilling story into the human significance of the events he portrayed. He failed in the opportunity to search deep into human nature.

What Wister does with the Boise "tempest in a teapot" is typical of his treatment of history.[6] Most modern Idaho histories have at least a comment on the notorious fourth Idaho territorial legislature, in which two men of northern sympathies, Governor Ballard and Secretary Howlett, clashed with a legislature composed mostly of southern sympathizers. Many of the members of that body were secessionists and ex-rebel soldiers who had not yet become reconciled to the outcome of the Civil War, which had ended the previous year.

When Howlett, the territorial secretary, informed the legislators that they must all subscribe to an oath of allegiance before they could be paid their per diem or travel money, a real "tempest" broke loose. Besides passing a law that repudiated the prescribed oath—a law which the Governor vetoed—the legislators organized a "rough house" and proceeded to break furniture and windows. Troops from the Boise barracks were called for and within an hour they appeared in front of the council chambers. Within the next half hour, the Idaho solons had all subscribed to the oath and received their pay.[7]

Wister's story follows the general outline of these events, but with enough change so that the incident fits it well. While adding a few names, changing the date of the legislature, reducing the number involved, and changing the place of the action, Wister condenses the real incident. He then has room within the confines of a short story to add the details which give the story immediacy. We hear, for example, the southern drawl and legislative rhetoric of the Missourians and see the weary councilmen slumped around the room, boots off and "for comfort, most of the pistols . . . on the table with the statutes of the United States."[8] The unwashed, unshaved legislators are vividly rendered: ". . . the member from

Silver City, for instance, whose day-old black growth blurred his dingy chin, or the member from Big Camas, whose scantier redcrop bristled on his cheeks in sparse wandering arrangements, like spikes on the barrel of a musical box."[9]

But Wister does more than give the real incident immediacy. He sacrifices the actual riot of the real incident to give his own imaginary hero a chance to shine in all his natural glory. Just as the crisis between the North and the South is coming to a head and the delegates are making dives for their guns, Corporal Specimen Jones steps into the room and says, "Don't nobody hurt anybody." He arrests the secretary, commandeers the strong box, and avoids a general disturbance.

Such a Wister treatment of the real incident and the thrilling story is typical. Working within the framework of a real incident, he has changed some names and by adding description and dialogue to the story has given it a sense of immediacy. But by supplying a hero from his own imagination he turns the story into a sort of melodrama instead of what it might have been, a significant examination of a national conflict in miniature. Wister lost an excellent opportunity to examine many of the significant post-Civil War problems which still concern us as individuals and as a nation; he contented himself with Specimen Jones and melodrama.

He realized, of course, that history need not always be treated seriously and in some stories he shaped the real incident into fiction, using a touch of comedy. Most of these thrilling stories are narrated from Wister's own point of view—that of the tenderfoot easterner traveling in the West. A good example of this is his rendering of the Wham payroll robbery, which forms the focal point of his story "A Pilgrim on the Gila."[10] Besides being almost pure comedy, the story gives us a good insight into the way Wister gathered up the real incidents that he put into his thrilling stories.

The official Army report records: "On May 11, 1889, Major Joseph W. Wham, paymaster, U. S. Army, was ambushed and robbed of $28,345.10 near Cedar Springs, between Fort Grant and Thomas, by a band of highwaymen, variously estimated to number from eight to twenty men."[11] The thieves were later caught and tried but were acquitted by an apparently bribed jury.[12] Four years later Wister traveled over the same road and heard the story of the robbery. He recorded in his journal: "We went over the road and up the hill, where a paymaster had been robbed of $28,000 to Cedar Springs and camped. . . . Barney Norton, of Cedar Springs, entertained

Edwards and me all evening with the paymaster robbery and old Tombstone days."[13] The next year, Wister was back in Arizona and recording in his journal: "Added to my general knowledge of Arizona matters . . . in particular about the Wham robbery."[14]

During both trips, he picked up other small details of local color: the clay-colored bodies and long black hair of the Indians, the voices of the stage drivers in the darkness of early morning calling, "All aboard for Bowie," and many other seemingly unimportant but nevertheless real details of life in Arizona. Interesting people were being treated in his notebooks and affecting his imagination. One of the most interesting to him was Bishop Leighton, the Mormon bishop of the Gila Valley, whom he met on his first trip west:

> At Thatcher I heard a lusty dominating voice outside giving the driver directions and chaffing the sheriff. "Who's riding in your bad company?" it inquired, and the canvas flap raised. "Why that's a decent man!" exclaimed the speaker seeing me. . . . He had a short gray beard and a strong shrewd face. This was the Mormon Bishop Leighton, owner of the stage line and of the whole Gila Valley community.[15]

Wister had more to say about the bishop to his mother. He tells her of meeting a "Mormon Bishop who has been in hiding for polygamy in his day on account of nine wives: he has forty-seven children and can't read or write but signs contracts and letters with an X. He is seventy-four and the other day had twins."[16]

The idea that all these ingredients would make one good story may very well have come from Captain Frank A. Edwards, Wister's good friend who was at that time stationed in Arizona. On January 7, 1894, Edwards wrote to Wister: "Word has reached us today that the stage from Bowie station to Thomas was held up yesterday when about nine miles out. Why could they not have done this when you were a passenger? . . . let us imagine that your friend the Mormon Bishop or my friend the Doctor had something to do with it?"[17] For Wister this was easily imagined. Whether Edwards' suggestion was the spark or not, before the month was out Wister was writing about the payroll robbery—an easy substitution for the stage robbery—and incorporating himself, many of his Arizona experiences, and the Mormon bishop into "A Pilgrim on the Gila."

This story is certainly not an attempt to render the robbery exactly as it happened. Though the scenery, the Indians, the stage coach, and other elements might be realistic, the participants in the thrilling story are for the most part imaginary. The narrator of the story—one part Wister and one part imagination—responds to the incidents in a typically unheroic fashion. The paymaster is pompous and absurd. Wister even adds an old colored woman, who plays the role of the comic servant in the robbery and trial scenes. The real incident has been remodeled by the imagination so that it becomes for the most part a vehicle for comedy.

Despite Wister's use of melodrama and comedy in turning real incidents into thrilling stories, in some stories Wister came surprisingly close to examining the western experience and saying something significant about its effects on the human consciousness. Sometimes it was only a phrase, sometimes only a sentence. But in at least one story—"Little Big Horn Medicine"—he made a conscious effort to render the experience in terms of its meaning to those involved.[18] In this story, he attempted to describe the rise and fall of a young Crow chief by the name of Chese-cha-pah-dish, or as he is referred to in some reports, the "Sword Bearer."

Two real incidents are involved in this thrilling story. In the first, two groups of Sioux Indians had come down from the Rosebud and Pine Ridge agencies to the Crow agency near Fort Custer. Sixty-five men and four officers were sent out to turn them back to their own reservation. The Indians were intercepted and were being escorted back by the troops when "Sword Bearer" rode up with his followers and attempted to stir up trouble for the troops. Before any harm was done, however, the young chief's old father rode up and, exerting his parental authority, sent the troublemakers home.[19]

The second incident took place in the autumn of the same year. "Sword Bearer" led a few of his followers on a horse-stealing expedition against the Piegans. When they returned and learned that the agent, Henry E. Williams, intended to arrest them for horse stealing, they made threats against him and fired at some agency buildings. In his official report, General Ruger ascribed this and the general unrest of the Indians to "Sword Bearer":

> This unsettled state of the tribe was principally brought about by a young medicine man, "Chese-cha-pah-dish," also called "The Sword Bearer," who was the principal actor in the disturbance at the agency, and had for some time before been defiant to the agent, and active in effort to supplant the older chiefs and become the principal man of the tribe. He had succeeded in getting the adherence of many of the young men, upon whom he imposed belief that he could prevent arrest of the offenders, and by intimidation and working upon their superstitious fears, had reduced the older and well disposed to a

passive state, so far as active interference with his schemes was concerned.[20]

The young chief did, indeed, have an old cavalry sword with which he was supposed to make such potent medicine that the white men would be rendered helpless. His stock as a medicine man rose even higher when, on several occasions, it seemed as if nature conspired with him and answered his commands for rain.

Finally, on November 5, all the Indians of the reservation having been brought into the agency, General Ruger gave them an hour and a half to deliver the troublemakers. He reported:

> At about the expiration of the time two Indians, one correctly presumed at the time to be "The Sword Bearer," and the other his submedicine man, rode out from the Indian camp, followed at a little distance by from one hundred to one hundred and fifty others. . . . Their movements presented necessity for action other than before intended, in case the Indians designated for arrest were not surrendered, and I directed Colonel Dudley to cut off the Indians in motion. He intercepted them by two troops of the First Cavalry; whereupon, a smart skirmish immediately ensued between the troops of the First Cavalry . . . and the Indians, principally the young men. . . . The Indians were soon driven back and over the Little Big Horn River, some escaping to the hills southeast of the agency and others taking refuge in the Indian village near the agency buildings. . . . "The Sword Bearer" and seven of his followers, as reported, were killed and a number wounded in the fight.[21]

Any summary of the real incident is in this Wister story a summary of the thrilling story. Very little of what actually happened failed to be described in Wister's version of the affair. He changed the names of some of the people involved and added one or two elements of minor importance. For instance, he has "Sword Bearer" perform magic tricks with Seltzer salts and water, and the agent's role in the affair is slightly altered. However, the whole thrilling story is remarkably close to the real incident.

One of the reasons for this close approximation of reality and fiction is the fact that Wister got most of his information about the incident from Edwards, who was very careful to see that Wister had all the details and had them right.[22] Wister told Edwards:

> I've dislocated history just at the start, but otherwise very little. If the whole thing lacks "artistic crescendo" it will be because I have tried to adhere to your own narration, which is really a series of events with stretches of weeks between. But damn artistic crescendo. Such a story as that should be tampered with as little as may be.[23]

How Wister would have altered the events to add artistic crescendo is a matter of speculation. The important thing in this instance is that he was so caught up in the real incident that he was unwilling to alter it even as a concession to a perhaps more thrilling story. Yet the story of "Sword Bearer" as Wister wrote it is still not history. What Wister was trying to make of this real incident is indicated in a comment that he made about it to his mother: "I undertook the difficult task of following the development of a state of mind and feeling by the objective method. And I wanted to know if the invisible had been made visible at all or not."[24]

In other words, he tried to follow, to see into, the mind of an individual. He tried to see how real incidents affected that mind. He tried to render the real incident in terms of what it might mean to that mind. By means of the imagination he made a conscious effort to probe deeper than history as incident and arrive at its fundamental meaning to the individual. Thus, when "Sword Bearer" apparently causes rain, Wister tries to render the incident in terms of its meaning to an individual who is beginning to think that he is endowed with supernatural powers.

Wister could have written a thrilling story that would have satisfied *Harper's* without trying to render the experience in terms of the Indian mind. But, at least in this instance, he was aware that the thrilling story could not by itself render the western experience in all its possible meanings for man. It was the meaning of the real incident to a deluded and primitive mind he was trying to describe.

This was, however, not the first time that he was confronted with the problem of rendering the real incident of the western experience in terms of its meaning to the individuals involved. His story "Balaam and Pedro" presented this problem.[25] It is based on one of his own striking experiences in which he had to watch his host beat a horse and gouge out its eye:

> . . . my own conduct in making no effort to prevent or stop this treatment of the horse has grown more and more discreditable to me. But, the situation was a hard one. Here was I, the guest, and the very welcome guest of a stranger, who had done all he could to make me at home because I had come to see his friend. He could have told me the horse was his horse, not mine, and I was riding another of his. And I should have done no good, and reduced the relation between us two solitary people to something pretty bad, with nothing to do but sit together, eat together, and sleep together.[26]

This incident reflects certain elements that are common in western experience—two men, isolated, one of them involved in a moral dilemma over his relationship with the other. In this case, one is the guest of the other, and as such bound by a certain code of conduct, but also committed to a certain moral code which called for an opposing course of action.

This was the real incident that Wister chose to make the central action in his thrilling story. However, in rendering that story suitable to himself and the editors of *Harper's*, he left out the real problems of the situation and reverted again to melodrama. There is no guest, struggling with a moral dilemma; instead there is the Virginian who fills the role of an avenger. "Then Balaam was rolled to the ground again by the towering Virginian, in whose brawn and sinew the might of justice was at work."[27] In this version and the final rendering in the novel, the complex moral problems with which the author was entangled are abandoned and replaced by melodrama. Any examination of the complexities of the real incident is pushed aside for the thrilling story.

To what degree does Wister succeed as a man of imagination in rendering the real incident and all its possibilities? For one thing, he had a good eye and a good ear. The landscape and setting that he paints are vivid as well as accurate, and his dialogues are well done. He is successful with the "you-are-there" feeling, the immediacy with which he colors history. But he does not probe beyond the real incidents of western experience and thoroughly explore their fundamental meanings for man.

Several things kept him from realizing his potential as an imaginative writer of the West. He told Edwards, for instance, that in some of his stories he felt "greatly hampered by Harper's demand for excitement and the exclusion of character study."[28] Then, too, the criticism of some of his literary friends was not very helpful. Wister recognized that "beneath the bright brave ripple [of the West] moved the groundswell of tragedy." [29] But, whenever he spoke of putting some of the darkness of that tragedy into his stories, his friendly critics discouraged him. Theodore Roosevelt, for instance, told him: "Let in some light. . . . Leave your reader with the idea that life, after all, does go on."[30]

Wister was also limited by the genteel attitude of his eastern audience. The murder of women and children, torturing, scalping, and many other such real incidents that were common in the West are noticeably absent from his stories. He never used them because they were too violent for his readers.

Finally, Wister's imaginative and critical abilities were often dulled by his own commitment to the thrilling story. As he told his friend Judge Holmes, "None of your 'at this point the conversation became both witty and brilliant' but *action*, sir, action and manifestation."[31] Action and the thrilling story were enough to hold the mundane, unliterary interests of the average train traveler, and too often this was as high as Wister aimed. He wrote in his journal, "If such as this will read me, I am secure."[32]

Had Wister lived in a later age, had his friends been more helpful, and had he sharpened his powers of self-criticism, he might have been more successful in rendering all the possibilities of the real incident instead of just writing thrilling stories. He knew the material, and he had the capabilities. But his commitment to the thrilling story prevented him from analyzing the great human problems that were involved in the real incidents of western life.

History as Melodrama: Theodore Roosevelt's "The Winning of the West"

MERRILL E. LEWIS
Western Washington College

The incongruity of Harvard-educated Theodore Roosevelt in the Bad Lands of North Dakota has been the source of numerous stories. As one of his biographers said: "His somewhat precise tones still flavored by exposure to Harvard culture rang strangely in [the ears of westerners]. He did not smoke or drink. His worst profanity was an infrequent 'Damn!' and his usual ejaculation was 'By Godfrey!' The first time he took part in a round up, sometime during the summer of 1885, one or two hardened cowboys nearly fell from their saddles as he called in his high voice to one of the men: 'Hasten forward quickly there!' " The phrase became a classic in the Bad Lands to express the westerner's view of eastern greenhorns.[1]

Conscious of some need to adjust to an image, Roosevelt worked hard at playing the role of the westerner, just as he had previously worked hard at playing the role of political reformer, and later would work hard at playing that of the African big-game hunter. In the Bad Lands, he dressed like a cowboy dandy, wearing a buckskin shirt and sporting a pearl-handled revolver. As a deputy sheriff, he prepared on one occasion to trail some thieves who had stolen his boat. The evening before leaving a friend overheard him in the kitchen practicing the lines he would use the next day: "I've got the gun on you," he repeated over and over. "I know you stole my boat and I'm here to claim it."[2] Paradoxically, he planned to take along on the chase Matthew Arnold to read for relaxation.[3] If Roosevelt, finally, out of dogged persistence and a sort of naive courage, succeeded in gaining acceptance as a westerner, his figure still remained essentially incongruous, even theatrical, against the western landscape.

He was saved from uniqueness only because role playing was becoming more and more the pattern in the West of the 1880's. He actually played many roles: cowboy, member of the cattlemen's association, deputy sheriff, chivalric gallant, and man of letters. All of them were dominated by the same general characteristics: a boyish robustness and athletic vigor of mind and body coupled with a sentimental attachment to the West as a place and with morality as a sentiment. All the roles championed Roosevelt's philosophy of the strenuous but moral life.

Most scholars conclude that Roosevelt's inveterate play acting merely illustrated his innate adolescence. Even Roosevelt's contemporaries saw him in this light. When he was elected to the White House for a second term in 1904, Cecil Spring Rice, an Englishman, wrote of him, "You must always remember that the President is about six." And Elihu Root wrote to Roosevelt on his forty-sixth birthday, "You have made a good start in life, and your friends have great hopes for you when you grow up."[4] To his friend Henry Adams, Roosevelt was exasperating. "What annoys me," Adams said, "is his childlike and infantile superficiality with his boyish dogmatism of assertion. He lectures me on history as though he were a high school pedagogue."[5] Dixon Wecter has summed up the nature of Roosevelt's private world in these words: "Like the world of adolescence, [it] was a place of high adventure, swagger, conspiracies, with a touch of melodrama, fierce loyalties, and equally fierce hates."[6]

Roosevelt the actor became Roosevelt the mythmaker. The kind of myths he was content to create is a fair measure of his intellectual achievements as well as his psychological makeup. More specifically, the philosophy of the strenuous life, filled as it was with strenuous loyalties to the West and the wilderness, suggests a mixing of matters subjective and objective, imaginative and factual. But sometimes the boundary line was fuzzy. At one of his interviews with Roosevelt, Hermann Hagedorn said, "I referred to his life in the Bad Lands as 'a kind of idyl.' 'That's it!' he exclaimed. 'That's it! That's exactly what it was!' "[7] Of course, Roosevelt's life in the Bad Lands was an idyl only in a highly subjective sense.

On yet another occasion, when there was talk of renominating him for President in 1916, he stated: "It would be a mistake . . . to nominate me unless the country has in its mood something of the heroic."[8] In light of such remarks, it is not surprising that, within a year after he left the ranch in North Dakota, he was at work on a history of the American West, as he announced to Lyman Copeland Draper, "from the days when Boone crossed the Alleghenies to the days of the Alamo and San Jacinto."[9] The first volume of *The Winning of the West* was published the next year. It was clearly an attempt to find a vehicle for the myth—to substantiate it in the solid matter of history. The result was a "literary" history.

Roosevelt had been formulating his views on the relationship of history and literature for some time. In a review of Francis Parkman's just-completed *France and England in North America* in 1892, he wrote, "Mr. Parkman would have been quite unequal to his task if he had not appreciated its romance as well as its importance." The importance which Roosevelt noted, of course, was the irrevocable march of the civilization of the Anglo-Saxon people against the lands of barbarism and savagery. The romance and color were to be found in the "incidents of wild and picturesque adventure" that accompanied the march. Coming as it did in the year that the second volume of *The Winning of the West* was published, the review is a candid confession of Roosevelt's own intellectual and emotional involvement in the westward movement. The wilderness, he said, "appeals to Parkman's very inmost soul."[10] The same could be said for Roosevelt. He even obtained permission to dedicate *The Winning of the West* to Parkman.

But a full development of Roosevelt's ideas had to await the famous presidential address, "History as Literature," before the American Historical Association on December 22, 1912. Roosevelt reaffirmed that history was devoted to actual facts, but he saw nothing incompatible between truthfulness and color.[11] History must be scientific and "accept what we now know of man's place in nature." But it should also be imaginative. The great historians must have the power to grasp "what is essential and to reject the infinitely more numerous non-essentials, the power to embody ghosts, to put flesh and blood on dry bones, to make dead men living before our eyes."[12] A "literary" history would not only render the scene, the incidents, and the characters of history, but it would also analyze their relative significance.

Yet history should also be moral. "It is no proof of impartiality," Roosevelt assured his audience, "to treat wickedness and goodness as on the same level." So literature also became the vehicle for educating its readers to "a broad human sympathy" and lifting them "out of their common selves to the heights of high endeavor." High moral truth could be taught only through concrete instances, and literature had the power to render life in concrete terms. No contradiction existed between moral truth and colorful adventure. It was only in some literary form that encompassed those elements that history "[pulsed] with immortal life."[13]

Roosevelt viewed the westward movement as a conquest—an

epic struggle—that pulsed with this "immortal life." In a letter to Frederic Remington, on December 28, 1897, he complimented Remington for his sketches of the West, and added that they, along with "the very best," would live on as the "cantos in the last Epic of the Western Wilderness."[14]

Roosevelt tried to capture the history of the West in epic terms in *The Winning of the West*. It was a heroic age, he stated in the opening volume.[15] But a history which merely renders the scene and elevates the soul cannot be epic; in *The Winning of the West*, Roosevelt did not render the scene, let alone write an epic or elevate the soul.

Certain limitations in Roosevelt's own literary taste foreshadowed the literary failure of *The Winning of the West*. Reading literature was, Roosevelt felt, a matter of taste. He liked books in which "something happened." He disliked introspective ones that were psychologically oriented or dealt with subtle social relationships. This may explain why he avidly read *Macbeth* and *Othello* and disliked *Hamlet* and *King Lear*, even though he knew "perfectly well the latter were wonderful." He felt that the novels of Henry James were "diseased"—nothing but "polished, pointless, uninteresting stories" that made "one blush to think that James was once an American." He enjoyed Chaucer, but found some of the tales "needlessly filthy," even unreadable; and he considered Tolstoi a great but decadent writer.[16]

Many of these attitudes simply show not only a lack of good judgment, but, even more important, a lack of sensibility. Roosevelt was contemptuous of the intellectual and esthetic in literature.[17] One of his problems as a writer was that he lacked any sense of literary esthetics. He could tolerate tragedy in certain of the great dramas and in some poetry, but not, he insisted somewhat unintelligibly "in good, readable novels of sufficient length to enable me to get interested in the hero and heroine." He read "to lose all memory of everything grimy" and did not "care to study suffering unless for some sufficient purpose." He further stated, "It is only a very exceptional novel which I will read if He does not marry Her; and even in exceptional novels I much prefer this consummation."[18]

His distaste for sordid details led him to censure his good friend Owen Wister for allowing Balaam, in the short story "Balaam and Pedro," to gouge out one of the eyes of Pedro, his horse, in a fit of violent anger. When Wister rewrote the scene for *The Virginian*, leaving that detail out, it lost what "meaning" it might have had and became a scene of melodramatic violence, in which the Virginian's "sledgehammer blows of justice" revenge the act and pound Balaam into "a blurred, dingy, wet pulp." Roosevelt did not object to the new version.[19]

The Winning of the West reflects Roosevelt's lack of literary sensibility. The participants in the action of the history are nothing less than the forces of good and the forces of evil—the forces of civilization and the forces of savagery. Good is personified in the deeds of the heroic Anglo-Saxon backwoodsman, and evil is personified in the Indian, his French and British allies, the Spanish, and such backwoodsmen as Simon Girty—all who turn their backs on destiny and side either directly or indirectly with savagery. On such a grandiose scale, the conquest of the West was "in its essence just and righteous." War was inevitable. Providence predestined victory.

"It is indeed," said Roosevelt, without a hint of irony, "a warped, perverse, and silly morality which would forbid a course of conquest that has turned whole continents into the seats of mighty and flourishing civilized nations."[20] The crises created by the conquest "demanded that the [backwoodsmen] should be both strong and good; but, above all things, it demanded that they should be strong." Because justice must prevail before mercy, it was the warlike qualities of the Long Knives that were truly admirable. Under existing conditions, it was perfectly proper for Bible-reading backwoodsmen to take Indian scalps.[21]

This confusion of muscle-flexing with moral righteousness turns *The Winning of the West* into a cosmic melodrama in which the forces of "dark death," "butchery," wantonness, and cruelty fight "ferocious wars" with the "hardy [and] strenuous band" of frontier Vikings in the midst of "dark and gloomy woods" and along "bloodstained rivers."[22] The situations in the history contain stock elements of melodrama: bloodshed, revenge, capture, escape, deception, and intrigue. Despite the appearance of realism—the attempt at the verisimilitude of historical facts—Roosevelt was often frustratingly vague and even ambiguous about significant events. He recommended to his friend Owen Wister in a letter: "Throw a veil over what Balaam did to Pedro, leave that to the reader's imagination, and you will greatly strengthen your effect."[23] The statement accurately describes Roosevelt's method in *The Winning of the West*. The history leaves all "conscientious descriptions of the unspeakable" to the reader's imagination. Like all melodramatists, Roosevelt relied on the imagination of his reader to supply the unpleasant details.[24] Even when he narrated grotesque events, emotional and moral conviction was lacking.

Roosevelt's awareness of the mind of his audience was a trait that his friend Brander Matthews admired: "Roosevelt . . . had imagination, and he knew that the American people also had it."[25] Though this trait may have made him a successful politician, it proved his undoing as a writer. He failed to discriminate between the masses' supposed awareness of high moral truth and elevated emotion, and their stock responses to patriotism, honor, race superiority, bravery, and women. He confused the triumph of virtue with "blood and thunder," and consequently was guilty of a series of literary and historical hypocrisies that mark his own peculiar insensibility to the absurd.

A passage describing the Indians during Clark's conquest of the Northwest illustrates Roosevelt's emotional treatment of his subject matter: "The darkbrowed, sullen-looking savages, grotesque in look and terrible in possibility . . . strutted to and fro in their dirty finery or lounged round the houses, inquisitive, importunate, and insolent, hardly concealing a lust for bloodshed and plunder that the slightest mishap was certain to render ungovernable."[26] A more open invitation to the imagination than "grotesque in look and terrible in possibility" cannot be imagined.

Despite these basic deficiencies in the history, Roosevelt seriously attempted to explain frontier character. He wrote to Frederick Jackson Turner, following Turner's review of *The Winning of the West*, that his purpose in writing the history was to "show who the frontiersmen were and what they did." In reply to Turner's specific criticism that he had failed to recognize the regional unity of the West, Roosevelt stated that separatist feeling made the various communities indifferent to one another, though "in type the men were the same."[27] It was a favorite theme with Roosevelt. In *Ranch Life and the Hunting Trail*, he distinguished between the cowboy and bad-man types in the prairie West. And, in his "Letter to John Hay," he wrote of possible new types developing in the Pacific coast regions.[28] Daniel Boone is described as the archetype of the "hunter and wilderness wanderer," a rather vague figure, in both *Hero Tales from American History* and *The Winning of the West*.[29] The latter book further identifies a distinctively American type, a strongly individualistic, self-reliant freeman, who is "produced" or "molded" by his frontier environment. A series of other types are also presented: hunter, hunter-settler, settler, and the like. The book also states that the frontier offered, pre-eminently, a "contrast in types."[30]

Roosevelt felt that the pressures of the frontier experience intensified and accentuated the qualities of "good" and "bad" (he often used just these terms). Though in *The Winning of the West* some attempt is made to render the Indian as a noble figure, as in the characterization of Cornstalk, and though savagery is presented in a repetitious catalogue of atrocities, the Indian is usually presented as a foil for the exploration of the character of the backwoodsmen. His fickleness, for example, is meant to stand in clear contrast to the unwavering steadfastness of the white man.[31] The pressure of Indian actions, like the primitiveness of the environment, accentuate the backwoodsman's tendencies toward good and evil and make him act in heroic or villainous fashion—in a rationale for melodrama.

Though Roosevelt examined the frontiersman in the traditions of the romantic hero-villain, in no sense did he seriously explore the real nature of heroism or villainy. His statement that "sharp dealing" in the East became "highway robbery" in the West appears to have been only an excuse for stressing the more colorful elements of the West.[32] When Roosevelt treated men whom he was forced both to admire and damn, such as George Rogers Clark and John Sevier, he actually created two characters to play each role, each representing the extremes he wished to portray. He could not wholly conceive Sevier because he did not understand him and could not accept him: "Sevier must be judged by another standard [than John Kirk, the brutal murderer of friendly Indians]. He was a member of the Cincinnati, a correspondent of Franklin, a follower of Washington. He sinned against the light, and must be condemned accordingly." Clark was "undone by his fondness for strong drink."[33]

Roosevelt clearly wrote in a literary as well as a historical tradition, owing as much to his literary predecessors James Fenimore Cooper and Sir Walter Scott as he did to the manuscripts and state papers which he studied. Early in the first volume of *The Winning of the West*, he describes a levy of frontier soldiers as "composed of men of the type of Leatherstocking, Ishmael Bush, Tom Hutter, Harry March, Bill Kirby, and Aaron Thousandacres." In the second volume, he compares Captain Kenton's running of the Indian gauntlet with *The Last of the Mohicans*.[34] He refers to Cooper again when he sums up a few of the most typical examples of frontier heroics from among the hundreds he has read about in contemporary manuscripts. The battle of the two Poe brothers with the seven Wyandot warriors is clearly told in the Cooper style.[35] Unlike Cooper, Roosevelt cannot be defended on the grounds of innovation.

At the ending of his account of the Poe-Wyandot episode, Roosevelt states: "It is curious how faithfully, as well as vividly, Cooper has reproduced these incidents. His pictures of the white frontiersmen are generally true to life; in his most noted Indian characters he is much less fortunate. But his 'Indian John' in *The Pioneers* is one of his best portraits; almost equal praise can be given to 'Susquesus' in the *Chainbearer*."[36] It is no wonder that many parts of *The Winning of the West* strongly resemble Cooper.

Allusions are also made to Scott. For example, Roosevelt compares the skirmishes between Indians and whites to the English-Scottish border wars fought two centuries before.[37] Because *Rob Roy* was one of his favorite novels, such allusions are not surprising.

Striving to make his history colorful and his color authentic, Roosevelt naively regarded the conflict between history and literature as potential rather than actual. He insists that the "silence . . . cunning and stealth . . . terrible prowess and merciless cruelty" of the Indians makes it no figure of speech to call them "the tigers of the human race." Elsewhere, he says that it is not a fanciful expression to say that Logan went for help with the "tireless speed of a wolf" because you cannot tire wolves. In fact, "too horrible to mention" was not a figurative expression because every white captive of the Indians suffered torture.[38] Certainly Roosevelt had a gross misunderstanding of the nature of figurative language.

He had two mistresses when he wrote *The Winning of the West*—history and literature—and his pleasures with one could not easily be reconciled with his pleasures with the other. For one thing, he was not very apt at telling them apart. Early in the history, Roosevelt makes it plain that he wishes to correct the inaccuracies of earlier writers like Haywood and Kirke. Kirke is criticized for stating that 15,000 Indians fought a single battle with the settlers. Yet only a few pages later Roosevelt tells a highly implausible story of the rescue of Kate Sherrill by her fiancé, John Sevier.[39] Within the matter of a few pages, then, Roosevelt defends authenticity and destroys plausibility.

Equally glaring is Roosevelt's failure to face the problem of sentimentalism squarely. Some of his most caustic criticism is aimed at Helen Hunt Jackson and all "sentimental" historians because they apologized for the conquest of the West. His own assertions that the white man had a legal and moral right to the West are tedious, repetitive, and in themselves sentimental.[40] But, while he exhibits such seeming tough-mindedness as a historian, he indulges in the most blatant sentimentalism as a creator of character and situation. To create the Indian in the role of villain, he stresses his indiscriminate cruelty to women and children—"the helpless non-combatants." He also dwells on emotional and spiritual dilemmas of the white captives, the situations arising from the marriage of Indian warriors and white women, and the tragedy of "half-breed" children.

Frequently, he insists, during the Indian retreats the captive women and children—and particularly "the women heavy with child"—were "tomahawked and scalped as soon as their steps faltered."[41] After narrating the Battle of Blue Licks, he indulges in bathos: "In every stockade, in almost every cabin, there was weeping for husband or father, son, brother or lover. The best and bravest in the land had been shed like water. There was no one who had not lost some close and dear friend, and the heads of all the people were bowed and their hearts sore stricken." Here, as elsewhere, the sentimental bias is inherent in the sometimes trite, sometimes stilted rhetoric. An additional example of sentimentalism is Roosevelt's reiteration of the "settler's fondness" for the "lonely life of the woods."[42]

Certainly Roosevelt lost many literary and historical opportunities. He could not conceive a complex character who had several sets of values, although he realized values clashed on the frontier. His own attraction to lawlessness was purely romantic. Temperamentally, he was drawn to admire physical prowess in any colorful form, but he could not conceive with any coherence or depth the conflict of values inherent in what he called savagery and civilization. He always felt most at ease characterizing men he could classify as pure villains—men like Aaron Burr.[43] He did not explore the paradox of Boone the Empire Builder and Boone the primitivistic child of nature. In fact, he did not even indicate that he was aware of the paradox, although he attributed both qualities to Boone.[44]

A greater literary capability would not have been enough to insure consideration of these themes; Roosevelt would have had to conceive a society much more complex than that described in *The*

Winning of the West. When the pattern of history shifted away from the frontiersmen toward the settlers, he lost interest, though admitting that the settlers were "the only part [of the community] worth taking into account" and that the "drifting element" was essentially unimportant.[45]

But did Roosevelt write good history? Macaulay, who defended "literary" histories, wrote that the historian who stated only facts might "produce the effect of grossest falsehood" unless he understood the "art of selection" and could, like the painter or writer, produce the effect of truth as well as the authenticity of truth.[46] Roosevelt tried to follow Macaulay's advice. He conceived an epic: the history of the westward movement illustrated the providential victory of civilization over savagery. But, when these abstractions were applied to the events and characters of history, history became melodrama. It is satisfying, he said, to find the stories of the prowess of heroes "attested by contemporary records."[47]

The very theories and principles propounded in Roosevelt's philosophy of history are literary as well as historical. But Roosevelt did not have the imaginative power—let alone the command of literary technique—to make *The Winning of the West* a notable literary achievement. Its failure as literature also accounts in part for its failure as history.

DIGGING FOR HISTORY—

THE ARCHAEOLOGICAL APPROACH

Historical Archaeology
on the Colorado River

C. GREGORY CRAMPTON
University of Utah

Man in the United States seems bent upon changing and re-
changing the face of nature, at a greater rate of speed than anywhere in the world. This is especially true in the West—still the
main frontier of America—where since 1890, and especially since
World War II, more millions have settled than ever before. As
cities sprawl over the countryside, they decay at the center. To
attract customers back to town and away from suburban shopping
centers, old buildings are being demolished to make way for parking
facilities.

Factories are burgeoning, smoke is filling the air, and waste is
polluting the water. A great network of super highways is en-
croaching on the land. Dams are being built, their reservoirs covering thousands of acres. Even in areas that might be expected to
escape spoilation by other means, retirement communities are being
established. The great changes being wrought are illustrated by recent activities on the Colorado River.

The Colorado has been, is, and will continue to be an important
force in the history of the seven states and Mexico that claim parts
of its basin. As a source in an arid region of water for domestic and
industrial use, for irrigation, and the generation of electrical energy,
it has long been the subject of individual, state, regional, national,
and international interest, planning, controversy, agreement, and
development. The signing of the Colorado River Compact in 1922
was a milestone in the development of the river's potential. It
eliminated most of the upper-lower basin rivalry and paved the
way for future agreements between the signatory states. It made
possible the big federal multipurpose projects, the first of which
was the Boulder Canyon Project, begun in 1928.

The Colorado River Storage Act, passed in 1956, authorized
many other important projects, the largest of which were the

Navajo Dam on the San Juan River in New Mexico, Flaming Gorge
Dam on the Green River in northern Utah, and the huge Glen
Canyon Dam on the Colorado River in northern Arizona. These,
and smaller projects, are now in various stages of construction. The
Bureau of Reclamation has listed 134 potential reclamation develop-
ment projects and sub-projects within the Colorado River Basin.[1]

The Glen Canyon project is of special interest. Fifteen miles
above Lee's Ferry in Arizona a huge concrete dam is being built,
which will rise 580 feet above the river bed. Its reservoir will cover
162,700 acres of incomparable natural beauty and extend 186 miles
upstream to near the junction of the Green and Colorado Rivers in
Utah. When the Colorado River Storage Act became law in July,
1956, recommendations were made to the National Park Service that
a historical program be inaugurated in the Glen Canyon region—the
study and charting of historic places and the removal of significant
relics from the reservoir area.

The National Park Service, through its Southwest Regional
Office at Santa Fe, had already begun to formulate broad plans for
both historical and archaeological salvage programs and for a number
of special studies in Glen Canyon. Contracts for these purposes were
negotiated in 1957 with the University of Utah and the Museum
of Northern Arizona. The historical salvage program in Glen Canyon
began in the summer of 1957 and will terminate in 1963.

At the outset, a decision was made to prepare a broad history
of the Glen Canyon region to assist others engaged in salvage studies
and to serve the public at large. Such a history would also provide
a regional perspective for the detailed data accumulated in the
canyon salvage operation. Preliminary study showed a certain unity
in the history of the country stretching from the Tavaputs Plateau
on the north to the San Francisco peaks on the south, and from Mesa
Verde on the east to the High Plateaus on the west—country
dominated by the river and the canyons and the spectacular plateau
geography. Yet, though this area is bigger than New England, its
general history had never been written. Historical studies had been
local, incidental, or had tended to follow the boundary lines of the
four states that share the region.

Hence, an *Outline History of the Glen Canyon Region* was prepared. Published in 1959, this volume broadly summarized the main
historical trends—from 1776, when the first significant Spanish
explorations were made, to 1922, when the Colorado River Compact
was drawn up—revealing a rich historical tapestry of Spanish friars,

Mexican traders, American fur men, government explorers, Indians, Mormon colonizers, cattlemen, outlaws, miners, and dam builders.[2] It also revealed that mining predominated in the occupation and use of the canyon. Placer mining for gold was confined almost wholly to the canyon floors in an area nearly identical with that of the future Glen Canyon reservoir, Lake Powell. Certainly Glen Canyon is of greater historical importance than any other canyon of the Colorado.

After the summary history was prepared, a listing was made of historic sites and remains threatened with loss through inundation. Especially because no history of the canyon was extant, any material remains needed to be examined that would throw light on the historical use and occupancy of the reservoir area. Documentary sources were also consulted for any historical information they would provide. Because much of the canyon's history dates within the last seventy-five years, living participants are important sources of information. Other investigators in the archaeological and biological phases of salvage operations in Glen Canyon have been cooperative in pointing out significant locations.

Another step was field exploration of the floor of the three main canyons of the Colorado River: the Cataract, Narrow, and Glen. These cover a distance of more than 216 river miles, not including the San Juan River, the main tributary within this distance, the bed of which for seventy-one miles above its mouth will be flooded by Lake Powell. For the most part, the canyons consist of precipitous walls rising as much as a thousand feet or more above the banks of the river. Because access is limited and difficult, nearly all field work was done in boats.

Information obtained from documents and informants not only facilitated the location of historic sites, but also to a great extent dictated the scope of field study. During the canyon exploration, many sites were found concerning which no documentary data had been discovered. Where possible, these were later checked against library and oral sources.

Site records include the following data: the exact location, the kind and degree of historical activity, the extent of historic remains, and any other information of possible interest to future investigators. They may include black and white and colored photographs, sketch maps, and special note of any remains of interest for museum purposes. Each site, which is precisely located on a large-scale map, is given a number; and records made in the field, as well as information subsequently obtained by documentary research, are filed under that number and become a part of the permanent project records, which will be retained by the University of Utah. Using these raw data, each site is described in a final published report. One volume of historic site studies for the Lake Powell area has already been published, and three more will be published before the project is completed.[3]

These volumes will contain descriptions of approximately 300 historic sites, nearly all of which will be flooded. These sites represent only a generous sampling of the area; a systematic mile-by-mile exploration was not possible. Thus, a body of knowledge about an important region is being preserved before it is forever lost.

It is doubtful that any of the findings will be of national importance, but the sum total of the historical evidence collected is impressive. It tells much about the few thousands of people who figure in the history of Glen Canyon up to about 1922—and who lived or passed through this remote and wild and rugged land, a deep canyon draining a wilderness of bare rock and little soil.

For example, the earliest date of apparent authenticity found on the walls of Glen Canyon, 1837, must have been inscribed by trappers during the heyday of the Rocky Mountain fur trade. A rusting dredge is a monument to the quest for gold. Historical evidence exists of the activities of Robert B. Stanton, an engineer who surveyed the line of canyons from Cataract through Grand to determine the feasibility of a railroad route from the coal fields of Colorado to the cities of the California coast. The network of Navajo stock trails, many of them crossing bald rock, steep slopes, and narrow side canyons, indicates the intensive use of the sparse grazing resources. The building of a spectacular wagon road across Glen Canyon at Hole-in-the-Rock by a Mormon colonizing expedition is dramatic testimony to the strength of a faith. Outlaw trails show that the users knew a good place to hide. The numerous places where toe-and-hand-hold steps, pecked and ground out with stones on the face of nearly vertical slopes, have been enlarged by steel picks demonstrate that modern men often followed the routes of prehistoric people.

A number of problems confront the historian when he leaves the library and the archives and goes into the field to study environmental and material remains. One of the more serious of these is the necessity for establishing suitable procedural techniques, about which handbooks on historical method say little. Fortunately, some archaeological methods can be adapted, such as the general sequence of approach for a prescribed salvage area: a reconnaissance, followed by systematic survey. Indeed, the final reports are so unlike historical treatises that it is not altogether inappropriate that they will be part of the *Anthropological Papers* published by the University of Utah Press. Historical archaeology, as its name implies, represents the bridging of historical and archaeological techniques.

It is a valuable discipline because of the destruction of historical data and monuments during the present rapid expansion of the West. Fortunately, this destruction is being resisted by individuals and organizations, public and private. The Federal Government, beyond its salvage programs, is concerned with places of outstanding national importance.[4] State governments have acknowledged their responsibility in the preservation of monuments, though budgets have frequently not been adequate. Other participating agencies are: state historical societies, municipalities, patriotic groups, professional associations, philanthropists, and others—though, unfortunately, the national historical associations have been very slow to participate. Much of this effort is being made to save the dramatic and the spectacular, the unique and the unusual.

One can easily applaud the preservation of Fort Vancouver, the California missions, the Alamo, Fort Laramie, and Tumacacori. But what of lesser monuments, even the commonplace? Who is preparing a systematic record of buildings, artifacts, roads, ranches, irrigation projects, Chinatowns, modern Indian villages, colonization projects that failed, churches, saloons, cemeteries, theaters, and monuments that illustrate movements, forces, styles, eras, regions, and other historical developments?

To the archaeologist, the preparation of such records is important; the location of surviving objects and a study of material culture are central to his discipline. Unfortunately, many disdainful academic and scholarly historians do not feel this way. They would very much like to leave these matters to the spades and brooms and the tape measures and cameras of the archaeologists. Because historians have been content to study history in the library, while archaeologists have studied prehistory in the field, a wide hiatus exists between the two disciplines—especially in the West.

As a result, the historical profession is neglecting one of its responsibilities. In the West, particularly, more scholarly practi-

tioners should be working in historical conservation and preservation—in historical societies, museums, city and state governments,
Federal Government, private organizations, and foundations. What
is called for is the establishment at the university level of a center
for the training of such people. New methods, especially in field
techniques, need to be formulated. A publication program would
make known new research in the area. The inauguration of such
programs would indicate that the historical profession is accepting
its responsibilities in the conservation of historical resources.

Salvage Archaeology Today
and the Glen Canyon Project

ROBERT H. LISTER
University of Colorado

The number of salvage archaeology programs that are being conducted today, not only throughout the West but elsewhere in the United States and abroad, is increasing at a rapid rate. These programs—which involve not only archaeological but also historical, paleontological, and ecological studies—have as their primary concern the collection of materials and data that would otherwise be destroyed by five major types of construction projects: reclamation, highway, gas and oil pipeline, power line, and urban expansion.

Reclamation projects involve the building of dams which create storage reservoirs that flood miles of river bottoms and adjacent lands, the construction of networks of canals and ditches, and the land-leveling operations associated with irrigation projects. Highway projects include the right-of-way and grading operations being performed during the rapid expansion of the state and federal highway systems. Gas and oil pipeline projects and power line projects involve thousands of miles annually of trenches, right-of-ways, and access roads. Urban expansion projects are associated with residential, recreational, business, and industrial expansion.

Prehistoric and early historic Indian sites, as well as historic sites, frequently have been destroyed by such projects; and, despite salvage activities, destruction will continue at a greatly accelerated pace in the future. For example, the Corps of Engineers' plans for reservoir construction in February of 1962 were as follows:

Year	No. of Reservoirs	Expenditure
1960	123	$ 99 million
1970	290	190 million
1980	450	300 million
2000	700	700 million

These are the plans of but one of two federal dam-building agencies.

The tremendous program of dam and reservoir construction throughout the United States is of special concern because such projects alter or flood miles of valley floors. It is in precisely these areas—along stream banks and in stream valleys—that the Indians lived, and where frontiersmen made their camps, forts, and homes. In these same areas, great modern cities have also grown. The cities are protected in the present water control planning, but this is not always true of the historic and prehistoric sites. Fortunately, salvage archaeology is doing something about the problem.

Its origins date back to the 1930's, when recovery of archaeological remains was undertaken by the Tennessee Valley Authority during the construction of dams and reservoirs. This work was supported by the Works Progress Administration. In 1935, the Historic Sites Act was passed by Congress. This authorized the National Park Service to "make necessary investigations and researches in the United States relating to particular sites, buildings, or objects to obtain true and accurate historical and archaeological facts and information concerning the same."

Recognizing the imperative need for a salvage program, authority for which was provided by the Historic Sites Act, the Director of the National Park Service, assisted by archaeologists of the Smithsonian Institution, proceeded to instigate cooperative agreements with the major governmental construction agencies—the Corps of Engineers and the Bureau of Reclamation.

In 1945, the threat to archaeological resources posed by the extensive plans for government-sponsored multipurpose dams and related projects led to the establishment of the Committee for the Recovery of Archaeological Remains, made up of representatives of the American Anthropological Association, Society for American Archaeology, and the American Council of Learned Societies. This committee developed a program, with the help of Smithsonian Institution scientists, and the Inter-Agency Archaeological Salvage Program was organized. The Smithsonian Institution and the National Park Service have administered the activities of this program, which involves the cooperation of numerous federal agencies, such as the Bureau of Reclamation, Corps of Engineers, Federal Power Commission, International Boundary and Water Commission, United States Geological Survey, and a great many state and local agencies, such as universities, museums, and archaeological societies.

Since 1945, the Inter-Agency Salvage Program has carried on intensive archaeological, historical, and paleontological surveys in more than 310 reservoir areas in 42 states. These surveys are initial investigations to determine if any significant remains are to be destroyed by flooding or construction; and, if so, which should be excavated. Surveys of many reservoir areas have shown that no loss to scientific knowledge would result and no salvage is needed. Others have shown that important losses would occur, and projects for archaeological salvage excavations are recommended.

More than 12,000 archaeological and historic sites have been located and recorded by these surveys. Excavations in recommended sites have been undertaken in more than seventy-five reservoir areas located in thirty-one states. These excavations and the surveys that preceded them have produced more than four million archaeological specimens. These become museum exhibit pieces and study collections in the United States National Museum, and at state and local museums and research centers. Results of these excavations, ranging from popular accounts to detailed technical reports, have been published in many journals, magazines, and bulletins.

Salvage of archaeological remains along right-of-ways of federal and state highway systems was stimulated in 1954 by the Museum of New Mexico, the State Highway Department of New Mexico, and the Bureau of Public Roads. In 1956, the Federal-Aid Highway Act authorized the use of Federal-aid funds to reimburse the states for a portion of the cost of archaeological salvage performed within the "road prism" on all Federal-aid projects. The spread of this activity has been slow, and many false starts have occurred and half-hearted plans made. Fairly extensive programs are now being carried out in twelve states, including California, Oregon, Utah, Nebraska, and New Mexico in the West. Limited programs are in effect in Colorado and Arizona.

Archaeological materials exposed by gas pipelines and the clearing of power line right-of-ways have been successfully recovered in some areas. Salvage programs in conjunction with urban expansion projects have been undertaken to a very limited degree. Salvage archaeology programs are being conducted elsewhere in the world, such as in Russia, Mexico, Peru, and along the Nile in Egypt and the Sudan.

The salvage archaeology program in Glen Canyon of the Colorado River demonstrates how effective such programs can be. When, after years of discussion and plans, funds were authorized for the construction of Glen Canyon dam and other dams in the Upper Colorado River Basin, the National Park Service concerned itself with the problem of salvage. It later contracted with the University of Utah's Department of Anthropology to perform salvage studies along the right bank of the Colorado River and its tributaries in Glen Canyon; the Museum of Northern Arizona had already been awarded a contract for work on the left bank of the canyon. The studies were initiated in 1957, under the direction of Dr. Jesse D. Jennings of the University of Utah's Department of Anthropology, who has continued to direct the project. The last field work was completed in the summer of 1961.

At the outset, the magnitude of the job was frightening. Glen Canyon dam will create a reservoir—to be named Lake Powell— which will extend from the dam site in northern Arizona 183 miles through Glen Canyon to above the river crossing at Hite, Utah. Also to be flooded are several hundred miles of right-bank tributary canyons.

The contract called not only for the salvage of remains lying within the reservoir proper but also, fortunately, all lands adjacent to the canyons which promised to be of importance in the field investigation. Many previous projects of this nature had been restricted solely to lands to be inundated; thus, if an important site was located just outside the reservoir it could not be investigated. Excavations at several villages outside the confines of the reservoir have helped interpret the cultures being studied in Glen Canyon.

Of basic concern in planning was the need for determining the most effective method of field operation. This is not normally a problem, but in the uninhabited, remote Glen Canyon country, logistics, supply, and communication constituted a special problem. Because a series of land and air reconnaissance trips indicated that access to the territory from the Colorado River was impractical except for those sites in the deeply incised Glen Canyon proper, the decision was made to use predominately land transportation. Four-wheel-drive vehicles were used when possible; sometimes pack animals were required. The surveyors, as is their normal lot, conducted the mile-by-mile search on foot. Boats were used only in the main stem of the canyon.

Because the University of Utah did not have sufficient special facilities to handle properly the materials and information that would accrue from a project of this magnitude, a two-story temporary building on the campus was modified and assigned exclusively to the project for laboratory use. All the necessary equipment was purchased.

The survey was started in June of 1957. That season involved much trial and error. The plan for the operation was tested and modified as necessary. The survey was completed in the summer of 1958. More than 1,100 archaeological sites in and adjacent to the reservoir area were located. These included pictograph panels, trails, areas where stone tools had been manufactured, simple camp sites, and small and large habitation sites—some located within the protective confines of shallow caves in the canyons' walls and others situated in the open on mesa tops, canyon bottoms, and flatlands adjacent to the canyons.

Even before the survey was completed, excavation teams took to the field and began their laborious task. Though the survey required only about six months, excavation and laboratory analysis of materials recovered have not yet been completed in the five years since the project began.

The laboratory work and report preparation, of course, consumes more time than the field work. All specimens must be identified, cleaned, repaired or preserved, measured, photographed, catalogued, described, and classified. Maps, charts, and illustrations must be drawn. Field notes must be transformed into readable accounts, edited, and printed. Specialists must study botanical, zoological, and mineralogical specimens and help date specimens and geological deposits with which cultural materials are associated. Comparative studies to relate findings to others previously made in the region need be accomplished.

More than seventy-five sites have been partially or thoroughly excavated in the process of sampling all prehistoric cultures represented in the area. Seven reports dealing with the results of these investigations have been published. Additional site reports and several comprehensive monographs summarizing data obtained during the project are forthcoming. These will discuss ecological and historical as well as archaeological findings.

The findings indicate the following Indian utilization pattern of the area:

The region was rarely visited by Indians prior to about A.D. 1000, and those who did visit were transient. However, between A.D. 1000 and 1300 predecessors of the modern Pueblo Indians, of the Anasazi culture, made considerable use of Glen Canyon and its tributary canyons. During this period, farming peoples from today's Hopi country of northeastern Arizona migrated to the Glen

Canyon area. They sought out locales such as rock shelters, shallow caves, and plateau tops where suitable habitations and storage granaries could be constructed and where arable lands were available for planting corn, beans, and squash. However, because the climate and the land along the Colorado River in those days was much like they are today, satisfactory locations for even small-scale farming operations were not numerous. Dry farming was the rule, but rudimentary irrigation works have been discovered in a few places. During the same period, migration to Glen Canyon also occurred from central Utah and the Mesa Verde villages in southwestern Colorado.

The lack of settlement in Glen Canyon prior to A.D. 1000 occurred because the surrounding areas were more attractive for settlement by agricultural peoples. Because the population in the surrounding areas reached a climax in the 300-year period following 1000, migration into the less desirable Colorado River canyon country may have been stimulated. Only in a few localities were found evidences of communities of any size, or occupations of any length of time. The usual settlement pattern consists of small, crude masonry houses and storage units. These were apparently used for short periods by small groups of transient people searching for favorable living areas.

By A.D. 1300 the area was largely abandoned, apparently for several reasons. The drought that hit the Southwest in the latter part of the thirteenth century may have forced the migration of the marginal farmers of Glen Canyon. The arrival of nomadic raiding groups in the Southwest—such as the ancestors of the modern Ute and Paiute—may have begun during this period. Or the resident Indians may have grown tired of attempts to make a living in the hostile land and returned to their former homeland.

Since the 1300's the area has been utilized by nomadic tribes, such as the Ute, Paiute, and Navajo, who have left little archaeological evidence of their presence.

Beyond the technical ramifications of the findings, the Glen Canyon salvage project has led to a thorough and comprehensive investigation of an area that certainly would never have been so completely and rapidly studied had it not been for the Glen Canyon dam and the Inter-Agency Salvage Program. Many of the more remote, inhospitable areas would probably never have been investigated at all had it not been for the project.

Despite the great progress that has been made in salvage archaeology, salvage operations need to be greatly expanded and many new programs established to keep pace with the onrushing bulldozer. A key factor in future programming is the lack of trained archaeologists to lead salvage expeditions. Our colleges and universities need to turn out trained archaeologists at a greatly accelerated rate to catch up with the demands. When this is done, our archaeological heritage will be further enriched.

Notes

CLIFFORD P. WESTERMEIER
The Modern Cowboy—An Image

1. Clifford P. Westermeier, *Trailing the Cowboy* (Caldwell, Idaho, 1955), pp. 381-382.
2. *Ibid.*, p. 382.
3. Mody C. Boatright, "The American Myth Rides the Range," *Southwest Review*, 36 (Summer 1951), p. 158.
4. Westermeier, *Trailing the Cowboy*, pp. 393-394; Clifford P. Westermeier, "Seventy-Five Years of Rodeo in Colorado," *Colorado Magazine*, 28 (January 1951), pp. 15-16, 21, 26; Thérèse S. Westermeier, "Colorado Festivals," *ibid.*, 30 (July 1953), pp. 193-215.
5. Owen Wister, *The Virginian* (New York, 1947), p. x.
6. Del Carnes, "On the Air—TV Adopts Film Classics," *Denver Post*, Aug. 7, 1962, p. 22.
7. Hal Bridges, "Roundup Time on the Western Range," *New York Times Book Review*, Aug. 17, 1958, p. 18; Irwin R. Blocker, *The Old West in Fiction* (New York, 1961), from "Notes for a Preface," unpaged.
8. Walter Manfried, "Fewer True Cowboys Ride the Range—But Their Imitators Are in Demand," *Buffalo Evening News* (Buffalo, New York), Nov. 1, 1950, p. 14.
9. Dick Spenser, "The Cowboy's Not for Vanishing," *Colorado Wonderland*, 8 (August 1950), pp. 1, 20; Walt Wiggens, "Northwest Cowpoke," *Argosy*, 346 (February 1953), p. 29; Lewis Nordyke, "Rugged Riders of Pitchfork Ranch," *Saturday Evening Post*, 232 (Oct. 3, 1959), p. 157; Frank X Tolbert, "Modern Cowboys Is Sissies," *ibid.*, 226 (Dec. 26, 1953), p. 57; Donald Wayne, "Cowpunching Doesn't Change," *Parade, Denver Post*, July 3, 1949, p. 18. See also Joe B. Frantz and Julian Ernest Choate, Jr., *The American Cowboy: The Myth and the Reality* (Norman, Oklahoma, 1955), p. 60.
10. *Ibid.*
11. Frank Farmer, "The Vanishing Cowboy," *Collier's*, 137 (May 25, 1956), pp. 33, 35; Tolbert, "Modern Cowboys Is Sissies," p. 18; K. C. Winchester, "Rangeland Revolution," *Home and Highway*, 4 (Autumn 1953), p. 21; Edwin V. Burkholder, "The Cowboy Who Never Lived," *Bluebook*, 93 (June 1954), pp. 75-141.
12. From stenographic notes taken during the program "Brinkley's Journal," National Broadcasting Company, July 4, 1962.
13. *Ibid.*
14. Edith Efron, "David of the Devastating Quip," *TV Guide*, 10 (July 14, 1962), pp. 24-25.
15. *Ibid.*, p.25.
16. Bern Keating, "How Do You Figure the Greatest Cowboy," *Show*, 2 (May 1962), p. 13; Donald Wayne, "Cowpunching Doesn't Change," *Parade, Denver Post*, July 3, 1949, p. 20.
17. E. C. Abbott ("Teddy Blue") and Helen Huntington Smith; *We Pointed Them North* (Norman, Oklahoma, 1955), pp. 99-112; Westermeier, *Trailing the*

Cowboy, pp. 189-212; Clifford P. Westermeier, "Cowboy Capers," *Annals of Wyoming*, 22 (July 1950), pp. 16, 17, 22, 25. See also Leonard McCombe and John Bryon, *The Cowboy* (Garden City, New York, 1951).

18. Clifford P. Westermeier, *Man, Beast, Dust: The Story of Rodeo* (Denver, Colorado, 1946), pp. 50-68; Westermeier, *Trailing the Cowboy*, pp. 395-396.

19. Philip A. Rollins, *The Cowboy—An Unconventional History of Civilization on the Old-Time Cattle Range* (New York, 1936), pp. 21-25; C. L. Sonnichsen, *Cowboys and Cattle Kings—Life on the Range Today* (Norman, Oklahoma, 1950), p. 88; Westermeier, *Man, Beast, Dust*, pp. 39-40; "Cattle-Herding in the Great West," *Littell's Living Age*, 18 (April 14, 1877), p. 126; "Among the Cowboys," *Lippincott's Magazine*, 27 (June 1881), pp. 568-569.

20. "Frontier Sketches," *Denver Field and Farm* (Denver, Colorado), July 8, 1899, p. 6; Westermeier, "Seventy-Five Years of Rodeo in Colorado," *Colorado Magazine*, 28 (January 1951), pp. 14-15.

21. "Self-Made Cowboy," *Time*, 61 (Jan. 5, 1953), p. 40; "Tompkins Gets Time Writeup," *Rodeo Sports News*, 1 (Jan. 15, 1953), p. 1. See also "The Western Horseman Portfolio of Champion Cowboys, 1929-1961," *Western Horseman*, 27 (July 1962), pp. 35, 39.

22. Westermeier, *Man, Beast, Dust*, p. 325.

23. Bill Butler, "King of the Cowboys," *Tulsa Sunday World Magazine*, Dec. 16, 1956, p. 18; Paul Friggens, "Rodeo's Rambling Wreck," *True*, 41 (August 1960), p. 97.

24. "1,800 Steers Punched Into Stock Pens," *Boulder Daily Camera* (Boulder, Colorado), Jan. 9, 1962, p. 15; "South Dakota—Tails to the Wind," *Newsweek*, 59 (Jan. 22, 1962), p. 20; "Old Time Drive Over Windy Western Trails," *Life*, 52 (Jan. 19, 1962), pp. 38-39. For modern cattle drives, see "Cattle Drives Not Extinct—Almost," *Denver Post*, Nov. 20, 1955, p. 16A; John Guernsey, "Oregon Cattle Drive," *Western Horseman*, 27 (August 1962), pp. 36-37, 88-89.

25. Harold Heffernan, "Heaven Bless the Cowboy," *Empire Magazine, Denver Post*, Aug. 6, 1950, p. 8; "Western Films Hailed As Top Entertainers," *Rocky Mountain News* (Denver, Colorado), Aug. 19, 1953, p. 35.

26. Westermeier, *Man, Beast, Dust*, pp. 30-37; Westermeier, *Trailing the Cowboy*, pp. 341-376.

27. Westermeier, *Man, Beast, Dust*, pp. 288-291. See also Thérèse S. Westermeier, "Colorado Festivals," pp. 193-215.

28. Westermeier, *Man, Beast, Dust*, pp. 94-100, 183-188.

29. *Ibid.*, pp. 100-127.

30. *Ibid.*, pp. 94, 100-127.

31. "*Rodeo Sports News* Declared Official Association Publication," *Rodeo Sports News*, 1 (Feb. 1, 1953), p. 1.

32. "Information Commission Incorporated Recently," *ibid.*, 3 (March 1, 1955), p. 1.

33. Clifford P. Westermeier, *Who Rush to Glory—The Cowboy Volunteers of 1898* (Caldwell, Idaho), pp. 252-257.

34. "Rodeo Cowboys' Association, Inc. Approved Rodeos of 1955," *Annual Edition, 1956, Rodeo Sports News* [January 1956], pp. 40-41.

35. "Rodeo Cowboys' Association, Inc. Approved Rodeos of 1961," *Annual Edition, 1962, Rodeo Sports News* [January 1962], pp. 73-81.

36. Joan Dickinson, "Jim Shoulders Tells How To Watch a Rodeo," *Sports Illustrated*, 11 (Dec. 21, 1959), p. 40; "Man, Beast, Dust," editorial in *Boulder Daily Camera* (Boulder, Colorado), July 27, 1957, p. 4; "Over 14 Million See 1958 Rodeos," *Rodeo Sports News*, 7 (May 15, 1959), p. 4.

37. "'Wall Street Journal' Article Emphasizes Economic Value of Professional Rodeos," *Rodeo Sports News*, 3 (Aug. 15, 1955), p. 1.

38. "First National's Rodeo Site Chosen," *Rodeo Sports News*, 7 (Nov. 15,

1958), p. 1; "What Will Be Needed To Get Full Benefit From the First 'World Series' of Rodeo?" *Annual Edition, 1959, Rodeo Sports News* [January 1959], p. 39; John VanCronckhite, "What the National Finals Rodeo Will Mean to the Sport," *ibid.,* p. 39.

39. Eddie O'Brien, "Rodeo Chat," *Hoofs and Horns,* 13 (March 1944), p. 8; "An Editorial," *ibid.,* 17 (January 1948), p. 17; "A Reply," *ibid.* (February 1948), p. 18; "The Spectator Speaks," *Rodeo Sports News,*" 1 (Dec. 1, 1952), p. 6; "Wyoming Paper First To Put Rodeo on Sports Page," *ibid.* (Dec. 15, 1952), p. 1; "Rodeo Hits Sports Page of Million Circulation Newspaper," *ibid.* (May 1, 1953), p. 1.

40. "London All Worked Up Over an American Rodeo," *Literary Digest,* 82 (July 27, 1924), pp. 42-47; Westermeier, *Man, Beast, Dust,* p. 337.

41. "Rodeo in France," *Hoofs and Horns,* 15 (October 1945), p. 14; "Ledo Road Rodeo," *ibid.,* 13 (June 1945), p. 15; "Rodeo in China," *ibid.* (October 1945), p. 13; "South Pacific Rodeo," *ibid.,* 14 (June 1945), 15; "European Rodeos," *ibid.,* 16 (August 1942), p. 15; "Rodeo in Honolulu," *ibid.,* 12 (September 1942), p. 10; "Honolulu Rodeo," *ibid.,* 14 (May 1945), p. 15; "AF Stages Rodeo in North Africa," *Rodeo Sports News,* 5 (Nov. 15, 1957), p. 2; "Rodeo on Guam," *ibid.,* 7 (July 1, 1959), p. 5.

42. "Cowboys-Indians Leave For Brussels," *Rodeo Sports News,* 6 (June 15, 1958), p. 9; "R.C.A. Not Connected With Ill-Fated Show at World's Fair," *Boulder Daily Camera* (Boulder, Colorado), July 21, 1958, p. 4.

43. "1956 Final Point Award Championship Standings," *Annual Edition, 1957, Rodeo Sports News* [January 1957], p. 5.

44. "1955 Final Point Award Championship Standings," *Annual Edition, 1956, Rodeo Sports News* [January 1956], p. 3.

45. "1961 Champion Standings," *Annual Edition, 1962, Rodeo Sports News* [January 1962], p. 4.

46. "Who Is the Average Rodeo Cowboy?" *Annual Edition, 1958, Rodeo Sports News* [January 1959], p. 122.

47. Westermeier, *Man, Beast, Dust,* pp. 131-136; "Who Is the Average Rodeo Cowboy?" *Annual Edition, 1958, Rodeo Sports News* [January 1959], p. 122.

48. "Rodeo Cowboys' Association, Inc. Approved Rodeos of 1961," *Annual Edition, 1962, Rodeo Sports News* [January 1962], p. 81.

49. "Who Is the Average Rodeo Cowboy?" *Annual Edition, 1958, Rodeo Sports News* [January 1959], p. 122.

50. Clifford P. Westermeier, "Roping and Riding—A School Sport," *Western Horseman,* 13 (March-April 1948), p. 29.

51. "The American Junior Rodeo Association," *Hoofs and Horns,* 22 (September 1952), p. 26; *ibid.,* 23 (July 1953), p. 17; "Youth Goes Rodeoing," *Rodeo Sports News,* 3 (July 1, 1955), p. 6; Carl Shephard, "AJRA Youth Rodeo," *Western Horseman,* 27 (August 1962), pp. 7, 89-90.

52. "National Intercollegiate Rodeo Association," *Rodeo Sports News,* 2 (March 1, 1954), p. 5; Jean Muir, "Cowboys on the Campus," *Saturday Evening Post,* 223 (Feb. 10, 1951), pp. 37, 138-141. See also Orville Rennie, "Intercollegiate Rodeo," *Western Horseman,* 27 (September 1962), pp. 21, 102-104.

53. The AJRA consists of High School Rodeo Clubs, Future Farmers of America, 4-H Clubs, and various Kid's Rodeos. The members must be under twenty years of age. See Lex Connelly, "Rodeo—1957," *Annual Edition, 1958, Rodeo Sports News* [January 1958], pp. 72-73.

54. "Roping School Opens," *Rodeo Sports News,* 6 (Sept. 1, 1958), p. 8. See also Dick Spencer, "Rodeo School," *Western Horseman,* 27 (September 1962), pp. 50-52.

55. "Westerns," *Time*, 73 (March 30, 1959), p. 52; "The Westerns," *Look*, 26 (March 13, 1962), p. 82.

56. "Westerns," *Time*, 73 (March 30, 1959), p. 53; George Eells, "TV Western Craze—How Long Will It Last?" *Look*, 24 (June 24, 1958), pp. 66, 71; John Hazard Wildman, "Hopalong to Heaven," *America*, 94 (March 17, 1956), pp. 666-667; Hal Boyle, "Views the World," *Northwest Arkansas Times* (Fayetteville, Arkansas), Jan. 11, 1958, p. 8.

57. "Westerns," *Time*, 73 (March 30, 1959), p. 57; Leonard Spinrad, "Boots and Saddles," New York *Times*, June 8, 1947, p. 4x. In 1958, Broncho Billy Anderson received an honorary "Oscar" for his pioneer work in the film industry. *Daily Oklahoman* (Oklahoma City, Oklahoma), April 7, 1958, p. 21.

58. "Westerns," *Time*, 73 (March 30, 1959), p. 57.

59. Fred Gipson, *Fabulous Empire—Colonel Zack Miller's Story* (Boston, 1946), pp. 233, 238.

60. *Ibid.*, pp. 224, 232-242.

61. Harold Heffernan, "Heaven Bless the Cowboy," *Empire Magazine, Denver Post*, Aug. 6, 1950, p. 8.

62. "Westerns," *Time*, 73 (March 30, 1959), p. 57.

63. Edward Abbey, *The Brave Cowboy* (New York, 1956).

64. "The New Westerns," *Time*, 80 (July 13, 1962), p. 66.

65. Alex Murphree, "New Film Candidly Probes Rodeo Life," *Denver Post*, Nov. 4, 1952, p. 26.

66. "Rodeo Hits National TV," *Rodeo Sports News*, 1 (Feb. 15, 1953), p. 1; "First TV Contract Signed," *ibid.*, 2 (Jan. 15, 1954), p. 6; "38 Million See Pendleton Rodeo," *ibid.*, 5 (Nov. 1, 1957), p. 1.

67. *TV Guide*, October 1961-September 1962.

68. Hans Plischke, *Von Cooper Bis Karl May* (Dusseldorf, Germany, 1951), pp. 5-8.

69. Karl May, *Winnetou* (Bamberg, Germany, 1950).

70. "Cowboys Abroad," *Time*, 80 (Aug. 3, 1962), p. 51.

71. Karl Kohrs, "German (!) Cowboys Ride Again," *Parade, Denver Post*, Oct. 26, 1952, pp. 18-19. "Flying Jack," a fictional cowboy, has become the hero of thousands of boys and girls in West Germany. He is the creation of Kurt Sellers, who makes the Old West live again in paperbound books. "West German Cowboy Hero," *Post-Dispatch* (St. Louis, Missouri), Oct. 5, 1952, p. 17.

72. Leslie Lieber, "Vive Le Cowboy!" *This Week Magazine, Sun* (Baltimore, Maryland), Sept. 16, 1951, pp. 20, 25; Charles J. Belden, "The Spirit of the Old West Still Lives in Paris," *Horse Lover's Magazine*, 27 (December 1961-January 1962), pp. 30-31; "Cowboy Craze in France," *Newsweek*, 52 (July 28, 1958), p. 54. Well known in France are the cowboys of Camargue, the Rhone Delta horse- and bull-raising area in southern France. About the only thing the Camargue cowboys have in common with the Texas variety are their horses and their sombreros. "They Marry From the Saddle," *Sign*, 35 (June 1956), pp. 46-47.

73. William Houseman, "The U. S. Is Going Cowboy Nutty," *Look*, 14 (July 18, 1950), pp. 63-64; "Cowboys Abroad," *Time*, 80 (Aug. 3, 1962) p. 51.

74. "Cowboy Represents U. S.," *Arkansas Gazette* (Little Rock, Arkansas), June 6, 1954, p. 2G.

75. Johann Wolfgang Goethe, *Goethe's Werke*, 3 (Leipzig, 1914), p. 438.

76. Paul Coze, *Rodeos de cow-boy et les jeux du lasso* (Paris, 1934), p. 35.

WILLIAM H. GOETZMANN

*The Wheeler Surveys and the Decline
of Army Exploration in the West*

1. See the very brief obituary in the *Army and Navy Journal,* May 6, 1905, which was copied from the New York *Times* of May 5, 1905.
2. Other Army officers who led exploring expeditions in the West during this period were: Maj. R. S. Williamson, Capt. D. P. Heap, Lt. G. C. Doane, Capt. J. W. Barlow, Capt. W. A. Jones, Capt. William Ludlow, Capt. G. J. Lydecker, Lt. E. H. Ruffner, Capt. W. S. Stanton, Lt. E. Maguire, and Lt. Col. G. A. Custer.
3. See W. H. Goetzmann, *Army Exploration in the American West, 1803-1863* (New Haven, Connecticut, 1959).
4. *Dictionary of American Biography.*
5. *Webster's Collegiate Dictionary,* 5th edition (Springfield, Massachusetts, 1947).
6. 1st Lt. George M. Wheeler, *Preliminary Report Upon a Reconnaissance Through Southern and Southeastern Nevada, Made in 1869* (Washington, 1875).
7. A picture of this vehicle appears in W. H. Rideing, "The Wheeler Survey in Nevada," *Harper's New Monthly Magazine,* 55 (June 1877) p. 68.
8. Thurman Wilkins, *Clarence King* (New York, 1958), pp. 112-131.
9. *Ibid.,* pp. 132-133.
10. George P. Merrill, *The First One Hundred Years of American Geology* (New Haven, Connecticut, 1924), p. 511.
11. Wallace Stegner, *Beyond the Hundredth Meridian* (Boston, 1954), pp. 127-145. See also Frederick Dellenbaugh, *A Canyon Voyage,* Yale Western Americana Series, No. 4 (New Haven, Connecticut, 1962).
12. Wheeler to O. C. Marsh, Washington, D. C., March 4, 1871, in the Marsh Papers, Peabody Museum, Yale University. For Humphreys' pride in Army achievements, see A. A. Humphreys to James A. Garfield, Washington, D. C., Feb. 5, 1873, in the Humphreys Papers, Pennsylvania Historical Society.
13. Capt. George M. Wheeler, *Report of the United States Geographical Surveys West of the One Hundredth Meridian,* 1 (Washington, 1889), pp. 166-168. Hereafter cited as *Final Report.*
14. Lt. George M. Wheeler, *Preliminary Report Concerning Explorations and Surveys Principally in Nevada and Arizona. . . .* 1871 (Washington, 1872), pp. 93-94. For Stansbury's description, see Howard Stansbury, "Exploration and Survey of the Valley of the Great Salt Lake of Utah," 32nd Cong., Spec. Sess., Sen. Exec. Doc. 3 (1851), p. 105. Henry Engelmann's remarks concerning the Great Basin are in James H. Simpson, *Report of Explorations Across the Great Basin of the Territory of Utah* (Washington, 1876), pp. 302-303. Though published as late as 1876, this report was actually written in 1859. For King's views on the Basin, see Wilkins, *Clarence King,* pp. 123, 213-215.
15. *Ibid.,* pp. 60, 61.
16. Weyss's work appears in *Final Report,* pp. 50-53. Compare this with the work of W. H. Holmes in the "Atlas" and with Clarence Dutton, *The Tertiary History of the Grand Canyon District* (Washington, 1882).
17. Wheeler to Humphreys, Washington, D. C., Feb. 3, 1873, in George M. Wheeler, *Notes Relating to Surveys in the Western Territories of the United States* (n.d., n.p.), Yale Collection of Western Americana, p. 7.
18. Statement of Lt. W. L. Marshall, March 1, 1874, in House Reports, 43d Cong., 1st sess., No. 612, pp. 71-72. Hereafter cited as *Townsend Report.*
19. *Ibid.*

20. *Ibid.*, p. 63. Dr. F. Kampf also supported this testimony.

21. See Letters Received File, United States Geographical and Geological Survey of the Territories (Hayden Survey), Interior Department Records, National Archives, for many examples of this practice.

22. Stegner, *Hundredth Meridian*, pp. 174-191. Wheeler also produced three collections of photographs, which he distributed to interested parties. See Wheeler Papers, Beinecke Collection, Yale University Library.

23. This famous fight is recounted in Henry F. Osborne, *Cope: Master Naturalist* (Princeton, New Jersey, 1931), pp. 402-413. Much of the controversy came to a head in the New York *Herald*, Jan. 12 and Jan. 19, 1890, which featured such headlines as "Scientists Wage Bitter Warfare" and "Marsh Hurls Azoic Facts at Cope."

24. *Townsend Report*, p. 18.

25. *Ibid.*, pp. 73-77.

26. *Ibid.*, p. 51.

27. *Ibid.*, p. 39.

28. *Ibid.*, p. 57.

29. *Ibid.*, pp. 73-77. For the Wheeler-Dana relationship, see Wheeler to Gen. A. A. Humphreys, Washington, D. C., Nov. 11, 1873, in the Wheeler Papers, Beinecke Collection, Yale University Library. Wheeler grants Dana permission to publish his material in preliminary reports in journals and "for insertoin [sic] in a new edition of his work on Geology."

30. See "Message of the President," May 2, 1874, House Executive Documents, 43d Cong., 1st sess., No. 240 (1874).

31. See Exhibit No. 11, "Disclaimer of Faculty of Yale College Concerning Geographical and Geological Surveys West of the Mississippi," June 9, 1874, House Reports, 43d Cong., 2d sess., No. 149 (1874).

32. *Townsend Report*, pp. 16-18.

33. Wheeler to Hon. James G. Blaine, Washington, D. C., Feb. 8, 1875, in the Wheeler Survey Records, RG 77, National Archives.

34. Lt. George M. Wheeler, *Annual Report* (Washington, 1875).

35. W. H. Emory, "Notes of a Military Reconnaissance From Fort Leavenworth, in Missouri, to San Diego, in California, Including Parts of the Arkansas, Del Norte, and Gila Rivers," Senate Documents, 30th Cong., 1st sess., No. 7 (1848), p. 98.

36. Wheeler, *Annual Report*, 1875.

37. E. D. Cope to father, Sept. 14, 1874, in the Cope Papers, American Museum of Natural History, New York, New York. Also quoted in Osborne, *Cope: Master Naturalist*, pp. 200-201.

38. Lt. George M. Wheeler, *Annual Report* (Washington, 1876).

39. *Ibid.*, 1877.

40. *Ibid.*, 1878, 1879.

41. *Ibid.*, 1879, p. 215.

42. W. H. Rideing, "The Wheeler Expedition in Southern Colorado," *Harper's New Monthly Magazine*, 52 (May 1876), p. 800.

43. Wilkins, *Clarence King*, p. 233. Between 1867 and 1878 Congress appropriated the following amounts to the four surveys: Hayden, $690,000; Wheeler, $550,000; King, $387,000; and Powell, $259,000. See William C. Darrah, *Powell of the Colorado* (Princeton, New Jersey, 1951), p. 243.

44. Wheeler to Humphreys, April 28, 1878, in the Wheeler Survey Records, RG 77, National Archives. Powell's admission of the excellence of Wheeler's astronomical work appears in *Townsend Report*, p. 51.

45. Wheeler to Humphreys, April 28, 1878, in the Wheeler Survey Records, RG 77, National Archives.

46. Darrah, *Powell of the Colorado*, p. 248. See also the speeches by western

congressmen Martin Maginnis (Montana), Thomas M. Patterson (Colorado), D. C. Haskell (Kansas), and John D. C. Atkins (Tennessee) of Feb. 18, 1879, in *Congressional Record*, 8, pt. 2, 45th Cong., 3d sess., pp. 1202-1211. See also Stegner, *Hundredth Meridian*, pp. 235-242.

47. Report of the Committee of the National Academy of Science, Nov. 6, 1878, Senate Misc. Documents, 45th Cong., 3d sess., No. 9. The members of the committee were: O. C. Marsh, James D. Dana, William B. Rogers, J. S. Newberry, W. P. Trowbridge, Simon Newcomb, Alexander Agassiz. See also Powell to Marsh, Sept. 24, 1878, in the Marsh Papers, Peabody Museum, Yale University, which reveals Powell's attempt to influence Marsh's Committee; and Powell to Secretary of the Interior Carl Schurz, pp. 971-975, Letters Sent, Jan. 2-Dec. 31, 1878, Rocky Mountain Survey, Interior Department Records, National Archives, in which Powell actually edits Marsh's report.

48. The effect of the post-Civil War explorations and surveys in creating the "tourist's frontier" in the West is a subject deserving of further investigation. Powell's association with various early touring parties such as that of Schuyler Colfax and Governor Hunt of Colorado is well known, as are Hayden's efforts to promote the scenic beauties of the Yellowstone and the ruins of Mesa Verde. King's celebration of "mountaineering in the Sierras" became famous. Wheeler's surveys were represented at the Philadelphia Centennial Exposition of 1876 by Indian artifacts, stereopticon slides, photographs, paintings, maps, and even a plaster model of the San Juan Mountains and the archaeological remains thereat. All of the survey operations were covered in popular magazines like *Scribners' Overland Monthly,* and *Harper's.*

RICHARD A. BARTLETT

John Wesley Powell and the Great Surveys:
A Problem in Historiography

1. The best sources of information on the 1869 river trip are the diaries of the men who made the journey, together with the excellent editorial comment of William C. Darrah in the *Utah Historical Quarterly,* 15 (1947).

2. For a good discussion of the problems of biography, see Allan Nevins, *The Gateway to History* (New York, Doubleday Anchor Books, revised edition 1962), pp. 347-369.

3. William C. Darrah, *Powell of the Colorado* (Princeton, New Jersey, Princeton University Press, 1951) treats Hayden and Wheeler and their surveys adversely and King negligibly. Wallace Stegner, *Beyond the Hundredth Meridian— John Wesley Powell and the Second Opening of the West* (Boston, Houghton Mifflin, 1954) treats the other men and their surveys with great fairness, though because of the biographical nature of the work Powell is naturally emphasized. Thurman Wilkins, *Clarence King* (New York, Macmillan, 1958) assumes all of Hayden's and Wheeler's vices and none of their virtues. A. Hunter Dupree, *Science in the Federal Government* (Cambridge, Massachusetts, Belknap Press of the Harvard University Press, 1947) relies heavily on the works of Stegner and Darrah.

4. Charles D. Walcott, "Ferdinand Vandiveer Hayden," U. S. Geological Survey, *Ninth Annual Report,* 1887-1889, p. 32; John M. Clarke, *James Hall of Albany, Geologist and Paleontologist,* 1811-1898 (Albany, New York, 1932).

5. The interesting details of this trip are described in the letters from Meek to Hall, in George P. Merrill, *The First One Hundred Years of American Geology* (New Haven, Connecticut, Yale University Press, 1924), pp. 699-707.

6. One of Hayden's finest pieces of work in these years, embracing not only geology but most of the natural sciences plus ethnology, is his extensive "On

the Geology and Natural History of the Upper Missouri," *Transactions of the American Philosophical Society*, New Series, 12 (1862).

7. *U. S. Statutes at Large*, 14, p. 470.

8. "James Stevenson," U. S. Geological Survey, *Ninth Annual Report*, 1887-1888, p. 42; "James Stevenson," *American Anthropologist*, New Series, 18 (1916), pp. 552-559.

9. *New York Times*, May 22, 1930, p. 29.

10. Hoffman to Hayden, Feb. 1, 1872, in the Hayden Survey, General Letters Received, RG 57, National Archives. See also "Henry Gannett," *National Geographic Magazine*, 26 (December 1914), p. 610.

11. *Dictionary of American Biography*, 7, p. 136.

12. William Henry Holmes, "Biography of William H. Holmes," Random Records, Volume I, in custody of the Director of the National Collection of Fine Arts, New Museum Building, Washington, D. C. These are scrapbook collections assembled by Mr. Holmes toward the end of his life.

13. *New York Times*, Nov. 14, 1946. Ingersoll published two books about his experiences with the Hayden survey: *Knocking Round the Rockies* (New York, Harper and Brothers, 1883) and *Crest of the Continent* (Chicago, R. R. Donnelley and Sons, 1885), and he wrote extensively for *Scribner's, Harper's*, and *St. Nicholas*.

14. Jackson's experiences are described in his autobiography, *Time Exposure* (New York, Putnam's, 1941), and Harold R. Driggs and William Henry Jackson, *The Pioneer Photographer* (New York, World Publishing Company, 1929).

15. The political appointees were, true enough, often the sons of important men in the government. W. S. Holman, Jr., was the son of Congressman William S. Holman of Indiana, and relatives of Senator Logan of Illinois and of Secretary of the Interior Columbus Delano were among the fortunate "pilgrims"—as the camp men called them—who went along.

16. *Geological and Geographical Surveys*, House Executive Documents, 45th Cong., 2d sess., No. 81, p. 5; *U. S. Statutes at Large*, 20, p. 230.

17. Publications are listed in Laurence F. Schmeckebier, *Catalogue and Index of the Hayden, King, Powell, and Wheeler Surveys*, U. S. Geological Survey, Bulletin No. 222 (Washington, Government Printing Office, 1904).

18. Richard A. Bartlett, "Clarence King's Fortieth Parallel Survey," *Utah Historical Quarterly*, 24 (April 1956), pp. 131-147.

19. The final reports are catalogued under *Professional Papers of the Engineer Department, U. S. Army*, No. 18. The quotation is from Clarence King, *Systematic Geology* (Washington, Government Printing Office, 1878), 1, p. xi.

20. "Copy Book of Letters," in the King Survey, RG 57, National Archives, Feb. 25, 1874.

21. Nov. 26, 1872.

22. "Copy Book of Letters," King Survey, RG 57, National Archives, March 20, 1878. King in this source gave $523,851.90 as the total cost, but he did not include the years 1867 or 1878, which would undoubtedly have brought total expenditures to about $600,000.

23. William C. Darrah, ed., "The Colorado River Expedition of 1869," *Utah Historical Quarterly*, 15 (1947), pp. 9-18.

24. Powell Survey, Letters Received, RG 57, National Archives, Jan. 11, 1873.

25. Gilbert's best known work is his *Report on the Geology of the Henry Mountains* (Washington, Government Printing Office, 1877); Dutton's works include his *Report on the Geology of the High Plateaus of Utah* (Washington, Government Printing Office, 1880). Major Powell's works were first published by the government in 1875, and have since been published in many private editions.

26. Darrah, *Powell of the Colorado*, p. 243.

27. Capt. George M. Wheeler, *Geographical Report*, Vol. I in *Report Upon United States Geographical Surveys West of the One Hundredth Meridian* (Washington, Government Printing Office, 1889), p. 45.

28. *Ibid.*, p. 692. The works of the scientists appear throughout the final reports.

29. Wheeler to Cope, Dec. 19, 1875, April 4, 1877, April 7, 1877, in the Wheeler Survey, Letters Sent, Stanford University Special Collections; Cope to Wheeler, Aug. 27, 1877, in Letters Received. These records were transferred to the National Archives about three years ago.

30. The following texts make no mention of the men of the Great Surveys: Harlow, *The United States—From Wilderness to World Power*, third edition, 1957; Dulles, *The United States Since 1865*, first edition, 1959; Malone and Rauch, *Empire of Liberty: The Genesis and Growth of the United States of America*, first edition, 1960; Bailey, *The American Pageant*, second edition, 1961; Hofstadter, Miller, and Aaron, *The American Republic*, first edition, 1959; Perkins and Van Deusen, *The United States of America—A History*, first edition, 1962. The following texts mention Powell: Morison and Commager, *The Growth of the American Republic*, fourth edition, 1958; Carman, Syrett, and Wishy, *A History of the American People*, second edition, 1961; Hicks, *The American Nation—A History of the United States From 1865 to Present*, third edition, 1955; Current, Williams, and Freidel, *American History—A Survey*, first edition, 1961. The latter and the volume by Carman, Syrett, and Wishy also mention King.

31. Billington, *Westward Expansion*, second edition, 1960, and Clark, *Frontier America*, first edition, 1959. Riegel, *America Moves West*, second edition, 1955, and Hafen and Rister, *Western America*, first edition, 1941, do mention Powell.

32. Howard D. Cramer, "The Scientist in the West, 1870-1880," *Pacific Historical Review*, 12 (September 1943), pp. 239-251.

33. *Ibid.*, pp. 246, 251.

GERALD D. NASH

*Research in Western Economic
History—Problems and Opportunities*

1. In this paper, the West is construed broadly as that portion of the United States lying between the Mississippi River and the Pacific Coast.

2. John Caughey, "The Mosaic of Western History," *Mississippi Valley Historical Review*, 33 (March 1947), pp. 595-606; Earl S. Pomeroy, "Toward a Reorientation of Western History—Continuity and Environment," *ibid.*, 41 (March 1955), pp. 579-600.

3. Robert G. Athearn, "Railroad Renaissance in the Rockies," *Utah Historical Quarterly*, 25 (1957), pp. 1-26, and "The Independence of the Denver and Rio Grande," *ibid.*, 26 (1958), pp. 1-21; Richard C. Overton, *Gulf to Rockies* (Austin, Texas, 1953); William S. Greever, *Arid Domain—The Santa Fe Railroad and Its Western Land Grants* (Stanford, California, 1954); Donald F. Pegrum, *Rate Theories of the California Railroad Commission* (Berkeley, California, 1932); James F. Doster, *Alabama's First Railroad Commission, 1881-1885* (University, Alabama, 1949).

4. Charles N. Dearing, *American Highway Policy* (Washington, 1941), a very general work; for California, see California Surveyor-General, *Report, 1856* (Sacramento, 1856), pp. 43-47, 247-249; California Bureau of Highways, *Report, 1895* (Sacramento, 1896), pp. 6-8, 35-36; Ben Blow, *California Highways* (Los Angeles, 1920), pp. 1-2, 27-31; California Bureau of Highways, *Report, 1920* (Sacramento, 1922), pp. 9-13; Wayne E. Fuller, "Good Roads and Rural Free

Delivery," *Mississippi Valley Historical Review*, 42 (June 1955), pp. 67-72.

5. California Railroad Commission, *Report*, 1920 (Sacramento, 1922), pp. 152-160; for a study of an individual truck line, see Wayne G. Broehl, *Trucks, Trouble, and Triumph: The Norwalk Truck Line Company* (New York, 1954); for airlines, see Frank J. Taylor, *High Horizons . . . the United Air Lines Story* (New York, 1951), and John H. and Peggy Hereford, *The Flying Years—A History of America's Pioneer Airline* [Western Air Lines] (Los Angeles, 1946).

6. C. Raymond Clar, *California Government and Forestry* (Sacramento, 1959), pp. 195-213; California State Board of Examiners, *Report*, 1905 (Sacramento, 1906), p. 23; E. A. Sterling, "The Attitude of Lumbermen Toward Forest Fires," U. S. Department of Agriculture *Yearbook*, 1904 (Washington, 1905), pp. 133-140.

7. Colorado State Forester, *Report*, 1887-88 (Denver, 1888), pp. 3-14, 39-72; California State Forestry Commission, *Report*, 1905 (Sacramento, 1906), pp. 24-26; Oregon State Board of Forestry, *Report*, 1907-08 (Salem, 1908).

8. American Fish Culturists Association, *Proceedings*, 1873 (Albany, New York, 1873), pp. 3-9; U. S. Commissioner on Fisheries, *Report*, 1871 (Washington, 1873), pp. vii ff.; California Fish and Game Commission, *Report*, 1871 (Sacramento, 1872), pp. 5-8; Nebraska Fish Commission, *Report*, 1883 (Lincoln, 1883), pp. 3-6; Utah State Department of Fish and Game, *Report*, 1897-98 (Salt Lake City, 1898), pp. 5 ff.

9. California State Engineer, *Report*, 1880 (Sacramento, 1881), 3; Montana State Engineer, *Report*, 1905 (Helena, 1905), pp. 3-12; Arizona State Engineer, *Report*, 1909-14 (Phoenix, 1914), pp. 56-64; Utah State Engineer, *Report*, 1897-98 (Salt Lake City, 1899), pp. 8-24; Wyoming State Engineer, *Report*, 1893 (Cheyenne, 1894), pp. 14-128; and *ibid.*, 1895-96 (Cheyenne, 1897), pp. 1-15.

10. Will R. King and E. W. Burr, *Handbook of the Irrigation District Laws of the Seventeen Western States of the United States* (Washington, 1920), pp. 7-12, 87-164; Frank Adams, "Irrigation Districts in California, 1887-1915," in California State Department of Engineering, *Bulletin*, No. 2 (Sacramento, 1916); 1887 Cal. Stats. 29; 1876 Utah Stats. 219.

11. Rodman Paul, *California Gold* (Cambridge, Masssachusetts, 1947), pp. 124-170; Eliot Lord, *Comstock Mining and Miners* (reprint, Berkeley, California, 1959); Grant H. Smith, *The History of the Comstock Lode, 1850-1920*, University of Nevada, *Bulletin*, 37, No. 3 (Reno, 1943); Harold F. Williamson and Arnold Daum, *The American Petroleum Industry—The Age of Illumination, 1859-1899* (Evanston, Illinois, 1959).

12. Leonard J. Arrington, *Great Basin Kingdom—An Economic History of the Latter Day Saints, 1830-1900* (Cambridge, Massachusetts, 1958); Edwin T. Coman and Katherine Gibb, *Time, Tide, and Timber—A Century of Pope and Talbot* (Stanford, California, 1949); William I. Parish, *The Charles Ilfeld Company—A Study of the Rise and Decline of Mercantile Capitalism in New Mexico* (Cambridge, Massachusetts, 1961).

13. Allan G. Bogue, *Money at Interest—The Farm Mortgage on the Middle Border* (Ithaca, New York, 1955); Glenn H. Miller, Jr., "The Hawkes Papers: A Case Study of a Kansas City Mortgage Broker's Business, 1871-1888," *Business History Review*, 55 (1960), pp. 18-39.

14. Albert O. Greef, *The Commercial Paper House in the United States* (Cambridge, Massachusetts, 1938); Charles Warren, *Bankruptcy in American History* (Cambridge, Massachusetts, 1935).

15. Wendell Paddock, *Fruit Growing in Arid Regions: An Account of Approved Fruit Growing Practices in the Intermountain Country of the Western United States* (New York, 1910); J. Hendricks, *Western Fruits and How To Grow Them* (Cawker City, Kansas, 1888); Rahno M. MacCurdy, *History of the California Fruit Growers Exchange* (Los Angeles, 1925); William W. Cumber-

land, *Cooperative Marketing: Its Advantages As Exemplified by the California Fruit Growers Exchange* (Princeton, New Jersey, 1917).

16. Samuel W. Geiser, *Horticulture and Horticulturists in Early Texas* (Dallas, 1945), pp. 5-28; Kansas State Horticultural Society, *Report*, 1867-72 (Topeka, 1872); Missouri State Horticultural Society, *Report*, 1859-60 (Jefferson City, 1860).

17. H. R. Shurtleff, *The Log Cabin Myth* (Cambridge, Massachusetts, 1939); Everett N. Dick, *The Sod House Frontier: A Social History of the Northern Plains* (New York, 1937); H. M. Bodfish, ed., *History of Building and Loan in the United States* (Chicago, 1931), pp. 307-624, includes brief outlines of developments in western states; H. M. Bodfish, *Money Lending Practices of Building and Loan Associations in Ohio* (Columbus, Ohio, 1927), is a model study; Marquis and Bessie H. James, *Biography of a Bank: The Story of Bank of America* (New York, 1954).

18. E. W. Patterson, *The Insurance Commissioner in the United States* (Cambridge, Massachusetts, 1927); Spencer L. Kimball, *Insurance and Public Policy . . . Based on Wisconsin Records, 1835-1959* (Madison, Wisconsin, 1960); Joseph B. McLean, *Introduction to Life Insurance* (4 vols., New York, 1948-51), 2; J. Owen Stalson, *Marketing Life Insurance—Its History in America* (Cambridge, Massachusetts, 1942).

19. John P. Young, *San Francisco—A History of the Metropolis* (2 vols., San Francisco, 1912), 1, pp. 383-387; Joseph L. King, *History of the San Francisco Stock and Exchange Board* (San Francisco, 1910), pp. 3-14; Salt Lake City Stock and Mining Exchange, *Constitution and By-Laws* (Salt Lake City, 1913); Louis Loss, *Blue Sky Law* (Boston, 1958), pp. 3-13; Louis Loss, *Securities Regulation* (3 vols., Boston, second edition, 1961), 1, pp. 23-63; Jacob M. Edelman, *Securities Regulation in the 48 States* (Chicago, 1942), pp. 11-28.

20. Hugh S. Hanna, *Labor Laws and Their Administration in the Pacific States*, U. S. Bureau of Labor Statistics, *Bulletin No. 211* (Washington, 1917); Carroll D. Wright, *Index of All Reports Issued by Bureaus of Labor Statistics in the U. S. Prior to March, 1902* (Washington, 1902).

LEE SCAMEHORN

The Development of Air Transportation in the West

1. In this paper, the West is defined as that area encompassing the six plains states, from the Dakotas to Texas, and the eight mountain states, from Montana and Idaho to New Mexico and Arizona.

2. *The Marietta Intelligencer* (Marietta, Ohio), March 8, 1849.

3. The extent of aeronautical experiments throughout the United States preceding and following the Wrights' triumph has not been appreciated by historians. Investigations of two widely separated states, Illinois and Colorado, have been completed by the author of this paper. See *Balloons to Jets—A Century of Aeronautics in Illinois, 1855-1955* (Chicago, 1957), pp. 13-73; "The First Fifty Years of Flight in Colorado," University of Colorado *Studies*, History Series, No. 2 (1961), pp. 102-121.

4. *The Rocky Mountain News* (Denver, Colorado), Jan. 22, 1902.

5. *The Denver Post*, May 7, 1908; May 24, 1908; Sept. 21, 1909; Oct. 28, 1910.

6. *Ibid.*, Aug. 11, 1909.

7. *The Denver Republican*, July 7, 1910.

8. *The Denver Post*, Nov. 29, 1909.

9. *The Rocky Mountain News*, Aug. 19, 1915, and Sept. 15, 1915; *The*

Denver Post, Jan. 20, 1916; Henry Ladd Smith, *Airways—The History of Com-mercial Aviation in the United States* (New York, 1942), p. 55.

10. Smith, *Airways,* p. 55.

11. World War I production and training achievements are discussed in Theodore Macfarlane Knappen, *Wings of War—An Account of the Important Contributions of the United States to Aircraft Invention, Engineering, Develop-ment, and Production During the World War* (New York, 1920), *passim,* and in Edgar S. Gorrell, *The Measure of America's World War Aeronautical Effort,* Norwich University, James Jackson Cabot Lecture, No. 6 (Burlington, Vermont, 1940), pp. 11-56.

12. Unsuccessful postwar airlines included the Apache Aerial Transportation Company of Phoenix, the Aerial Transportation Company of New Jersey, and Alfred W. Lawson of Milwaukee—all of which were projected as transcontinental enterprises. See the New York *Times,* March 14, 1919; *Aviation and Aeronautical Engineering,* 6 (March 15, 1919), p. 229, and 8 (June 1, 1920), p. 362; *Aerial Age Weekly,* 11 (March 22, 1920), p. 51.

13. Manufacturers Aircraft Association, *Aircraft Year Book,* 1921 (Boston, 1921), pp. 15-21; Aeronautical Chamber of Commerce of America, *Aircraft Year Book,* 1924 (New York, c. 1924), pp. 20-26.

14. For the achievements and failures of the government service, see Smith, *Airways,* pp. 60-93; Benjamin B. Lipsner and Leonard Finley Hilts, *The Airmail—Jennies to Jets* (New York and Toronto, c. 1951), pp. 1-211; Paul T. David, *The Economics of Air Mail Transportation* (Washington, 1934), *passim.*

15. *U. S. Statutes at Large,* 43, Pt. 1, p. 805.

16. Aeronautical Chamber of Commerce of America, *Aircraft Year Book,* 1926 (New York, c. 1926), pp. 292-293.

17. Frank J. Taylor, *High Horizons—Daredevil Flying Postmen to Modern Magic Carpet—The United Air Lines Story* (New York, c. 1951), pp. 39-40.

18. U. S. Postmaster General, *Annual Report,* 1934 (Washington, 1935), p. 111. See also David, *The Economics of Air Mail Transportation,* pp. 105-134.

19. U. S. Postmaster General, *Annual Report,* 1934, p. 116; Federal Aviation Agency, *Statistical Handbook of Aviation,* 1960 (Washington, 1961), p. 78; Aeronautical Chamber of Commerce of America, *Aircraft Year Book,* 1928 (New York, c. 1928), p. 450.

20. Thirty years ago, more so than today, airlines could be classified as na-tional, regional, and local. The first two classifications, the trunk lines of the present domestic system, performed essentially the same functions as the trunk lines of today, but on different scales. Both served major traffic centers. The third classification was limited in scope geographically and served few large cities. In the prewar period, regional carriers such as Western Airlines and Continental Air Lines, in the absence of local service companies, provided local service. See Jack Hereford and Peggy Hereford, *The Flying Years—A History of America's Pioneer Airline* ([Los Angeles], c. 1946), *passim;* Lee Scamehorn, "The Air Transport Industry in Colorado," in Carl Ubbelohde, ed., *A Colorado Reader* (Boulder, Colorado, 1962), pp. 308-321.

21. Hereford and Hereford, *The Flying Years,* pp. 20-21; Scamehorn, "The Air Transport Industry in Colorado," p. 312.

22. Smith, *Airways,* p. 140; David, *The Economics of Air Mail Transporta-tion,* pp. 121-122.

23. Smith, *Airways,* pp. 110-111; David, *The Economics of Air Mail Trans-portation,* p. 131; U. S. Postmaster General, *Annual Report,* 1933 (Washington, 1934), p. 103.

24. David, *The Economics of Air Mail Transportation,* p. 132.

25. In 1934, five members of the Independent Scheduled Air Transport Operator's Association were located in the plains states. See Smith, *Airways,* p. 261.

26. U. S. Postmaster General, *Annual Report*, 1934, pp. 114-115.

27. *Ibid*. See also Scamehorn, "The Air Transport Industry in Colorado," pp. 314-315.

28. U. S. Postmaster General, *Annual Report*, 1934, pp. 114-115.

29. For the evolution of modern transport aircraft, see Richard G. Hubler, *Big Eight—A Biography of an Airplane* (New York, c. 1960), pp. 34-49; Harold Mansfield, *Vision—A Saga of the Sky* (New York, c. 1956), *passim*.

30. The trend away from local-stop operations to limited- and one-stop flights is traced with respect to the Watres Act and the efforts of the Post Office Department to create a more stable industry in David, *The Economics of Air Mail Transportation*, pp. 105-157.

31. For Denver's dissatisfaction with the original transcontinental system, see *The Rocky Mountain News*, Oct. 21, 1926; Oct. 23, 1926; June 17, 1927; *The Denver Post*, Dec. 30, 1926; March 19, 1927; May 6, 1937.

32. *The Denver Post*, Feb. 19, 1937; April 19, 1937.

33. Smith, *Airways*, pp. 299, 385, 387.

34. U. S. Interstate Commerce Commission, *Annual Report*, 1941 (Washington, 1941), p. 9.

35. The inadequacy of surface transportation in the West was particularly apparent in the case of railroads. Colorado, which led the eight mountain states, had 5.32 miles of railroad per 100 square miles of territory, in contrast to the national average of 8.5. See U. S. Interstate Commerce Commission, *Annual Report on the Statistics of Railways in the United States*, 1920 (Washington, 1922), p. xi.

36. The number and type of aircraft produced for the armed forces in World War II are listed in U. S. Civil Aeronautics Authority, *U. S. Military Aircraft Acceptances, 1940-1945* (Washington, n.d.). For a discussion of the wartime military air transport effort, see Oliver La Farge, *The Eagle and the Egg* (Boston, 1949), and Reginald M. Cleveland, *Air Transport at War* (New York and London, 1946).

37. 1,056 DC-4 (C-54) planes were produced during the war. U. S. Civil Aeronautics Authority, *U. S. Military Aircraft Acceptances, 1940-1945*, pp. 24, 27, 30.

38. Specifications for the DC-4, the Boeing 307, and the Lockheed Constellation are listed in Leonard Bridgman, ed., *Jane's All the World's Aircraft, 1943-1944* (New York, 1945), pp. 167C, 187C, 209C.

39. Otis F. Bryan, "Technical Developments in Air Transport," *Social Science*, 20 (October, 1945), pp. 272-273; Railroad Committee for the Study of Transportation, *Air Transportation* ([Washington], 1947), pp. 8-9.

40. Federal Aviation Agency, *Statistical Handbook of Aviation*, 1961 (Washington, 1961), p. 85.

41. Henry Ladd Smith, *Airways Abroad—The Story of American World Routes* ([Madison], 1950), pp. 270-274, 278.

42. *American Aviation*, 15 (Feb. 18, 1952), pp. 15-16; (March 17, 1952), p. 72; 16 (June 9, 1952), p. 22.

43. See Air Transport Association brochure, "Better Than a Magic Carpet—Local Service Airlines, Pathways of Movement and Growth," (Washington, [1958]).

44. *Ibid*.

45. Pioneer Air Lines operated in the Southwest until merged with and absorbed by Continental Air Lines in 1955. See Scamehorn, "The Air Transport Industry in Colorado," p. 318.

46. U. S. Interstate Commerce Commission, *Annual Report*, 1961 (Washington, 1961), p. 15.

47. Aeronautical Chamber of Commerce of America, *Aircraft Year Book*, 1927 (New York, c. 1927), p. 317.

48. *Ibid.*, 1931 (New York, c. 1931), p. 40.

49. New York *Times*, April 16, 1961. See also time tables of the appropriate airlines.

50. *The Rocky Mountain News*, Oct. 7, 1962.

51. *The Boulder Daily Camera* (Boulder, Colorado), Jan. 9, 1962; New York *Times*, July 8, 1962.

RAYMOND W. SETTLE

The Role of Russell, Majors & Waddell in Western Overland Transportation

1. Kearny, born in Newark, New Jersey, August 30, 1794, led the Army of the West in the Mexican War. See his recent biography, D. L. Clarke, *Stephen Watts Kearny, Soldier of the West* (Norman, Oklahoma, 1961).

2. Walker D. Wyman, "The Military Phase of Santa Fe Freighting, 1846-1865," *Kansas Historical Quarterly*, 1 (1931-32), pp. 415, 420-422.

3. *Ibid.*, p. 418.

4. Senate Executive Documents, 31st Cong., 1st sess., No. 26, p. 12.

5. Wyman, "The Military Phase of Santa Fe Freighting, 1846-1865," p. 425; Raymond W. and Mary L. Settle, *Empire on Wheels* (Stanford, California, 1949), p. 7.

6. *Lexington* [Missouri] *Weekly Express*, Feb. 23, 1853; Jan. 10, 1855.

7. House Executive Documents, 33d Cong., 1st sess., No. 63, pp. 33-34.

8. Alexander Majors, *Seventy Years on the Frontier* (Columbus, Ohio, 1950), pp. 139-140.

9. "Contract Between William H. Russell, Alexander Majors, and William B. Waddell," Dec. 28, 1854.

10. House Executive Documents, 34th Cong., 1st sess., No. 17, p. 9.

11. "The United States Dr. to Majors & Russell," February 1860.

12. Majors, *Seventy Years on the Frontier*, pp. 141-142.

13. "Articles of Agreement Between Quartermaster Captain Thomas L. Brent and Majors & Russell, February 25, 1857."

14. Majors & Russell, "A Brief Statement of the Claim of Majors & Russell, Also the Evidence upon Which It Rests," p. 26.

15. *Ibid.*, p. 34.

16. *Ibid.*, p. 6; "The United States Dr. to Majors & Russell," February 1860.

17. "Articles of Agreement Between Quartermaster General Thomas S. Jesup of the Army and Russell, Majors & Waddell," Jan. 16, 1858.

18. Charles R. Morehead, "Personal Narrative," in William E. Connelley, *Doniphan's Expedition* (Kansas City, 1907), pp. 611-614.

19. House Reports, 36th Cong., 2d sess., No. 78, p. 302.

20. *Ibid.*, pp. 78-80, 82-83.

21. *Ibid.*, pp. 343, 345.

22. George A. Root and Russell K. Hickman, "Pike's Peak Express Companies," *Kansas Historical Quarterly*, 13 (1944-45), pp. 167-168.

23. Jones, Russell & Company, "Balance Sheet," November 1859; "Articles of Agreement Between Russell, Majors & Waddell and Jones, Russell & Company, October 28, 1859."

24. "An Act to Incorporate the Central Overland California & Pike's Peak Express Company," 1860, *Laws of Kansas, 1859*, pp. 254-259.

25. Root and Hickman, "Pike's Peak Express Companies," pp. 487-488.

26. *Ibid.,* p. 486 and note. Chorpenning, a Pennsylvanian, traveled to California with three companions in 1849. On April 25, 1851, he and Absalom Woodward were awarded the first mail contract for service from Sacramento to Salt Lake City. Woodward was killed by Indians in November of that year. Chorpenning continued to fulfill the mail contract until 1859. See LeRoy R. Hafen, *The Overland Mail* (Cleveland, Ohio, 1926).

27. Raymond W. and Mary L. Settle, *Saddles and Spurs* (Harrisburg, Pennsylvania, 1955), pp. 35-51.

28. "Articles of Agreement Between Quartermaster Captain Stewart Van Vliet and Russell, Majors & Waddell," April 11, 1860.

29. House Reports, 36th Cong., 2d sess., No. 78, is a complete record of the hearings of the Select Committee appointed to investigate Russell, Majors & Waddell's acceptances and the abstracted Indian Trust Fund bonds. For a resumé of the whole case, see Settle and Settle, *Empire on Wheels,* Chapter 12.

30. Post Office Appropriation Bill, March 2, 1861, providing for the Daily Overland Mail; "Contract Between William H. Russell representing the Central Overland California & Pike's Peak Express Company and William B. Dinsmore representing the Overland Mail Company," March 16, 1861.

CLARK C. SPENCE

The Mining Engineer in the West

1. *The Autobiography of John Hays Hammond* (New York, 1935), 1, pp. 63-73; Thomas T. Read, *The Development of Mineral Industry Education in the United States* (New York, 1941), p. 28; Thomas A. Rickard, ed., *Rossiter Worthington Raymond* (New York, 1920), pp. 4-5; Frederick G. Corning, *A Student Reverie* (New York, 1920), p. 35; Edwin Wildman, *Famous Leaders of Industry,* Second Series (Boston, 1921), p. 123.

2. Read, *Development of Mineral Industry Education,* pp. 47, 84-90.

3. *Who's Who in Mining and Metallurgy* (London, 1908), pp. 42, 84; *Who's Who in Engineering, 1922-1923* (Brooklyn, 1922), p. 64; Franklin Harper, ed., *Who's Who on the Pacific Coast* (Los Angeles, 1913), p. 300.

4. *Who's Who in Engineering, 1922-1923,* pp. 1020-1021; Press Reference Library, *Notables of the West* (New York, 1913), 1, p. 409; *Mining and Scientific Press* (San Francisco), 77 (Aug. 6, 1898), p. 135; 79 (Sept. 9, 1899), p. 292; Hammond, *Autobiography,* 2, p. 209; Thomas A. Rickard, *Retrospect* (New York, 1937), pp. 8-9; Thomas A. Rickard, *Interviews With Mining Engineers* (San Francisco, 1922), p. 255.

5. Rickard, *Interviews,* pp. 188, 224-226, 230-236; Mary L. Benn, "Mary Hallack Foote," *The Colorado Magazine,* 33 (April 1956), pp. 97-108; *Mining and Scientific Press,* 48 (June 14, 1884), p. 397.

6. Hammond, *Autobiography,* 1, pp. 83-84.

7. For comments on the superior attitude of the trained engineer, see *ibid.,* 1, p. 147; Richard B. Hughes, *Pioneer Years in the Black Hills,* edited by Agnes W. Spring (Glendale, California, 1957), pp. 288-290; *Mining and Scientific Press,* 47 (Dec. 15, 1883), p. 382. For the running verbal battle between practical and "educated" engineers, see *The Silver Standard* (Silver Plume, Colorado), March 5, 1887; *Anglo-Colorado Mining and Milling Guide* (London), 4 (Jan. 30, 1901), pp. 9-10; *Mining and Scientific Press,* 19 (Dec. 4, 1869), p. 354; 20 (May 28, 1870), p. 360; 26 (June 21, 1873), p. 306; 39 (July 12, 1879), p. 18; 53 (July 17, 1886), p. 34; 66 (Jan. 28, 1893), pp. 52, 53.

8. *Black Hills Pioneer,* quoted in *Mining and Scientific Press,* 60 (Feb. 15, 1890), p. 110. See also 41 (Aug. 21, 1880), p. 120; 53 (July 10, 1886), p.

20; 75 (Dec. 4, 1897), p. 523; *Anglo-Colorado Mining and Milling Guide,* 1 (Oct. 19, 1898), p. 141.

9. See Rickard, *Interviews,* pp. 255, 351; Hammond, *Autobiography,* 1, pp. 86, 106-107; *The Memoirs of Herbert Hoover* (New York, 1951), 1, pp. 17-20; Thurman Wilkins, *Clarence King* (New York, 1958), p. 97; *Who's Who in Mining and Metallurgy,* pp. 5, 6, 9, 19, 23, 29, 37, 67, 77, 87; *Who's Who in Engineering, 1922-1923,* pp. 95, 649; *Dictionary of American Biography,* 3, p. 511; 4, p. 103; 5, pp. 27, 396; 17, p. 263.

10. Copy, Box I, T. J. Lamoureaux Manuscripts, Huntington Library. See also John C. Bloomer, *Pacific Cryptograph . . .* (San Francisco, 1874).

11. *Mining and Scientific Press,* 65 (Aug. 13, 1892), p. 106; 78 (June 3, 1899), p. 582.

12. Rickard, *Retrospect,* pp. 81-82; Robert M. Brereton, *Reminiscences of an Old English Civil Engineer* (Portland, Oregon, 1908), p. 34.

13 *Mining and Scientific Press,* 66 (Jan. 28, 1893), p. 52. For the Camp Bird case and others where engineers ran into difficulties from relying on information furnished by others, see *Mining and Scientific Press,* 42 (April 9, 1881), p. 232; Rickard, *Retrospect,* p. 76; Rickard, *R. W. Raymond,* p. 56; *Financial Times* (London), Dec. 8, 1900; William N. Symington, *Report on the Quality and Value of the Ore in Sight in the Robinson Mine, Summit County, Colo.* (n.p., 1881), pp. 2-4.

14. For Janin and the great diamond fraud, see Wilkins, *Clarence King,* pp. 159-168; *The Times* (London), Dec. 2, 1872; *Bulletin of the American Institute of Mining Engineers,* No. 53 (May 1911), pp. xxviii-xxxvi; Henry Janin, *A Brief Statement of My Part in the Unfortunate Diamond Affair* (San Francisco, 1873).

15. *Henry v. Mayer, et al.,* 53 *Pacific Reporter* (1898), p. 590; *Mudsill Mining Company, Ltd., et al. v. Watrous, et al.,* 61 *Federal Reporter* (1894), pp. 164-190; Charles Siringo, *A Cowboy Detective* (Chicago, 1912), pp. 74-84; Brereton, *Reminiscences,* p. 38; *Mining and Scientific Press,* 69 (July 28, 1894), p. 50.

16. *The Silver Standard,* Sept. 10, 1887.

17. *Mining and Scientific Press,* 52 (April 10, 1886), p. 238; 95 (Sept. 7, Oct. 17, 1907), pp. 286, 522; *Lindemann v. Belden Consolidated Mining & Milling Company,* 16 *Colorado Appeals* (1901), pp. 342-348.

18. *Mining and Scientific Press,* 66 (Jan. 7, 1893), p. 4.

19. Quoted in *ibid.,* 70 (Jan. 12, 1895), p. 23.

20. *Ibid.,* 95 (July 20, 1907), p. 79. For a humorous, tongue-in-cheek, fictitious mine report by "Professor Noncommital," see *The Nevada Monthly* (Virginia City), 1 (July 1880), p. 247.

21. *Engineering News,* 28 (Oct. 6, 1892), p. 328.

22. *Mining and Scientific Press,* 75 (Oct. 30, 1897), p. 406.

23. *Ibid.,* 95 (Aug. 24, 1907), p. 237.

24. James P. Whitney, *Colorado, in the United States of America* (London, 1867), p. 57. For other comments on this problem, see John Wetherbee, *A Letter on Colorado Matters to the Stockholders of Excelsior Co.* (Boston, 1867), p. 47; Samuel Cushman and J. P. Waterman, *The Gold Mines of Gilpin County, Colorado* (Central City, Colorado, 1876), pp. 32-33.

25. Rickard, *Interviews,* pp. 433-434; Harry J. Newton, *Pitfalls of Mining Finance* (Denver, 1904), pp. 64, 141; Henry B. Clifford, *Rocks in the Road to Fortune* (New York, 1908), pp. 77-78.

26. Rickard, *Interviews,* p. 408; J. C. Bayles, "Professional Ethics," *Trans. A.I.M.E.* (1885-86), p. 611; John Hays Hammond, "Professional Ethics," *Trans. A.I.M.E.* (1908), pp. 623-624.

27. *Mining and Scientific Press,* 73 (Sept. 29, 1896), p. 234.

28. *Ibid.,* 35 (Aug. 25, 1877), p. 121; 66 (June 3, 1893), p. 340.

29. Wilkins, *Clarence King*, pp. 350-351; Rickard, *Interviews*, p. 306; Thomas A. Rickard, *A History of American Mining* (New York and London, 1932), p. 364.

30. Rickard, *Interviews*, pp. 76, 78-80; *Dictionary of American Biography*, 3, pp. 186-187; 20, pp. 374-375.

31. Rickard, *Interviews*, p. 106; Rickard, *R. W. Raymond*, pp. 10-11; Rickard, *Retrospect*, pp. 66-67; *Mining and Scientific Press*, 44 (Feb. 11, 1882), p. 96; 79 (Feb. 6, 1897), p. 110; Kahn v. Old Telegraph Mining Company, et al., 2 *Utah Reports* (1877), p. 174.

32. From "Lawyers and Experts," quoted in Rickard, *R. W. Raymond*, p. 95.

33. G. T. Ingham, *Digging Gold Among the Rockies* (Philadelphia, 1881), pp. 196, 199; *Mining and Scientific Press*, 25 (Dec. 7, 14, 1872), pp. 360, 380; Joshua E. Clayton to J. H. Stallan, Salt Lake, Feb. 20, 1873, copy in Letterbook III, Joshua E. Clayton Manuscripts, Bancroft Library.

34. Hammond, *Autobiography*, 1, p. 149; Rickard, *Retrospect*, p. 81.

35. Hammond, *Autobiography*, 1, p. 145; *Dictionary of American Biography*, 17, pp. 273-274. See also Joshua E. Clayton to [?] Brown, Salt Lake, Jan. 15, 1883, copy, in Letterbook II, Clayton Manuscripts; Henry Janin to James D. Hague, London, April 4, 1899, Box 12, and James D. Hague to R. J. Wilson, New York, May 15, 1890, copy, in Letterbook XIII, James D. Hague Manuscripts, Huntington Library.

36. Rickard, *History of American Mining*, p. 324; *Who's Who in Engineering*, 1922-1923, p. 179.

37. *Democrat* (Baker, Oregon), quoted in *Mining and Scientific Press*, 79 (Sept. 2, 1899), p. 257.

38. Hammond, *Autobiography*, 1, p. 148. For examples of fees and salaries, see Hoover, *Memoirs*, 1, p. 27; *Mining and Scientific Press*, 42 (April 9, 1881), p. 232; 53 (Nov. 13, 1886), p. 309; 95 (Aug. 10, 1907), p. 173; *Report of Committee of Investigation Appointed by Stockholders of the Wide West Mining Company, January 25th, 1864* (San Francisco, 1864), p. 7; Cash Statement from Sept. 1870, to Oct. 1871, of the Eberhardt and Aurora Mining Company, Ltd., in the William Read Manuscripts, Bancroft Library; business diary of James Thomson, entry for Nov. 6, 1872, in the Bodleian Library, Oxford University; "Emma Mine Investigation," House Reports, 44th Cong., 1st sess., No. 579 (1875-1876), pp. 126, 669; *Anglo-Colorado Mining and Milling Guide*, 5 (Oct. 31, 1902), p. 150; Stratton's Independence, Ltd., *Annual Report*, year ending June 30, 1901.

39. Edward T. McCarthy, *Further Incidents in the Life of a Mining Engineer* (New York, n. d.), p. 58.

40. Rickard, *Retrospect*, p. 53; Rickard, *Interviews*, pp. 535-536.

41. Raphael Pumpelly, *My Reminiscences* (New York, 1918), 1, pp. 182-197; Rickard, *Retrospect*, pp. 54-55, 61; *Mining and Scientific Press*, 38 (Aug. 24, 1878), p. 114.

42. Hammond, *Autobiography*, 1, pp. 90-91, 172-175.

43. *Mining and Scientific Press*, 43 (Aug. 6, 1881), p. 86.

44. Pumpelly, *My Reminiscences*, 1, pp. 200, 202-205, 218, 226.

45. New Colorado Silver Mining Company, Ltd., *Directors' Report*, Nov. 15, 1892, to May 31, 1894. See also Rickard, *Retrospect*, p. 54.

46. *Mining and Scientific Press*, 95 (Dec. 14, 1907), p. 727.

47. Hoover, *Memoirs*, 1, p. 27; Hammond, *Autobiography*, 1, p. 86.

48. *Ibid.*, 1, p. 179. See also Rickard, *Interviews*, p. 377; McCarthy, *Further Incidents*, p. 290; Robert M. Brereton to James D. Hague, London, Jan. 9, 1886, in Box 22, Hague Manuscripts.

49. *Mining and Scientific Press*, 68 (June 2, 1894), p. 339; 69 (Nov. 17, 1894), p. 311; 70 (March 9, 1895), p. 151; 78 (April 29, 1899), p. 459.

50. For a typical expression of such views, see Brereton, *Reminiscences*, p. 5.

51. *Mining and Scientific Press,* 70 (April 13, 1895), p. 227; 75 (Nov. 29, 1902), p. 319; Rickard, *Retrospect,* pp. 56, 57, 300, 304; Rickard, *Interviews,* pp. 99-100, 395; Rickard, *Across the San Juan Mountains* (San Francisco, 1907), pp. 41-43; Hammond, *Autobiography,* 1, pp. 188-191; 2, pp. 492-494; Vernon H. Jensen, *Heritage of Conflict* (Ithaca, New York, 1950), pp. 28-36, 74-86, 112, 266-269; *Trans. A.I.M.E.* (1903), pp. 835-838.

52. *Who's Who on the Pacific Coast,* pp. 191, 222-223, 300; *Who's Who in Engineering, 1922-1923,* pp. 117, 811, 1000, 1026, 1412; Amanda M. Ellis, *The Strange, Uncertain Years* (Hamden, Connecticut, 1959), p. 201; *Biographical Directory of the American Congress* (Washington, 1950), p. 1113.

53. Hammond, *Autobiography,* 2, pp. 527-531, 534, 633.

54. *Mining and Scientific Press,* 30 (June 19, 1875), p. 304; 39 (Aug. 2, 9, 1879), pp. 66, 86; 44 (June 24, 1882), p. 416; *United States Annual Mining Review and Stock Ledger . . . for the Year 1879* (New York, 1879), pp. 27-28; William P. Blake, *A Winter Trip to the Mines of the West* (New York, 1880), pp. 1-11; Robert W. Sloan, ed., *Utah Gazetteer and Directory of Logan, Ogden, Provo, and Salt Lake Cities* (Salt Lake, 1884), p. 604.

55. *A History of American Mining* (1932). *His Man and Metals* (1932) and *The Romance of Mining* (1945) are also of historical interest.

56. Rickard, *Retrospect,* p. 60; *Who's Who on the Pacific Coast,* p. 339; *Mining and Scientific Press,* 28 (May 9, 1874), p. 289; 41 (Sept. 25, 1880), p. 200; 44 (March 18, 1882), p. 187; 48 (March 8, April 5, 1884), pp. 171, 240.

57. *Ibid.,* 54 (April 23, 1887), p. 268; 72 (Jan. 4, 1896), p. 16; *Who's Who in Mines and Metallurgy,* pp. 17, 20, 34; Read, *Development of Mineral Industry Education,* p. 98.

58. For example, Americans had difficulty in constructing a workable mining dredge until Robert H. Postlethwaite of New Zealand came to San Francisco in 1896 and helped the Risdon Iron Works produce a successful machine patterned on those in operation in his homeland. Subsequently, Risdon and the Union Works produced the dredges for export—even to New Zealand. *Engineering and Mining Journal,* 64 (Dec. 11, 1897), p. 699; *Who's Who in Engineering, 1922-1923,* p. 1009.

59. *Mining and Scientific Press,* 72 (Jan. 18, 1896), p. 43; 76 (Jan. 1, 1898), p. 4; Rickard, *Interviews,* pp. 242, 245-246, 249.

DONALD C. CUTTER
Spanish Scientific Exploration Along the Pacific Coast

1. José Luis Benítez Miura, "El Doctor Francisco Hernández, 1514-1578," *Anuario de Estudios Americanos,* 7 (Sevilla, 1950), pp. 367-405.

2. Published as *De Historia Plantarum Novae Hispaniae* (3 vols., Madrid, 1790).

3. Sessé to Ortega, Havana, Jan. 30, 1785, in Archives of the Real Jardín Botánico, Madrid, 4ta División, legajo 19.

4. The career of Malaspina is summarized in "Antiguidades de los oficiales de guerra de la Armada," Museo Naval, Madrid, tomo 1161 bis. Museo Naval hereafter cited as MN.

5. Lt. José Espinosa y Tello had extracted the narrative of Ferrer Maldonado from the Archivo General de Indias prior to departure of the expedition. See "Correspondencia relativa al viage de Malaspina," hereafter cited as Malaspina Correspondencia, Tomo A, ff. 47-48, MN 583.

6. Half-pay Captain John Meares and Ensign Esteban José Martínez were the principal catalytic agents in the controversy.

7. Documents on the observation of the transit of Venus by Medina and Doz are found in "Papeles Apreciables," II, MN 147.

8. A list of equipment is in "Viaje al Estrecho de Fuca," Tomo II, MN 144. Manifests of the Sutil and Mexicana upon departure from San Blas are contained in Archivo Histórico Nacional, Madrid, Estado 4290, as are also Malaspina's instructions to the crews (Estado 4288). Archivo Histórico Nacional hereafter cited as AHN.

9. For biographical data on Cardero, see Donald C. Cutter, *Malaspina in California* (San Francisco, 1960), pp. 12-16.

10. To name a few: Galiano Island, Valdés Island, Quadra Island, Maurelle Island, Tejada Island, Tofiño Inlet, Salamanca Canal, Cardero Island, Vernacci Sound, Toba Inlet, and Haro Strait.

11. Published in Spanish in *Relación del viage hecho por las goletas Sutil y Mexicana en el año de 1792*, as well as in an atlas on the voyage published in Madrid in 1802 and again in 1958; and in English in Cecil Jane, ed., *A Spanish Voyage to Vancouver and the Northwest Coast of America* (London, 1930) and in Henry R. Wagner, *Spanish Explorations in the Strait of Juan de Fuca* (Santa Ana, California, 1933).

12. "Vargas Ponce," MN 1060, seemingly in the hand of José Cardero. Manuscript copies of the shortened version of the "Voyage of the Sutil and Mexicana" are located in AHN, Estado 4290; Archivo General de la Nación, Mexico, Historia 31; MN 143, 144; MN 468. Archivo General de la Nación hereafter cited as AGN.

13. Lesley B. Simpson, trans. and ed., *Journal of José Longinos Martínez* (San Francisco, 1961). For a scholarly treatment of Longinos' activities, see Iris H. Wilson, "Scientific Aspects of Spanish Exploration in New Spain During the Late 18th Century" (Ph.D. Dissertation, University of Southern California, 1962).

14. "Viaje a la Costa N. O. de la America Septentrional por Don Juan Francisco de la Bodega y Quadra. . . ." [1792], Manuscript No. 145, in Archivo del Ministerio de Asuntos Exteriores, Madrid; also in Vol. XXX, Revilla Gigedo Collection, in Bancroft Library.

15. Sessé to Revilla Gigedo, Mexico, May 9, 1793, in AGN, Historia 527.

16. The dictionary is available in many places in manuscript; Alberto M. Carreño edited a version which was published in Mexico in 1913. Though of great interest for its anthropological information, it has never been published in English. Manuscript copies can be found in MN 142 and 468; Vol. XXXII, Revilla Gigedo Collection, in the Bancroft Library; in the Beinecke Collection, Yale University Library; in the Sociedad Mexicana de Geografía y Estadística; and in the AGN. The original illustrations have never been discovered. Only recently did some copies come to light. A copy of the entire series became available in the Revilla Gigedo Collection in the Bancroft Library, and a second copy (Manuscript No. 146) was discovered by the author of this paper in the Archivo del Ministerio de Asuntos Exteriores, in Madrid.

These two sets had been executed with considerable care at the Academia de San Carlos by Echeverría's associates: Tomás Suria, José Cardero, Gabriel Gil, Julián Marchena, J. Vicente de la Cerdá, José María Montes de Oca, Francisco Lindo, José María Guerrero, José María Vásquez, M. García, José Castañeda, Mendoza, Nicolas Moncayo, José Mariano de Aguila, Miguel Albián, and Manuel López; Suria, Cardero, Lindo, and Cerdá all had been associated with the Malaspina enterprise. Some of these drawings doubtless were sketched during an excursion Echeverría made with Naturalist José Maldonado on a side trip out of Nootka under the command of Lt. Jacinto Caamaño in 1792. The journal of this expedition is presented in "Extracto del Diario de Navegaciones, exploraciones y descubrimientos hechos en la America Septentrional por D. Jacinto Caamaño. . . . del año de 1792," Manuscript No. 10, in Archivo del Ministerio de Asuntos Exteriores, Madrid.

17. Chief of Charts and Maps Felipe Bauzá of the Malaspina expedition was particularly proficient at coastal profiles. Most of the profiles are on file in the Museo Naval.

18. Almost a century afterwards, some of the results of the Malaspina expedition were published in Pedro de Novo y Colson, ed., *La Vuelta al Mundo por las corbetas DESCUBIERTA y ATREVIDA al Mando del Capitán de Navío D. Alejandro Malaspina desde 1789 a 1794* (Madrid, 1885). Hereafter cited as *Vuelta al Mundo*.

19. Malaspina Correspondencia, Tomo A, ff. 12-16, MN 583.

20. Ibid., f. 48.

21. Haenke has recently been treated extensively by Joseph Kuhnel, in *Thaddaeus Haenke: Leben und Wirken eines Forschers*.

22. Malaspina Correspondencia, Vol. I, f. 81, MN 278.

23. Valdés to Malaspina, Madrid, July 21, 1789, in *ibid*.

24. Table of apparent altitudes of Mt. St. Elias is in "Curiosidades Sueltas," MN 169.

25. The simple pendulum experiments are described in "Papeles Apreciables," III, MN 148.

26. "Relación de maderas de Mulgrave, de Nutka, de Monterey in Pacífico América," Tomo I, MN 126.

27. "Descripciones del Sr. Gonzáles hechas en el viage a los 60° N," in Pineda Notes in Archivo del Museo de Ciencias Naturales, Madrid.

28. "Libro de Guardias, Descubierta," MN 729; "Libro de Guardias, Atrevida," MN 755.

29. Malaspina Correspondencia, Tomo A, ff. 98-99, MN 583.

30. "Noticias que nos dió Maquina," in California y Costa N. O. de America, Tomo I, MN 330.

31. A copy of the purchase of land from the Nootkans, appropriately notarized, is in AHN, Estado 4290.

32. Justino Fernández, *Tomás de Suria y su viage con Malaspina, 1791* (Mexico, 1939). The original journal is in the Yale University Library.

33. Alcalá Galiano and Valdés to Revilla Gigedo, Mexico, March 3, 1793, in AGN, Marina 82; Joseph Cardero, "Expediente matrimonial," in Archivo General Militar, Segovia.

34. Malaspina to Josef Espinosa, Nutka, Aug. 17, 1791, in "Apuntes, Noticias y correspondencias pertenecientes a la Expedición de Malaspina," MN 427.

35. "Libro de Guardias, Descubierta," MN 729.

36. Willis L. Jepson, *The Silva of California* (Berkeley, California, 1910), p. 138.

37. *Anales de Ciencias* (Madrid, 1801), 3.

38. All the California drawings are published in Cutter, *Malaspina in California*.

39. *Vuelta al Mundo*, p. 447.

40. Felipe Bauzá, "Viaje alrededor del Mundo, 1789-96," MN 749.

41. Ibid.; Cutter, *Malaspina in California*, p. 31.

42. Baron A. de Humboldt, *Ensayo Político sobe Nueva España* (Jalapa, 1869), 1, p. 261.

43. The appropriate document is entitled "Relativo a la causa reserbada que se les formo a Don Alejandro Malaspina, P. Manuel Gil, Sra. Marquesa de Matallana," in AHN, Estado 3150.

HOWARD R. LAMAR

The Reluctant Admission: The Struggle
To Admit Arizona and New Mexico to the Union

1. The Arizona statehood movement is treated briefly in Frank C. Lockwood, *Pioneer Days in Arizona* (New York, 1932), pp. 368-378; that of New Mexico more thoroughly in Marion Dargan, "New Mexico's Fight for Statehood, 1895-1912," *New Mexico Historical Review*, 14 (January 1939), pp. 1-33, 121 ff.; 15, pp. 133 ff.; 16, pp. 70-103, 379-400. See also Claude G. Bowers, *Beveridge and the Progressive Era* (New York, 1932), pp. 182 ff.

2. Dargan, "New Mexico's Fight"; and the following University of New Mexico Master's Theses, housed in the Coronado Room of the University Library: Archie M. McDowell, "The Opposition to Statehood Within the Territory of New Mexico, 1888-1903" (1939); Beatrice A. Cottrell, "Senate Action on the Omnibus Bill of 1902" (1938); Charles E. Maddox, "The Statehood Policy of Albert J. Beveridge, 1901-1911" (1938); Dorothy E. Thomas, "The Final Years of New Mexico's Struggle for Statehood, 1907-1912" (1939); Mary J. Masters, "New Mexico's Struggle for Statehood, 1903-1907" (1942).

3. LaMoine Langston, "Arizona's Fight for Statehood in the Fifty-Seventh Congress" (Master's Thesis, University of New Mexico, 1939), pp. 11 ff.

4. Lockwood, *Pioneer Days*, pp. 368-369.

5. See discussion in *Journals of the Constitutional Convention for the State of Arizona* (Phoenix, 1891), pp. 56 ff.

6. McDowell, "Opposition to Statehood," pp. 13, 23, 25, 29-52 passim, 54.

7. Langston, "Arizona's Fight," p. 5.

8. George H. Kelly, *Arizona Legislative History, 1864-1912* (Phoenix, 1920), p. 302.

9. Will H. Robinson, *The Story of Arizona* (Phoenix, 1919), p. 173.

10. *Ibid.*, pp. 176-177.

11. Lockwood, *Pioneer Days*, p. 369.

12. McDowell, "Opposition to Statehood," pp. 76, 82 ff., 88 ff.

13. Masters, "New Mexico's Struggle," pp. 2-4.

14. See Cottrell, "Senate Action on the Omnibus State Bill of 1902."

15. Beveridge's career as Chairman of the Committee on Territories is summarized in Maddox, "Beveridge." See also Bowers, *Beveridge and the Progressive Era*, p. 194.

16. During the congressional debates in 1902 and 1903 it was stressed that Oklahoma was not arid, illiterate, or underpopulated.

17. Maddox, "Beveridge," p. 11.

18. *Ibid.*, pp. 12-13, 43-46, 57; Langston, "Arizona's Fight," pp. 33, 35-36; Bowers, *Beveridge and the Progressive Era*, pp. 195-197.

19. Maddox, "Beveridge," pp. 47-50.

20. Quoted in Langston, "Arizona's Fight," p. 49.

21. Maddox "Beveridge," pp. 69, 72.

22. Waldemar Westergaard, "Senator Thomas R. Bard and the Arizona-New Mexico Controversy," *Annual Publications, Historical Society of Southern California*, 11 (Los Angeles, 1919), pp. 11-12.

23. Maddox, "Beveridge," p. 85.

24. This fact becomes apparent in a perusal of the Official Papers and Letterbooks of Governors M. A. Otero, W. J. Hagerman, and George Curry, which in 1959 were still maintained by the New Mexico State Historical Society, in Santa Fe.

25. See, for example, George Curry to Theodore Roosevelt, Aug. 14, 1907, copy in Official Papers. See also Thomas, "The Final Years of New Mexico's Struggle," pp. 65-68.

26. Maddox, "Beveridge," pp. 90-92.

27. Masters, "New Mexico's Struggle," p. 20.

28. Ibid., pp. 123-127.

29. Ibid., p. 110; Donald B. Leopard, "Joint Statehood, 1906" (Master's Thesis, University of New Mexico, 1958), pp. 11, 24, 33.

30. Maddox, "Beveridge," pp. 85-92.

31. Leopard, "Joint Statehood" is based on a study of the Bursum Papers. See especially pp. 1.ʳ-18.

32. Ibid., pp. 61-62.

33. Ibid., p. 62.

34. Curry to Jefferson Raynolds, Jan. 16, 1908, copy in Official Papers.

35. Andrews to Curry, Dec. 31, 1907, copy in Official Papers.

36. Andrews to Curry, Dec. 23, 1908, telegram in Official Papers; Bowers, Beveridge and the Progressive Era, p. 301.

37. Arizona Journal-Miner, Oct. 14, 1909.

38. For an excellent day-to-day account of the statehood crusade and the 1910 constitutional convention, see the George W. P. Hunt Scrapbooks in the Special Collections Room of the University of Arizona Library.

39. See Curry to Andrews, Feb. 16, 1910, copy in Official Papers.

40. Thomas, "Final Years," p. 79.

41. Daily Globe (Arizona), July 19, 1910, and Daily Silver Belt, undated, in the Hunt Scrapbooks.

42. Arizona Gazette (Phoenix), Feb. 10, 1911, in the Hunt Scrapbooks.

43. Andrews to Curry, Feb. 4, 1909, in Official Papers.

44. L. B. Prince, "Statehood Pamphlet," in Official Papers of Governor Otero.

ALSO CONSULTED

The Statehood Letters of Harvey B. Fergusson. University of New Mexico Library, Albuquerque.

Miscellaneous Manuscripts and Documents Relating to the New Mexico Constitutional Convention of 1910. New Mexico Historical Society.

Private Letterbooks of M. A. Smith, 1900-1905. Special Collections Room, University of Arizona Library.

Journals of the Constitutional Convention for the State of Arizona (Phoenix, 1891).

Proceedings of the Arizona Convention for Statehood (Phoenix, 1893).

Arizona Pioneers Historical Society folders on Statehood.

GUSTIVE O. LARSON

Brigham Young and the Indians

1. "L.D.S. [Latter-day Saints] Journal History," July 31, 1847.

2. Howard Stansbury, Exploration and Survey of the Valley of the Great Salt Lake (Philadelphia, 1852), pp. 148-149.

3. Wilford Woodruff in Journal of Discourses, 4, p. 231.

4. Journal of Discourses, 1, pp. 106-107.

5. Ibid., 4, p. 41.

6. "History of Brigham Young," manuscript in Latter-day Saints Church Historian's Office, Salt Lake City, Utah, 1850, p. 121.

7. Journal of Discourses, 6, p. 328.

8. "History of Brigham Young," 1852, p. 51.

9. Ibid., 1849, p. 155.

10. Thomas D. Brown, "Journal," quoted by Juanita Brooks in *Utah Historical Quarterly*, 12, p. 11.

11. *Book of Mormon*, II Nephi 20:5-6.

12. R. G. Cleland and Juanita Brooks, *A Mormon Chronicle Diaries of John D. Lee* (2 vols., San Marino, California, 1955), 1, p. 108.

13. "History of Brigham Young," 1851, p. 846.

14. *Deseret News* (Salt Lake City), Jan. 10, 1852.

15. *Territorial Papers*, Department of State, Utah Territory, in National Archives, p. 11.

16. Letter on file at Utah State Historical Society.

17. *Western Humanities Review*, 6, p. 253.

18. "History of Brigham Young," Feb. 6, 1855.

19. Letters Received and Letters Sent, Utah Superintendency, 1849-80, RG 75, Records of the Office of Indian Affairs.

20. House Executive Documents, 35th Cong., 1st sess., No. 71, pp. 128-130.

21. *Ibid.*, Dec. 28, 1851, pp. 133-136.

22. *Ibid.*, pp. 138-139.

23. Young to Lea, May 28, 1852, in the Utah Superintendency files, Office of Indian Affairs.

24. Dale Morgan, "Indian Affairs in Utah," *Pacific Historical Review*, 27, p. 389.

25. House Executive Documents, 35th Cong., 1st sess., No. 71, p. 176.

26. Some typical sermons are in *Journal of Discourses*, 1, pp. 106-107, 171; 4, p. 231; 15, p. 282; 17, p. 300.

27. "History of Brigham Young," 1853, pp. 149-152.

28. Hurt to Manypenny in the *Report of the Commissioner of Indian Affairs*, 1855, p. 201.

29. Quoted by Andrew L. Neff in *History of Utah*, p. 383, without a source cited, which is probably "History of Brigham Young."

30. Letters Sent, Office of Indian Affairs, 1855, Vol. 52, p. 2.

31. Young's Quarterly Report to Commissioner, June 30, 1856.

32. Hurt to Manypenny, March 30, 1857, in Letters Received, Office of Indian Affairs.

33. Senate Executive Documents, 35th Cong., 1st sess., No. 11, pp. 7-8.

34. *Journal of Discourses*, 7, p. 58; 5, p. 236.

35. *Ibid.*, 10, p. 107.

36. Unratified Treaties File, Department of Indian Affairs.

37. Original in Unratified Treaties File, Department of Indian Affairs.

NEAL LAMBERT

Owen Wister—The "Real Incident" and the "Thrilling Story"

1. Fanny K. Wister, "Letters of Owen Wister, Author of the Virginian," *The Pennsylvania Magazine of History and Biography*, 83 (1959), p. 8.

2. *Ibid.*, p. 21.

3. *Ibid.*, p. 7. Italics supplied.

4. Owen Wister, *Red Men and White* (New York, Harper and Brothers, 1896), pp. viii-ix. Italics supplied.

5. Fanny K. Wister, ed., *Owen Wister Out West* (Chicago, University of Chicago Press, 1958), p. 256.

6. Owen Wister, "Second Missouri Compromise," *Harper's*, 90 (March 1895), pp. 534-545.

7. Thomas Donaldson, *Idaho of Yesterday* (Caldwell, Idaho, Caxton Printers,

Ltd., 1941), pp. 247-251. See also W. J. McConnell, *Early History of Idaho* (Caldwell, Idaho, Caxton Printers, Ltd., 1913), pp. 344-349.

8. Owen Wister, *Red Men and White*, p. 132.

9. *Ibid.*

10. Owen Wister, "Pilgrim on the Gila," *Harper's,* 91 (November 1895), pp. 837-864.

11. Secretary of War, *Annual Report,* 1889, pp. 186-187.

12. Fanny K. Wister, *Owen Wister Out West*, p. 226.

13. *Ibid.,* p. 191.

14. *Ibid.,* p. 220.

15. *Ibid.,* p. 188.

16. *Ibid.,* p. 192.

17. Capt. Frank A. Edwards to Owen Wister, Jan. 7, 1894. This and the other letters that Edwards wrote to Wister are in the files of the Historical Society of Pennsylvania.

18. Owen Wister, "Little Big Horn Medicine," *Harper's,* 89 (June 1894), pp. 118-132.

19. Secretary of War, *Annual Report,* 1887, p. 146. See also Edwards to Wister, Feb. 11, 1894.

20. *Ibid.,* 1888, p. 148.

21 *Ibid.,* p. 149.

22. Edwards to Wister, Jan. 7, 1894.

23. Fanny K. Wister, "Letters of Owen Wister," p. 14.

24. Fanny K. Wister, *Owen Wister Out West*, pp. 193-194.

25. Owen Wister, "Balaam and Pedro," *Harper's,* 88 (January 1894), pp. 293-307.

26. Fanny K. Wister, *Owen Wister Out West*, p. 110.

27. Owen Wister, "Balaam and Pedro," p. 303.

28. Fanny K. Wister, "Letters of Owen Wister," p. 19.

29. Owen Wister, *Members of the Family* (New York, Macmillan, 1911), p. 11.

30. Owen Wister, *Roosevelt—The Story of a Friendship* (New York, Macmillan, 1930), p. 319.

31. Fanny K. Wister, *Owen Wister Out West*, p. 16.

32. *Ibid.,* p. 197.

MERRILL E. LEWIS

History as Melodrama: Theodore Roosevelt's
The Winning of the West

1. Henry F. Pringle, *Theodore Roosevelt* (New York, Harcourt, Brace, 1931), p. 97.

2. Dixon Wecter, *The Hero in America* (New York, Charles Scribner's Sons, 1941), pp. 376-377.

3. Elting E. Morison, ed., *The Letters of Theodore Roosevelt* (Cambridge, Massachusetts, Harvard University Press, 1951), 1, p. 95. He actually took *Anna Karenina.*

4. Quoted by Wecter in *The Hero in America*, p. 374.

5. Quoted by Charles Fenton in "Theodore Roosevelt as an American Man of Letters," *Western Humanities Review,* 13 (Autumn 1959), p. 272.

6. Wecter, *The Hero in America*, pp. 374-375.

7. Hermann Hagedorn, *Roosevelt in the Bad Lands* (Boston, Houghton Mifflin, 1921), p. x.

8. Quoted by Wecter in *The Hero in America*, p. 389.

9. Morison, ed., *Letters*, 1, p. 94.

10. Theodore Roosevelt, *Literary Essays*, National Edition (New York, Charles Scribner's Sons, 1926), p. 247.

11. *Ibid.*, p. 5.

12. *Ibid.*, pp. 10-11.

13. *Ibid.*, pp. 12-13, 17.

14. Morison, ed., *Letters*, 1, p. 749.

15. *Ibid.*, pp. 120-123; Theodore Roosevelt, *The Winning of the West* (New York, G. P. Putnam's, 1900), 1, pp. 221-222.

16. Theodore Roosevelt, "Books for Holidays in the Open," *Works*, Elkhorn Edition, 27 (New York, Charles Scribner's Sons, 1920), pp. 261, 263; Morison, ed., *Letters*, 2, pp. 276-277, 390.

17. Fenton, "Theodore Roosevelt as an American Man of Letters," p. 372.

18. Roosevelt, "Books for Holidays in the Open," pp. 264, 266.

19. See the excellent discussion of the incident by Don D. Walker in "Wister, Roosevelt and James—A Note on the Western," *American Quarterly*, 12 (Fall 1960), pp. 358-366.

20. Roosevelt, *The Winning of the West*, 2, pp. 33, 73; 4, pp. 52, 54-56. Elsewhere Roosevelt describes the opposing forces as the "rifle-bearing freemen" pitted against the "polished old-world powers" and the "wild and squalid warriors of the wilderness." He contended that the British failed to hold the Old Northwest because they "fought against the stars in their courses, while the Americans battled on behalf of the destiny of the race." *Ibid.*, 4, pp. 6-8, 65. The alliteration is a typical stylistic device.

21. See, for example, *ibid.*, 2, pp. 84, 89.

22. To sample only one volume, see *ibid.*, pp. 53, 67, 83-84, 129-130. The backwoodsmen are called "iron-willed, steel-sinewed" and the Indians "savage lords." *Ibid.*, pp. 67, 220.

23. Owen Wister, *Roosevelt—The Story of a Friendship* (New York, Macmillan, 1930), p. 55.

24. Maurice Disher, *Blood and Thunder* (London, Frederick Muller, 1949), p. 12. The imagination of the masses in the nineteenth century, says Disher, was "like the feelings of crowds, an entity."

25. Brander Matthews, "Theodore Roosevelt as a Man of Letters," *Literary Essays*, National Edition (New York, Charles Scribner's Sons, 1926), p. xii.

26. See the discussion of nineteenth-century melodrama in Disher, *Blood and Thunder*, p. 14; Roosevelt, *The Winning of the West*, 2, p. 195.

27. Morison, ed., *Letters*, 1, pp. 196, 440-441.

28. Theodore Roosevelt, *Ranch Life and the Hunting Trail*, Elkhorn Edition (New York, Charles Scribner's Sons, 1906), pp 8, 12-13; Theodore Roosevelt, *Cowboys and Kings* (Cambridge, Massachusetts, Harvard University Press, 1954), pp. 15-16.

29. Theodore Roosevelt, *Hero Tales From American History*, Elkhorn Edition (New York, Charles Scribner's Sons, 1906), p. 19; *The Winning of the West*, 1, pp. 176-178.

30. *Ibid.*, 4, pp. 237-241.

31. *Ibid.*, 2, p. 194. Contrast the "perseverance" of Clark, p. 233.

32. See his discussion of frontier "dandies" and "bullies," *ibid.*, 1, pp. 152-153, 213-214. Roosevelt had a keen interest in lawlessness. See *The Winning of the West*, 2, p. 117; 4, pp. 28, 32-33; 1, pp. 167-168.

33. *Ibid.*, 4, pp. 218-219, 246.

34. *Ibid.*, p. 163; 2, p. 166.

35. *Ibid.*, pp. 291-294.

36. *Ibid.,* p. 296. Another Cooper touch is provided by Roosevelt's description of the prowess of the Indians: "With moccasined feet they trod among brittle twigs, dried leaves, and dead branches as silently as the cougar, and they equalled the great wood-cat in stealth and far surpassed it in cunning and ferocity." *Ibid.,* 1, pp. 108-109.

37. *Ibid.,* 4, p. 219.

38. *Ibid.,* 1, pp. 109, 125; 2, p. 151.

39. *Ibid.,* 2, pp. 92-93.

40. The Indians "roamed" the West, but in no sense "owned" or "occupied" it. *Ibid.,* 4, p. 52.

41. See, for example, *ibid.,* 1, pp. 125, 127; 2, pp. 140-142.

42. *Ibid.,* 3, pp. 80-81. See also 6, p. 160.

43. *Ibid.,* 6, p. 223.

44. *Ibid.,* 1, p. 176; 4, pp. 34-35. "Boone, the typical frontiersman, embodied in his own person the spirit of loneliness and restlessness which marked the first venturers into the wilderness." *Ibid.,* 6, pp. 159-160.

45. *Ibid.,* 2, p. 111.

46. Thomas Babington Macaulay, "History," reprinted in Fritz Stern, ed., *The Varieties of History* (Cleveland, Ohio, The World Publishing Co., 1956), p. 76.

47. *The Winning of the West,* 4, p. 69.

C. GREGORY CRAMPTON

Historical Archaeology on the Colorado River

1. U. S. Department of the Interior, Bureau of Reclamation, *The Colorado River . . . A Comprehensive Report on the Development of the Water Resources of the Colorado River Basin for Irrigation, Power Production, and Other Beneficial Uses in Arizona, California, Colorado, Nevada, New Mexico, Utah, and Wyoming . . . March 1946* (Washington, 1946).

2. C. Gregory Crampton, *Outline History of the Glen Canyon Region, 1776-1922,* University of Utah Anthropological Papers, 42 (Salt Lake City, 1959).

3. C. Gregory Crampton, *Historical Sites in Glen Canyon, Mouth of San Juan River to Lee's Ferry,* University of Utah Anthropological Papers, 46 (Salt Lake City, 1960). Subsequent reports will be published in this series of papers.

4. A comprehensive and significant program of historic site archaeology has been undertaken in the upper Missouri River Basin by the National Park Service and the Smithsonian Institution. Merrill J. Mattes, who has taken part in this program, has written extensively about it. See especially his "Historic Sites Archeology on the Upper Missouri," *Bureau of American Ethnology Bulletin* 176, pp. 1-23, which summarizes this program and presents a bibliography.

Appendix

THE WESTERN HISTORY ASSOCIATION

A significant new national organization, the Western History Association, is a manifestation of the recent surge of interest on the part of scholars and the general public alike in the history and development of the American West. It grew out of two conferences on the history of western America, the first held at Santa Fe in 1961 and the second at Denver in 1962. The great success of these conferences led to the formal organization of the Association at the Denver conference.

The new surge of interest in western America had been recognized by John Alexander Carroll of the University of Arizona, K. Ross Toole of the Museum of New Mexico, and a small group of western history devotees. Motivated by a belief that this interest existed in such depth that a national meeting was clearly in order—similar to the one sponsored by the University of Colorado at Boulder in 1929—in the spring of 1961 they called the First Conference on the History of Western America. The overwhelming response to this conference—held in Santa Fe October 12-14, 1961, and hosted by the Museum of New Mexico—far exceeded expectations. The Second Conference on the History of Western America, which convened in Denver October 11-13, 1962, and was hosted by the University of Denver, culminated in the organization of the Western History Association.

The Association was formed in the belief that interest in the American West is broad and deep as well as national and international in scope. Because it is dedicated to fostering the interdisciplinary approach to the study of the West, it defines "history" and "West" in the broadest possible sense. It welcomes the membership of anyone interested in the West.

252

Officers of the Association elected at the Denver conference include:

PRESIDENT:	Ray A. Billington
VICE PRESIDENT:	Oscar Osburn Winther
SECRETARY-TREASURER:	John Porter Bloom
COUNCIL:	Robert G. Athearn
	John F. Bannon, S. J.
	W. Eugene Hollon
	Walter Rundell, Jr.
	Don Russell
	Robert M. Utley

Annual meetings of the Association were projected for October of each year. One was planned for Salt Lake City in 1963 and another for Oklahoma City in 1964.

At the council meeting at Omaha in May 1963, plans were completed for publication of the Association's official quarterly journal, *The American West*. The council accepted the offer of the University of Utah to publish the journal and appointed A. Russell Mortensen as editor and C. Gregory Crampton as associate editor. The first issue was scheduled for January 1964. Selected papers presented at the Salt Lake City and other future meetings of the Association will be published in *The American West*. Papers from the two conferences on the history of western America were published by the Museum of New Mexico Press, the first volume being entitled *Probing the American West*.

Index

Abbey, Edward, author, 32
Absolutism, Spanish, 150
Academy of Science of St. Louis, founded, 136
Acapulco, port, 153
Adams, Andy, author, 26
Adams, Henry, friends of, 51, 202
Advertising, and cowboy image, 26; in rodeo, 29
"Aerial Railway," proposed, 71
Aeronautical Chamber of Commerce, directory of, 73
Africa, hunting in, 201
Agents, Indian: 149; and fur trade, 133; in Utah, 182-185
Agrarian movement, and state railroad boards, 62; and Turner, 69
Agriculture, and Indians, 136, 146, 185, 187; and passing of cowboy, 25; and rodeos, 26; and Spanish missions, 149; and transportation, 70; and Turner, 69; aspects of needing study, 67; at fur posts, 131; fairs and exhibits for, 26; in Aztec Empire, 147; in eastern U.S., 143; in England, 144, 145; in Glen Canyon region, 223-224; in Spain, 145; on Anglo-American and Spanish frontiers, 141, 142, 143, 144, 146, 148; produce of, displayed, 96; transition to, 137. See also Agrarian movement; Cattle industry
Air France, forerunners of, 73
Air transportation, see Aircraft; Airlines
Aircraft, development of, during World War I, 72-73; early experiments with, 70, 71; military, used by private airlines, 77; types of, introduction and use of, 71, 75, 77, 78, 79; used by cowboys, 26
Airlines, commercial: and other forms of transportation, 70, 75, 76, 77, 79; attempts to establish, 70; company turnover among, 73; development of, in West, 70-80; "feeder lines" of, 74, 78, 79; international service of, 77; phases in development of, 70-71;

reorganized by U. S. Post Office Department, 75; use military aircraft, 77; various aspects of needing study, 63
Airmail service, and private companies, 74, 75; payments for, 70; provided by U. S. Post Office Department, 70, 73, 74, 79
Alabama, railroad commission in, 62
Alamo, history of, 202; preserved, 217
Alarcón _____, memorials of, sought, 156
Alaska, air service in, 72, 77; Army interest in, 46; explored, 157
Albany Medical School, 49
Albuquerque, N. M., airline service at, 76
Alcohol, see Drinking
Alden, Henry Mills, editor, 191
Alfalfa, introduced in Nebraska, 96
Allegheny Mountains, crossed, 202
Allen, J. A., scientist, 51
Alliance, Nebraska, railroad survey at, 97
Amarillo, Texas, railroad service at, 98
America, Central, Spanish in, 148; character of, and its survival, 6; civil-military tradition of, 37; contested, 145, 152, 153, 154, 158; cowboy considered representative of, 34; cowboys from various parts of, 28; fads, issues, and unrelated crusades of, affect local wishes, 163, 174; imperialism of, 37, 167; interested in Colorado River, 213; interested in cowboys and rodeos, 29; international role of, 6, 11; interplay of, with regions and states, 38, 163-164; Latin, air service to, 77; lured by West, 3-4; people in, and Turner's frontier hypothesis, 6; people in, attitude of, toward Southwest, 163-167; pioneering past of, and present, 12; prejudices and preoccupations of, at turn of century, 175; problems of today, and western studies, 6, 12; relation of, to West, 38; responsibilities to,

of historians, 6, 8, 10; social structure of, and new western social order, 3-12; society of, and "History of the Frontier" school, 10

American Airways, activities of, 74

American Anthropological Association, 220

American Council of Learned Societies, 220

American Fish Culturists Association, 64

American Fur Company, activities of, 128, 129; needs study, 9

American Historical Association, as publisher, 7; T. Roosevelt addresses, 203

American Institute of Mining Engineers, activities and membership of, 101, 110

American Journal of Science and Arts, The, content of, 50

American Junior Rodeo Association, 31

American Protective Association, supported by mining engineers, 109

American Sugar Refinery, 102

American West, The, journal of Western History Association, 253

Anaconda Company, and apex mining litigation, 105-106; establishes geological department, 106; maps mines, 106

Anaku, Indian chief, 157

Anasazi culture, in Glen Canyon region, 223

Andrews, William H. ("Bull"), politician, 168, 171, 172, 175

Anglo-American frontier, contrasted with Spanish, 141-150

Anglo-Saxons, and T. Roosevelt, 203, 205; civilization of, in America, felt to be threatened, 169

Anthropological Papers, of University of Utah, 217

Anthropology, and new western social order, 4; social, and history students, 4; studied by Spanish, 154, 158. *See also* Archaeology; Artifacts; Ethnology; Fossils

Antiquarianism, and "History of the West" school, 8-9

Anza ———, journals of, 156

Apache Indians, and Spanish, 149; chief of, as fictional character, 33; in raid, 108; unsubdued, 40

Apex law, and mining industry, 105-106

Aragon, Spain, 152

Archaeology, collections on, made for

U. S. Smithsonian Institution, 44; historical, 213-218; personnel trained in, needed, 225; salvage, 219-225; societies in, 220; works on, published, 45. *See also* Anthropology; Artifacts, Ethnology; Fossils

Architecture, at fur posts, 131

Archives, studies in, by Spanish, 155, 156

Arguello, Lt. José Darío, commander of presidio, 159

Arid lands, Anglo-Americans and Spanish in, 144; book on, 44, 54; settlement in, 44

Arikara Indians, and fur trade, 119-120, 121

Arizona, 191, 192, 195; airline service in, 78, 79; business connections of, with California, 169, 170; constitution of, 165, 166, 173-174; dam projects in, 214-222; economic framework of, 164, 165; explored, 38, 39, 41, 45, 53; granted land, 175; highway salvage archaeology in, 221; horticulture in, 67; Indians in, 166, 223; industrial development of, 166; irrigation in, 164; labor unions in, 166, 173; military posts in, 38; mining in, 108, 164, 165, 173; name of, proposed for joint Arizona-New Mexico state, 170; population of, 166; statehood drive of, 163-175; termed "mining camp," 168; transportation in, 164. *See also* Museum of Northern Arizona; University of Arizona

"Arizona Boys," German club, 34

Arizona Enabling Act, 165

Arizona Gazette, quoted, 174

Arkansas, Confederates in, 87

Arkansas River, headwaters of, explored, 42; source of, sought, 116

Army, U. S., *see* United States Government agencies and departments, Army

Army and Navy Journal, on Wheeler death, 37

"Army of the West," occupies New Mexico, 81

Army of Utah, supplied, 83, 84, 85

Arnold, Matthew, author, 201

Arrapeen, Ute chief, 181

Art, *see* Artists

Arthur, Pres. Chester A., 110

Artifacts, Indian, and fur trade, 136; Indian, on Pacific Coast, 157, 159; record of, 217

new western social order, 3-12; changes in, during Depression, 5; interest of, in subject, 252; migrate to West, 4. See also specific fields

Schools, see Education

Science and scientists, and forest development, 64; and fur trade, 133, 135-136, 137; and Great Surveys, 38-57 passim; and mining litigation, 105, 106; and Spanish artists, 155; historical coverage of, 51, 53, 55-57; latest techniques of, used by Wheeler survey, 44; societies of, 110; Spanish, explore Pacific Coast, 151-160; terms of, and mining engineers, 104; works on, published, 45, 50, 51, 54, 151, 154, 160, 216, 218, 221, 223

"Scientist in the West, 1870-1880 (The)," article in historical journal, 56

Scott, Sir Walter, influences T. Roosevelt, 207, 208

Scottish-English border wars, 208

Scranton, Pa., 101

Seattle, Wash., airline service at, 74, 78

Secession movement, in California, 88; in Idaho, 193

Sectionalism, and historiography, 10

Securities, railroad, 90

Semantics, and historiography, 10

Senseve, Jayme, explorer, 154

"Separ's Vigilante," Wister story, 192

Serra, Junípero, biography of, 156

Sessé, Dr. Martin, scientist, 152

Settlement, of West: and fur trade, 128; era of, 62; hastened by improved transportation, 70; in arid lands, 44; information on, 56; map for, 45; plan for, 46; sparse, ends, 47. See also Frontier

Sevier, John, frontiersman, 207, 208

Shaler, Nathan, scientist, 105

Shaw, Albert, and Sen. Beveridge, 168

Sheffield Scientific School, of Yale University, 51

Sherill, Kate, frontierswoman, 208

Shiloh, Battle of, 53

Shivwit Indians, hill explorers, 48

Shoshone Indians, and Mormons, 176, 183; chief of, fictional, 33; steal horses, 177

Shoshone River, thermal phenomenon at, 122

Shoulders, Jim, rodeo performer, 28, 30

Shumerd, Benjamin F., scientist, 136

Sierra Mountains, explored, 45, 52

"Significance of the Frontier in American History (The)," Turner paper, 10

Silver, and Arizona-New Mexico statehood, 165, 166, 174; and Comstock Lode, 164; sought, by Spanish, 148. See also Mining-mineral industry

Silver City, Idaho, 194

Simpson, Capt. James H., explorer, 41

Singing, among cowboys, 17-19

Sioux City, Iowa, as fur trade boundary, 128; boat service at, 131

Sioux Indians, 196; and fur trade, 119, 120; wars of, 4

Siringo, Charles A., author, 25

Sites, see Historic sites

Slavery, among Indians, 180; among Spanish, 149; Mexican trade in, 180-181

Smith, Hamilton, Jr., mining entrepreneur, 106-107

Smith, Marcus Aurelius, politician, and Arizona-New Mexico statehood, 164-175 passim

Smithsonian Institution, see U. S. Smithsonian Institution

Snake Indians, trade with Spanish, 124

Social life, at fur posts, 131

Social order and structure: in England, 145; in Spain, 144; new western, and synthesis of western scholarship, 3-12; of Aztec Empire, 147; on Anglo-American and Spanish frontiers, 143, 148; studies on, during Depression, 5; western, complexity and nature of, 4, 56; western evolution of, 4, 6

Social science, and cowboy, 32; and frontier history, 7; and new western social order, 3-12. See also specific fields

Socialists, and Arizona constitution, 173

Society, see Social order and structure

Society for American Archaeology, 220

Sociologists, and frontier history, 7, 12; and history students, 5; and new western social order, 3-12; on cowboy, 32; and Turner's frontier hypothesis, 7

Soil, of West, considered inadequate, 168, 216

Sonora, map of, 156

Sorbonne University, 100

Source materials, for western history, scarce, 9

South, 63, 164; historians of, 61; sympathizers with, in Idaho, 193, 194,

and in California, 88; U. S. senators from, 167. *See also* Confederates
South Africa, mining in, 101, 111
South America, 151
South Dakota, airline service in, 78, 79; Black Hills of, mining engineers in, 102; joint statehood proposed for, with North Dakota, 170; modern trail drive in, 28-29. *See also* Dakota Territory; Dakotas; North Dakota
"Southern Indian Mission," of Mormons, 179
Southern Pacific Railroad, and Arizona-New Mexico statehood, 164, 168
Southwest United States, acquired by U. S., 144; airline service in, 72, 75, 78; Army posts in, supplied, 82, 86; drought in, 224; environment of, Spanish adapt to, 149; mining in, 108; national attitude toward, 167, 175; need for military information on, 40; nomadic raiding groups in, 224; settlement patterns in, 44; Spanish missions in, 131; statehood drive of territories in, 163-175; termed "great American desert," 167
Spain, 205; and Aztec Empire, 147; and fur trade, 124, 128; and Moors, 145, 147; arid-land methods of, borrowed by Anglo-Americans, 144; claims of, in Pacific, abandoned, 160; Colonial empire of, 141-150 *passim*; culture of, 144; drives out Jews, 145; explores Pacific Coast, 151-160; frontier of, in U. S., as second American frontier, 141-150; heresy in, 145; in Glen Canyon region, 214; increasing commitments of, in Europe, 160; Inquisition in, 145; mapping of, 155; missions of, 131, 143, 149, 159, 217; rivalry of, with England, 152, 153, 154, 158; seapower of, in Pacific, declines, 160; social and economic structure of, in fifteenth and sixteenth centuries, 145; training of mining engineers in, 100. *See also* Spanish-American War; Spanish-Americans,
Spanish-American War, and Arizona-New Mexico statehood, 166, 167, 168
Spanish-Americans, and Arizona - New Mexico statehood, 165, 166, 167, 170, 173
Spanish Fork, Utah, treaty signed at, 187
Spanish language, in Southwest, 167, 168
Speculation, in West: 67, 68; in com-

mercial aviation, 72; in Dakota lands, 130; in educational lands, 169; in mines, 39, 106; in railroads, 94, 97
Spengler, Oswald, historical theorist, 137
Sportsmen, and fish conservation, 64; cowboys as, 29. *See also* Rodeos
Sprague, Isaac, artist, 135
Stage lines, 85, 86, 87, 88; hasten settlement of West, 70; in Arizona, 195
Stansbury, Capt. Howard, geologist, 41, 175
Stanton, Robert B., railroad engineer, 216
State of Deseret, and Indians, 177
Statehood drives, of Arizona and New Mexico, 163-175
States, in West: and fur trade, 133; and mining engineers, 102, 110; and national attitudes, 174; aspects and activities of needing study, 62-69; building of, 61; create railroad commissions, 62; funds of, and Indian Trust Fund, 87; governors of, and Indians, 176; Granger laws of, 94; highway salvage archaeology programs of, 217, 219-225; historians of, 6; historical activities of, 217, 218; histories of, 214; interested in Colorado River, 213; interplay of, with regions and nation, 38, 163-164; population of, 4; regulate railroad rates, 95; rodeos in, 30. *See also* Statehood drives
Statistical techniques, and historians, 56; and Turner's frontier hypothesis, 12
Statistics, labor, state bureaus for, created, 69
Steam engines, railroad use of, ends, 66
Steamboats, design and use of, 131, 134, 135
Steeple Rock, New Mexico, lawlessness in, 108-109
Stevens, Isaac, surveyor, quoted, 134
Stevenson, James, government executive, 50
Stevenson, John J., geologist, 46, 54
Stocks, exchange for, 68; holders of, in railroads, 92; of Burlington Railroad, 96; speculation in, in West, 68; used as compensation for mining engineers, 106. *See also* Business; Capital; Corporations; Economic; Economic history; Finance
Stone Age, technology of, and Indians, 146
Stores, general, in West, 67

Townsend Committee, *see* United States House of Representatives

Toynbee, Arnold, historian, 137

Trade, among Indians, 146, 148, 157; favorable balance of, 132; in Aztec Empire, 147. *See also* Fur trade

Trail drive, modern, 28-29

Transcontinental & Western Air, activities of, 74, 79

Transcontinental service, air, 74-75, 76, 77; airmail, 70, 73; railroad, 39, 76; telegraph, 86

Transportation, in West: air, 63, 70-80; and salvage archaeology, 222; chamber of commerce interested in, 66; changes in, 70; histories of, 62; impact of, 63; improvements in, as theme in U. S. history, 70; improvements in, hasten settlement, 70; in Arizona, 164; overland, and wagon freighting, 81-88; patterns in, affected by bus and truck lines, 63; provided for surveyors, 134; river system for, 128. *See also* Bus lines; Railroads; Trucking industry

Trans-Texas Airways, activities of, 78

Trappers, *see* Fur trade

Trigonometry, used by Great Surveys, 41, 44

Trinidad, Colo., railroad service at, 98

Trinity and Brazos Valley Railroad, successor of, 98

"Triumvirate of settlement," on Spanish frontier, 142, 148

Trucking industry, aspects of needing study, 63; share of traffic, 70, 77

Tucson, Ariz., 107; and Arizona-New Mexico joint statehood, 171; mining oligarchy in, 164

Tudors, and English middle class, 145

Tulsa, Okla., rodeo performer from, 28

Tumacacori, preserved, 217

Turner, Frederick Jackson, historian, and T. Roosevelt, 206; frontier hypothesis of, 6, 7, 141; generation of, compared to today's historians, 61, 69; influence of, 9-12, 69; outlines economic study areas, 61; "safety-valve" theory of, tested, 12

Turnpikes, *see* Highways

Twin Cities, railroad service at, 92, 94, 96, 97. *See also* Minneapolis; St. Paul

Twin Lakes region, explored, 42

Uinta Valley, Indian lands in, 187

Uintah Indians, lands of, 183

Uintah Valley, 185

Union, U. S., admission of states to, 163-175; in Civil War, 50, 53

Union Fur Company, activities of, 129-130

Union Pacific Railroad, connections of, 90; expansion of, sought, 94; exploration south of route of, 42; goes into receivership, 98; officials of, 97; route of, completed, 92

Unions, labor, and Arizona constitution, 173; and mining engineers, 109; aspects and activities of needing study, 68-69; in Arizona, 166, 173; railroad, 95

United Air Lines, activities of, 74, 75, 76

United States, *see* America; government of, *see* United States Government

United States Airways, activities of, 75

United States Congress, and airmail service, 72; and Arizona-New Mexico statehood, 163-175; and commercial aviation, 73, 78; and fur trade, 133; and Great Surveys, 42-44, 53; and Indians, 177, 184, 185, 186; and Interstate Commerce Act, 95; and railroads, 95; and wagon freighting claims, 84; extends Intercourse Act, 181; mining engineers serve in, 110; passes Historic Sites Act, 220; passes Kelly Act, 73; passes Omnibus Bill, 164, 167, 169

United States Geographical and Geological Survey of the Rocky Mountain Region, *see* Powell, Maj. John Wesley

United States Geographical Surveys West of the One Hundredth Meridian, *see* Wheeler, Lt. George M.

United States Geological and Geographical Surveys of the Territories, *see* Hayden, Ferdinand Vandiveer

United States Geological Exploration of the Fortieth Parallel, *see* King, Clarence

United States Government, and Arizona-New Mexico statehood, 163-175; and fur trade, 133-134, 136; and Great Surveys, 37-57; and Indians, 130, 182-187 *passim;* and wagon freighting, 84; aspects and activities of needing study, 63, 64, 67; branches of, competition between, 43; clashes with Manuel Lisa, 116; explores Glen Canyon region, 215; forest reserves of, in New Mexico, 169; funds of, used to publish